Frederick William Robertson

The Human Race and Other Sermons

Preached at Cheltenham, Oxford, and Brighton

Frederick William Robertson

The Human Race and Other Sermons
Preached at Cheltenham, Oxford, and Brighton

ISBN/EAN: 9783337154929

Printed in Europe, USA, Canada, Australia, Japan

Cover: Foto ©Lupo / pixelio.de

More available books at **www.hansebooks.com**

"THE HUMAN RACE"

AND

OTHER SERMONS

PREACHED AT

Cheltenham, Oxford, and Brighton

BY THE LATE

REV. FREDERICK W. ROBERTSON, M.A.

INCUMBENT OF TRINITY CHAPEL, BRIGHTON

NEW YORK

HARPER & BROTHERS, FRANKLIN SQUARE

1881

CONTENTS.

Fifth Series.

SERMON I.
Cheltenham, April 26, 1846.

THE HUMAN RACE TYPIFIED BY THE MAN OF SORROWS.

ISA. liii. 3.—"A man of sorrows, and acquainted with grief: and we hid as it were our faces from him"......Page 9

SERMON II.
Cheltenham, May, 1846.

DEGREES IN GLORY.

MATT. xx. 23.—"And Jesus saith unto them, Ye shall drink indeed of my cup, and be baptized with the baptism that I am baptized with: but to sit on my right hand, and on my left, is not mine to give, but it shall be given to them for whom it is prepared of my Father". 23

SERMON III.
Oxford, June 13, 1847.

THE PHARISEE AND THE PUBLICAN.

LUKE xviii. 9.—"And he spake this parable unto certain which trusted in themselves that they were righteous, and despised others"...................... 34

SERMON IV.
Oxford, June 20, 1847.

THE CHRISTIAN'S HOPE AND DESTINY HEREAFTER.

1 JOHN iii. 2, 3.—"Beloved, now are we the sons of God, and it doth not yet appear what we shall be: but we know that, when he shall appear, we shall be like him; for we shall see him as he is. And every man that hath this hope in him purifieth himself, even as he is pure".................................. 39

SERMON V.
Oxford, June 27, 1847.

NATIONAL EDUCATION.—CHARACTER OF MOSES.

ACTS vii. 20–22.—"In which time Moses was born, and was exceeding fair, and nourished up in his father's house three months: and when he was cast out, Pharaoh's daughter took him up, and nourished him for her own son. And Moses was learned in all the wisdom of the Egyptians, and was mighty in words and in deeds"..................Page 44

SERMON VI.
Oxford, July 11, 1847.

THE KINGDOM OF HEAVEN.

LUKE xvii. 20, 21.—"And when he was demanded of the Pharisees, when the kingdom of God should come, he answered them and said, The kingdom of God cometh not with observation: Neither shall they say, Lo here! or, Lo there! for, behold, the kingdom of God is within you"...................... 52

SERMON VII.
Oxford, July 15, 1847.

THE SECRET GROWTH OF THE SEED.

MARK iv. 26.—"And he said, So is the kingdom of God, as if a man should cast seed into the ground".............. 58

SERMON VIII.
Brighton, September 19, 1847.

THE LAW OUR SCHOOLMASTER.

GAL. iii. 24, 25.—"Wherefore the law was our schoolmaster to bring us unto Christ, that we might be justified by faith. But after that faith is come, we are no longer under a schoolmaster" 62

SERMON IX.
Brighton, September 25, 1847.

ELIJAH ON MOUNT CARMEL.

1 Kings xviii. 21.—"And Elijah came unto all the people, and said, How long halt ye between two opinions? If the Lord be God, follow him; but if Baal, then follow him. And the people answered him not a word".............Page 69

SERMON X.
Brighton, October 3, 1847.

GROWTH INTO CHRIST IN LOVE AND TRUTH.

Eph. iv. 15.—"But speaking the truth in love, may grow up into him in all things, which is the head, even Christ"..... 74

SERMON XI.
Brighton, October 10, 1847.

(1.) SPIRITUAL WORSHIP.

John iv. 21-24.—"Jesus saith unto her, Woman, believe me, the hour cometh, when ye shall neither in this mountain, nor yet at Jerusalem, worship the Father. Ye worship ye know not what: we know what we worship: for salvation is of the Jews. But the hour cometh, and now is, when the true worshippers shall worship the Father in spirit and in truth: for the Father seeketh such to worship him. God is a Spirit: and they that worship him must worship him in spirit and in truth"..... 79

SERMON XII.
Brighton, March 5, 1848.

TEARS OF JESUS.

John xi. 35.—"Jesus wept"........... 84

SERMON XIII.
Brighton, April 7, 1850.

(2.) SPIRITUAL WORSHIP.

John iv. 23, 24.—"But the hour cometh, and now is, when the true worshippers shall worship the Father in spirit and in truth: for the Father seeketh such to worship him. God is a Spirit: and they that worship him must worship him in spirit and in truth"................ 89

SERMON XIV.
Brighton, November 10, 1850.

THE CONVICTION OF SIN IN THE MIND OF PETER.

Luke v. 8.—"When Simon Peter saw it, he fell down at Jesus' knees, saying, Depart from me; for I am a sinful man, O Lord"....................Page 96

SERMON XV.
Brighton, November 24, 1850.

GUILT OF JUDGING.—CONTEMPTUOUSNESS.

Rom. xiv. 10.—"But why dost thou judge thy brother? or why dost thou set at nought thy brother? for we shall all stand before the judgment-seat of Christ"........................... 102

SERMON XVI.
Brighton, December 15, 1850.

THE CHRISTIAN MINISTRY.

Matt. xi. 9, 10.—"But what went ye out for to see? A prophet? Yea, I say unto you, and more than a prophet. For this is he of whom it is written, Behold, I send my messenger before thy face, which shall prepare thy way before thee"................................ 108

SERMON XVII.
Brighton, December 22, 1850.

THE THREE CROSSES ON CALVARY.

Luke xxiii. 33.—"And when they were come to the place which is called Calvary, there they crucified him, and the malefactors; one on the right hand, and the other on the left"............... 115

SERMON XVIII.
Brighton, January 26, 1851.

THE STATE OF NATURE AND THE STATE OF GRACE.

Eph. ii. 3-5.—"Among whom also we all had our conversation in times past in the lusts of our flesh, fulfilling the desires of the flesh and of the mind; and were by nature the children of wrath, even as others. But God, who is rich in mercy, for his great love wherewith he loved us, even when we were dead in sins, hath quickened us together with Christ (by grace ye are saved)"..... 123

SERMON XIX.
Brighton, February 23, 1851.

THE CHURCH OF EPHESUS.

Rev. ii. 1-4.—"Unto the angel of the church of Ephesus write: These things saith he that holdeth the seven stars in his right hand, who walketh in the midst of the seven golden candlesticks; I know thy works, and thy labor, and thy patience, and how thou canst not bear them which are evil; and thou hast tried them which say they are apostles, and are not; and hast found them liars: and hast borne, and hast patience, and for my name's sake hast labored, and hast not fainted. Nevertheless, I have somewhat against thee, because thou hast left thy first love".........Page 130

SERMON XX.

Brighton, March 9, 1851.

(1.) WISDOM JUSTIFIED OF HER CHILDREN.

MATT. xi. 19.—"But wisdom is justified of her children"...................... 137

SERMON XXI.

Brighton, March 16, 1851.

(2.) WISDOM JUSTIFIED OF HER CHILDREN.

LUKE v. 33.—"And they said unto him, Why do the disciples of John fast often, and make prayers, and likewise the disciples of the Pharisees; but thine eat and drink?"........................ 143

SERMON XXII.

Brighton, March 23, 1851.

THE WISDOM OF CHRIST AND THE WISDOM OF SOLOMON.

LUKE xi. 31.—"The queen of the south shall rise up in the judgment with the men of this generation, and condemn them; for she came from the utmost parts of the earth to hear the wisdom of Solomon; and, behold, a greater than Solomon is here"................... 149

SERMON XXIII.

Brighton, August 3, 1851.

THE LAW OF SELF-SACRIFICE EXEMPLIFIED IN THE DEATH OF CHRIST.

JOHN xii. 23-28.—"Jesus answered them, saying, The hour is come, that the Son of man should be glorified. Verily, verily, I say unto you, Except a corn of wheat fall into the ground and die, it abideth alone: but if it die, it bringeth forth much fruit. He that loveth his life shall lose it; and he that hateth his life in this world shall keep it unto life eternal. If any man serve me, let him follow me; and where I am, there shall also my servant be: if any man serve me, him will my Father honor. Now is my soul troubled; and what shall I say? Father, save me from this hour: but for this cause came I unto this hour. Father, glorify thy name"........................Page 156

SERMON XXIV.

Brighton, November 2, 1851.

PURE RELIGION.

JAMES i. 27.—"Pure religion and undefiled before God and the Father is this, To visit the fatherless and widows in their affliction, and to keep himself unspotted from the world"................... 161

SERMON XXV.

Brighton, November 30, 1851.

(1.) THE PROGRESS OF REVELATION.

1 PETER i. 10-13.—"Of which salvation the prophets have inquired and searched diligently, who prophesied of the grace that should come unto you: searching what, or what manner of time the Spirit of Christ which was in them did signify, when it testified beforehand the sufferings of Christ, and the glory that should follow. Unto whom it was revealed, that not unto themselves, but unto us they did minister the things, which are now reported unto you by them that have preached the Gospel unto you with the Holy Ghost sent down from heaven; which things the angels desire to look into. Wherefore gird up the loins of your mind, be sober, and hope to the end for the grace that is to be brought unto you at the revelation of Jesus Christ"........................ 169

SERMON XXVI.

Brighton, December 7, 1851.

(2.) THE PROGRESS OF REVELATION.

GAL. iii. 24.—"Wherefore the law was our schoolmaster to bring us unto Christ, that we might be justified by faith". 176

SERMON XXVII.

Brighton, December 24, 1849, and December 14, 1851.

(1.) CHARACTER AND MISSION OF THE BAPTIST.

JOHN i. 22, 23.—"Then said they unto him, Who art thou? that we may give an answer to them that sent us. What sayest thou of thyself? He said, I am the voice of one crying in the wilderness, Make straight the way of the Lord, as said the prophet Esaias"................. 186

SERMON XXVIII.

Brighton, December 21, 1851.

(2.) CHARACTER AND MISSION OF THE BAPTIST.

LUKE iii. 3, 4.—" And he came into all the country about Jordan, preaching the baptism of repentance for the remission of sins: as it is written in the book of the words of Esaias the prophet, saying, The voice of one crying in the wilderness, Prepare ye the way of the Lord, make his paths straight"......Page 197

SERMON XXIX.

Brighton, March 28, 1852.

CHRISTIAN FORGIVENESS.

MATT. xviii. 32, 33.—" Then his lord, after that he had called him, said unto him, O thou wicked servant, I forgave thee all that debt, because thou desiredst me: shouldest not thou also have had compassion on thy fellow-servant, even as I had pity on thee?"............ 204

SERMON XXX.

Brighton, Christmas-day, 1852.

THE LIGHT OF THE WORLD.

JOHN i. 9.—" That was the true Light, which lighteth every man that cometh into the world "................... 210

SERMON XXXI.

Brighton (date unknown).

RIGHTEOUSNESS.

MATT. xv. 3–9.—" But he answered and said unto them, Why do ye also transgress the commandment of God by your tradition ? For God commanded, saying, Honor thy father and mother: and, He that curseth father or mother, let him die the death. But ye say, Whosoever shall say to his father or his mother, It is a gift, by whatsoever thou mightest be profited by me, and honor not his father or his mother, he shall be free. Thus have ye made the commandment of God of none effect by your tradition. Ye hypocrites, well did Esaias prophecy of you, saying, This people draweth nigh unto me with their mouth, and honoreth me with their lips; but their heart is far from me. But in vain they do worship me, teaching for doctrines the commandments of men"..........Page 217

SERMON XXXII.

Brighton (date unknown).

THE PEACE OF GOD.

ISA. lvii. 19, 20.—" Peace, peace, to him that is far off, and to him that is near, saith the Lord; and I will heal him. But the wicked are like the troubled sea, when it cannot rest, whose waters cast up mire and dirt. There is no peace, saith my God, to the wicked "............... 223

SERMONS.

Fifth Series.

I.

TYPIFIED BY THE MAN OF SORROWS, THE HUMAN RACE.

(FROM AUTOGRAPH MS.)

Preached for the Hospital. Christ Church, Cheltenham, April 26, 1846.

"A man of sorrows, and acquainted with grief: and we hid as it were our faces from him."—Isaiah liii. 3.

THERE are two aspects in which we may consider the Redeemer of the world. We may think of Him as the Christ, or we may think of Him as the Son of Man. When we think of Him as the Christ, He stands before us as God claiming our adoration. When we think of Him in that character in which He so loved to describe Himself, as the Son of Man, He stands before us as a type or specimen of the whole human race.

There is something exceedingly emphatic in that expression, Son of Man; it is a most wide and extensive appellation. Our Master is not called the Son of Mary; but, as if the blood of the whole human race were in His veins, He calls Himself the Son of Man. There is a universality in the character of Christ which you find in the character of no other man. If you take, for example, the life of Abraham, you have a man with all the peculiarities of that particular age belonging to him. You have a man moulded into a particular character with particular habits, particular prejudices. Abraham is by no means one to whom the whole human race can lay claim, and say he is our countryman.

He was the son of Terah, the offspring of a Syrian stock, the child of that generation. Abraham is full of rigid individual peculiarities. You have a distinct portrait that represents that one man, and no man else. Take, again, the character of David. It is a life of eminent saintliness, but you cannot mistake the Jew. There is Jewish exclusiveness, a Jewish way of looking at the world, Jewish faults, Jewish narrowness. He is not the son of man, but the child of Israel. Take, once more, the character of Paul, a man, if ever there was one, emancipated from exclusive feelings; generous, universal, catholic in his character. And yet it is not possible to take the portrait of the Apostle Paul and mistake for one moment to what age and nation he belonged. You could not for an instant say the man was born a Grecian; you could not take his character and say it is a character of the nineteenth century. You have unmistakably the disciple of Gamaliel, the man of peculiar education, the man of peculiar temperament; not the son of man, but the son of a certain father and a certain mother, the disciple of a certain school, with the peculiarities and the phraseology of that school. But when you take the character of Christ, all this is gone. Translate the words of Christ into what country's language you will, He might have been the offspring of that country. Date them by what century of the world you will, they belong to that century as much as to any other. There is nothing of nationality about Christ. There is nothing of that personal peculiarity which we call idiosyncrasy. There is nothing peculiar to any particular age of the world. He was not the Asiatic. He was not the European. He was not the Jew. He was not the type of that century, stamped with its peculiarities. He was not the mechanic. He was not the aristocrat. But He was the man. He was the child of every age and every nation. His was a life world-wide. His was a heart pulsating with the blood of the human race. He reckoned for His ancestry the collective myriads of mankind. Emphatically, He was the Son of Man.

The task which the master painters of the Middle Ages for centuries proposed to themselves as the highest aim of art was to realize on canvas the conception of the Anointed One of God. It was their grand work to paint a Christ. And what they made their business was not to turn off a portrait, but to embody the highest idea which genius could conceive of glorious humanity.

If the Italian painter or if the Spanish painter produced a form which bore the peculiar national lineaments worn by the humanity in his own climate, so far he had failed. He might have idealized the grandeur of the Italian form or the grandeur of the Spanish form, but he had not given to men's eyes that grandeur of the human species which belonged to a conception of the Son of Man. He had got a portrait to which a nobly formed individual of one nation might have sat, but an individual of no other. He had got the perfection of the Italian or of the Spanish type, but not the perfection of manhood. Now, that which the painter aimed at in the outward form, that Christ was in inward character. He was the type of the whole human race. He was the essence, the sublimation, of humanity. It was a noble endeavor of the Apostle Paul to be all things to all men. To the Gentile he became as a Gentile, that he might gain the Gentiles; to the Jew as a Jew. But in all this he was acting a single part for a time. He made it his business while the Jew was with him to try to realize the feelings and enter into the difficulties of a Jew. He laid it upon himself as a Christian duty while he was reasoning with a Gentile to throw himself into the Gentile's position, to try to look at things from his point of view, and even to fancy himself perplexed with his prejudices. But directly he had done with the man he wished to win, he threw himself out of his constrained position, he laid aside his part. He was neither Jew nor Gentile; but he was Paul again, with all Paul's personality and all Paul's peculiarities. That which Paul was for a time, Christ is forever. That which Paul was by effort and constraint, Christ is by the very law of His nature. He is all things to all men. He is the countryman of the world. He is the Mediator, not between God and a nation, but between God and man. He was the Jew and the Gentile, and the Greek and the Roman, all in one. He can sympathize with every man because He has, as it were, been every man. There is not a natural throb which ever agitated the bosom of humanity which Christ has not felt. The aspirations of loftiest genius and the failure of humblest mediocrity, the bitterness of disappointment and the triumph of success, the privations of the poor man and the feebleness of corporeal agony, Christ knew them all. He came into this world the Son and the Heir of the whole race of man.

It is for this reason that the passage before us is selected for our peculiar purpose to-day. It is our business to dwell to-day upon some of the sufferings common to the human species. And, therefore, we take up words belonging especially to Him who was the type of the human species. They were peculiarly true of Him. But they are in their measure true of every one whom the world can class as a son of man: "a man of sorrows, and acquainted with grief."

Here are two distinct facts which require consideration:

I. The lot of humanity in this world. This is the portrait of the species—"a man of sorrows, and acquainted with grief."

II. The treatment which depressed humanity commonly experiences—"we hid as it were our faces from Him."

I. The lot of humanity in this world was the position which Jesus occupied on earth. For the most part, that lot is one of suffering. But suffering is of two kinds: pain which we endure in our own persons—Christ was "a man of sorrows;" and pain which we know by familiarity with others' sufferings—Christ was "acquainted with grief."

1. First of all, then, we are to consider the personal trials of a son of man upon this earth—"a man of sorrows."

He that doubts whether we live in a ruined world or not has to account for this fact, that man's universal heritage is woe. Men of poverty we are not all, men of weak ability we are not all; but the man not of sorrows is yet unborn. It is the result of a universal survey of human life—"man is born to trouble." Therefore trial fell to the lot of Christ, and simply for this reason, that He was man—a man, therefore "a man of sorrows." In this time-world those two things shall not be severed. Bodily and mentally, the constitution of a son of man is such that escape is impossible. Look at that surface of the human frame which is exposed to outward injury. There runs beneath it, crossed and recrossed in windings inconceivable, a network of nerves, every fibre of which may become the home of pain. There is no interstice large enough to admit between them, in a space that does not feel, the finest needle's point. Beneath all that there is a marvellous machinery. Man anatomized is like an instrument of music. The combined action of ten hundred thousand strings, each moving in its moment and in its place, is the melody and the harmony of health; but if one chord vibrate out of tune, you have then the discord of the harp, the derangement of disease. Our bodies are strung to suffering. That we suffer is no marvel, that we want the repair of the physician is no wonder; the marvel is this—that a harp of so many strings should keep in tune so long.

Look next at the mental machinery of a son of man. These incomprehensible hearts of ours, my Christian brethren, have their liability to a derangement infinitely more terrible than bodily disorganization. The spirit of a man will sustain his infirmity, but a wounded spirit who can bear? The inner mind, wrapped up, as it seems, by impenetrable defences, is yet more exposed to shocks and wounds than the outward skin tissue; and the sensitive network which encompasses that mind is a thousandfold more alive to agony than the nerves that quiver when they are cut. There is such a thing as disappointment in this world. There is such a thing as affection thrown back upon itself. There are such things as slight and injury and insult. There is such a thing as an industrious man finding all his efforts to procure an honest livelihood in vain, and looking upon his pale children with a heart crushed, to feel that there is nothing for them but the poor-house. There is such a thing as a man going down the hill that leads into the sepulchre, and acknowledging, as the shadows darken around him, that life has been a failure. All this is sorrow; and just because of the constitution with which he is born. In some form or other, this is the portion of the son of man.

And, brethren, we remark this—the susceptibility of suffering is the lot of the highest manhood. Just in proportion as man is exquisitely man, he is alive to endurance. There is a languid, relaxed frame of body in which pain is not keenly felt. The more complete the organization, the severer the endurance. Strong and able manhood suffers more the division of the nerve than softened and debilitated frames. So it is with the spirit. The more emphatically you are the son of man with human nature in its perfection in you, the more exquisitely can your feelings bleed. That which a base and a craven spirit smiles at is torture to the noblest and the best. It was for this reason that Christ was in a peculiar sense the "Man of sorrows." Things which rough and scornful men would have shaken from them without feeling went home sharp and deep into His gentle and loving heart. The perfection of His humanity insured for him the perfection of endurance—"Behold and see if there be any sorrow like unto My sorrow."

There is another reason why a son of man is "a man of sorrows"—because labor is his heritage. Our Master came into this world to do a work. In sore toil, in weariness, in an unresting perseverance, which wore life away and made him seem fifty years of age when he was but thirty, that work had to be accomplished. It was forever pressing upon our Redeemer's spirit that he was here to labor. At an age when the boy has scarcely awakened to the reality of life, when the world is still a playground, at twelve years old, this was Christ's feeling when they found him at work, "Wist ye not I must be about My Father's business?" Later on in life we have him putting out the same perpetual conviction in words more pressing as his life was waning to a close—"I must work the work of Him that sent Me." Lastly, his career was closed with this profession, "I have finished the work which Thou gavest Me to do." In all this there is one idea—work—unresting work; and for the Son of Man no repose until the grave. He submitted himself to the universal law in all its rigor, "In the sweat of thy face shalt thou eat bread." His was the agony of bloody sweat which all men have agreed to call Divine—sweat of brow, sweat of brain, and sweat of heart, through life—that was the Redeemer's sorrow of labor.

Now, in this, my Christian brethren, Christ was a type of humanity. Labor is the destiny which binds us with the iron chain of a law. There are just a few—a luxurious, pampered few—who have emancipated themselves from this law, and given up life to idleness; and so, in escaping real distresses, they have found themselves, to their astonishment, the victims of distresses no less miserable—the fanciful, imaginary, nervous wretchedness of too abundant blessings. But when we have put out of sight these few exceptions, the mass of mankind are forced to drink their cup. Let us not overstate this—there is a blessing in labor, gladly we acknowledge that. There is no health either for mind or body without it. Nothing good was ever done without toil. No book worth the reading was ever written without it. No work that was meant to last but cost the happy man who did it toil. But it is true for all that labor is sorrow. Labor is enjoyment when you have just so much of it as is needful for exercise, and no more. Labor is well when you are not forced beyond your strength, and can get relaxation when the strength of frame gives way.

But it is seldom that labor of that kind falls to the lot of the son of man. It is all well for those of us who are in easy life to speak of the blessing of having something to do; but, my beloved brethren, it is a very different tale when we have something, as the laboring man has, that we *must* do. To him labor is sorrow all through. It is labor like his Master's from very childhood. The grim, earnest work of life-labor begins in the cottage at an age when the rich man's child has not thrown aside his toys. It is sorrow to be looking for employment; it is sorrow, often and often it is sorrow, to be doing it, sick or well, languid or vigorously fresh; when the head is aching and the heart is sick, still the laboring man must be up and doing. There will be famished lips and tearful eyes next week round an empty grate if he allows himself the luxury of rest. It is all this which makes the son of man, because born to labor, therefore "a man of sorrows."

There is one more ingredient in the cup which Christ drank which made Him "a man of sorrows." He was born poor. He knew what it was to want those solaces of life which alleviate pain. "Foxes have holes, and the birds of the air have nests, but the Son of Man hath not where to lay His head." And now, brethren, it is part of our special business to-day to recollect what sorrow and sickness are when they come into the cottage of the poor. There are, it may be, in this congregation several who have scarcely had it forced upon their contemplation. Living in sufficiency themselves, they have not suspected how others of the family of man struggle on. Brethren, let us contrast these things. When illness makes its appearance in the dwellings of the upper classes, there is a rich abundance of resources to mitigate the suffering. There is all the repose which can be secured by subdued light, and curtained windows, and muffled knockers, and noiseless steps. There is a smoothed pillow, there is a warm room, there are contrivances to suit and stimulate the sickly palate; the invalid reigns a kind of monarch in his chamber, every arrangement of the house giving way to the arrangements and the hours of his sick-room. Pass on from the comfortable mansion to knock at the low door in the next street. Sickness there exhibits itself in very different attire. Have we ever looked at the poor man's cottage, and pictured to ourselves how that almost den, small and comfortless as it is, can become the sick-room of the invalid? There is no securing repose, for all the domestic work of the family must be done within a few feet of the bed. The noise of footsteps entering and retiring goes on all day long, scarcely divided by a thin partition from the sick man's ear. We guard our delicate consumptive ones fearfully and affectionately so that not a breath of heaven's air shall play too roughly on the frame. Look at consumption in the cottage. Through the perpetually opening door, and through the broken window, and through the unguarded chimney the death-draughts pour down hour by hour upon the sufferer, till the fell and painful malady has done its work, and the rough, wretched coffin lies prematurely on the bed. The damp strikes through the brick or the mud floor, till rheumatism has stiffened the joints into contracted uselessness for life. Water from the pond is often all they have to wet the lips of the dying. There is not always one free from work to perpetually wet those hot lips. There is no fire in the bedchamber. Fuel costs too much; therefore to produce an artificial heat in the depth of winter, every aperture must be closed and pasted up, and so in the stifling, unwholesome warmth of an overheated cell, which takes away the very breath on entering, human life is gasped away. It is in all this that the poor man lives. It is in all this that the invalid must be nursed. Let but the sentimentalist go to the sick-bed of poverty, where there is scarcely bread in the closet for a meal, and no surplus money in the drawer to pay the physician's fees, and he will know what awful significance may be crowded into that one sentence—"a man of sorrows."

2. There was another feature in the lot of the Son of Man on earth, that He was familiar with the griefs of others—"He was acquainted with grief." Not merely by personally bearing it, but by continually coming in contact with it.

Now this acquaintance of Christ with grief was of two kinds. He knew it by passive and He knew it by active familiarity. When Jesus relieved distress, His acquaintance with it was of the active kind. When distress was simply in His presence, obtruding itself face to face, then His acquaintance with it was only passive. The Son of Man knew sadness passively by sympathy; He knew it actively by benevolence. Concerning both which parts of our human life we have a few remarks to make.

Christ's first acquaintance with sorrow was by sympathy. To sympathize is simply this, to feel with those that suffer. It is the instinct of a kindly heart. It is the obedience to that law of

Christian duty which bids us "rejoice with them that do rejoice, and weep with them that weep." It is the rising, the almost spontaneous rising, of the emotion of pity in the bosom. You do not bid the feeling come. It comes. That is passive knowledge of misery. When we have thrilled over the anguish that we see, there is a sense in which we are acquainted with grief.

And in this knowledge, brethren, our Redeemer's heart was rich. We will take but two cases which belong to our present purpose—the case of poverty and the case of corporeal maladies. It was a most distinguishing feature of the life of Jesus, the compassion which He felt for the degraded, neglected, unbefriended poor. It was not, except by invitation, in the rich man's house that Christ was found; it was not for his ears that His instructions were framed. It was His passion to teach those who were forgotten by the national instructors. There was a burning, almost passionate, indignation in His language whenever it came in His way to rebuke their oppressors, who shut up knowledge from them, and would have kept them uneducated, who overreached them (in Bible phraseology, "devouring widow's houses"), who lived in purple and fine linen, while Lazarus lay forgotten at their very threshold. Political economy has spoken its fine lessons of philanthropic humanity. Demagogues have courted the popular voice by loud harangues against what they call the oppression of the rich. Sentiment has taken poverty under its patronage, and adorned the cottage in touching stories with imaginary graces and purities that are never found there. But no man ever stood up the poor man's champion but Christ, and those who, like Christ, have lived with the poor and for them. Read the ninth chapter of St. Matthew. It is filled with tales of human suffering and human ignorance. At last there comes before the Redeemer a vast crowd of these poor and ignorant ones. When He saw the multitude, "He was moved with compassion on them, because they fainted, and were scattered abroad as sheep having no shepherd." That was not the glow of a demagogue's indignation against the rich venting itself in cheap words. It was not the sickly sigh of a novel-reader repining that this world is full of woe. It was the loving tenderness of the Son of Man, identifying Himself with the poor, and in deep emotion becoming acquainted with their sorrows.

Once more, our Lord sympathized with bodily anguish. He

was walking almost all His life through the wards of a vast hospital. The hospital was the world; the sick, the dying, and the mad were lying on their beds on both sides of Him. At evening "they brought unto Him many that were sick;" and, it is written again and again, "He was moved with compassion."

This, brethren, is an acquaintance with grief which most of us have not. Men are not acquainted with the pain which this world contains because it is not brought to them, and they do not go to look for it. There is a drapery of life which curtains away from us the loathsome parts of existence. You pass down the gay and glittering streets where almost all the forms which present themselves are forms of busy, strong, active humanity. Out of doors in the public thoroughfares you see the holiday of life. There is squalid poverty in the by-lanes and the alleys. There is sickness in the upper chambers. But you do not see that. It is not brought out as it was before Christ, bed after bed lining the pavement as you pass on. You cannot count the houses as you go along, and say this has its one dead and this has its two diseased. But the physician and the minister can. They can tell you what there is behind the scenes. They can say that within a few yards of where you stand there is one smarting under the torture of an amputated limb, and another stricken by the death-call of incipient decline, and farther on another feeding with his heart's best blood a disease which is eating life away, and for which there is no chance of ease except in the grave. We see it not. It is shut decently out of sight. The sick man does not sadden the street to-day in which he was walking blithely yesterday. All this is withdrawn from public scrutiny. To become vividly aware of it is to feel the emotion of sympathy. To have it perpetually and familiarly before the mind is to be acquainted with grief, but acquainted only passively.

In Christ's acquaintance there was something infinitely more. His love did not end with a passing sigh. It did not die with a keen emotion. His knowledge of human agony went deeper by the active benevolence of relieving it. When He was troubled by the tears of Martha and of Mary, He felt the sensation of sympathy; but when He went with them to the revolting grave, and gave back the dead man to their embrace, it was another kind of knowledge altogether which He possessed. It was the acquaintance got by active benevolence. This was the reason for which

Christ acquainted Himself with grief, not to nurse His own emotions, but to relieve it. He was perpetually in the presence of the miserable. Why? For this purpose: "The blind receive their sight and the lame walk, the lepers are cleansed, and the deaf hear, the dead are raised up, and the poor have the gospel preached to them." And here, brethren, we make a most important practical distinction. There is something dangerous in benevolence which is only emotional; there is something ennobling and something godlike in active kindness. This is the law of our nature, from which there is no escaping: impressions which are made upon us in the way of feeling get weaker and weaker the oftener they are repeated; but the habits of love which you get by being useful and active in doing others good get stronger and stronger the oftener you practise them. We read, it may be, a touching passage in our favorite author. The first time it thrills us. The second time it moves us less. The tenth time all emotion is gone, except that of mere admiration. The first death-bed you see haunts your recollection all night. See a hundred, and the startling power is gone. You reproach yourself. You think your heart is harder than it was. Marvel not! There is no preventing it. That acquaintance with sorrow which is only passive loses its sharpness every time you see it. And if a man wanted to have a thoroughly callous and hardened heart, we can tell him of no way so sure as this: Let him become familiar with the distresses of his fellow-men, and do nothing to relieve them; let him read of pauper misery, and content himself with theorizing about the improvidence of the poor; let him listen to appeals from the pulpit which attempt to move his charity, and pass the plate without a sacrifice—we will promise him his sensibilities shall soon be placed beyond the power of wounding; he shall have a heart as cold and dead as if he had been born without human sympathies.

Let us put this before us, brethren, in an illustration connected with to-day's subject. There are two epochs in the career of medical life. There is a period in the surgeon's existence when he occupies the position of a student, and belongs to a class of men proverbially reckless. And there is another period in his life when he belongs to a class which all experience forces us to place among the most devoted, the most tender, the most sympathetic of his species. How comes it that the young experimentalist is so marvellously transformed into the benevolent physician? The secret lies in this: In the outset of the profession a man has to look as a bystander on suffering. The recoil and the faintness of human sensitiveness pass off. He becomes familiar with human anguish. He looks upon the contortions of agony with the cold eye of a theorist. The human frame into which the sharp knife is passing is nothing to him but the material for a lecture. Emotion has dulled itself by repetition. This is the passive acquaintance with sorrow. It would be a miracle, indeed, if all this did not blunt sensibility. For if by God's wise law it did not blunt it, and if the emotion remained as keen as ever, how could the human heart bear perpetual laceration? That is the first stage. But as medical life goes on it becomes a duty not to look on, but to relieve. And then he begins to feel the blessedness of benevolence, and once more his heart expands when he sets about doing good. And year by year the habit deepens: the shudder of inexperience, and the mere emotional, useless sickening of the heart, which comes from witnessing an operation—all that is gone. It was worth nothing, after all; and in its place there has come something nobler, something that can be made use of in this work-day world, something even in its way Christ-like— that habit of prompt love which will enable a man to put up with much that is disgusting, and much that would shock the false delicacy of mere feeling, in order to do good.

Brethren, all this is practical. If we would acquaint ourselves with sorrow to any purpose, we must relieve it. Christian love is an active, hardy thing. Let a Christian familiarize himself with the trials of the poor. Let him hear their tales of distress. Let him see them in their malady. But unless he wishes to ruin his own heart, let him do as the Samaritan did, bind up the wounds, and not pass by on the other side.

II. We say but two things respecting the treatment which depressed humanity meets with in this world: "We hid as it were our faces from Him." It is the common lot of the sad to be forgotten by the light-hearted.

1. We hide our faces from the "man of sorrows" when we wish to make this world a paradise of rest; when we neglect the duty of knowing and acquainting ourselves with the burdens which are borne by men, and begin to plan for this world as if it were a place for happiness and repose. There is no rest here: woe

to the man who attempts to make it a place of rest. Oh! there is a false view of things which we get when we try to shut out the thought of suffering. Think of the young man and the young woman who make gayety their home day after day and night after night, and think of Christ with the sick and the maimed around Him; think of one who surrounds himself with the entertainment of this world, and think of one whose day is spent in passing from one sick-chamber to another. Observe the infinite difference in the views which they respectively form of life: one sees it all bright, the other sees it (not dark only, and not bright only) bright and dark together. Shut out suffering, and you see only one side of this strange and fearful thing, the life of man. Brightness and happiness and rest—that is not life. It is only one side of life. Christ saw both sides. He could be glad, He could rejoice with them that rejoice, He could bid men be merry at the marriage, He could take His part naturally in convivial conversation; and yet he has entered little into the depths of our Master's character who does not know that the settled tone of His disposition was a peculiar and subdued sadness. Take the two brightest moments of His career. When glory encircled Him on the mountain where His form was clothed in the radiance of a supernal cloud, what was His conversation with Moses and Elias? They spake to Him of His decease. When a multitude escorted Him triumphantly into Jerusalem, in the very midst of all that merriment His tears were flowing for Jerusalem. Not the splendor of a transfiguration, and not the excitement of a procession, could dazzle the view which the Son of Man had formed of life. Life was too earnest for deceiving Himself; He knew that the son of man is "a man of sorrows, and acquainted with grief." He had been behind the gaudy scenes. He stood in the very midst of a wretched and ruined world; and when death and retribution were so near, what had He to do with a gleam of momentary sunshine? That gave the calm depth to the character of Christ; He had got the true view of life by acquainting Himself with grief. Life is not for rest, but for seeking out misery.

And now, brethren, would we counteract the false glare and glitter of life? Would we escape that selfish hardness which the heart gets from not being personally exposed to want? Would we be calm and wise and loving, not depressed by misery, and not over-hypelated by gladness? Acquaint yourselves with sorrow;

know something of the way in which the poor man lives. Association with the poor is a marvellous corrective of the evils of easy circumstances. Real sorrows make us ashamed of imaginary ones; they force us out of ourselves; they make us feel that there is an infinite voice in the suffering of which the world is full, calling out Shame upon the way in which the rich man surrounds himself with indulgences. Brethren, but how much know ye, how much reck ye, of the suffering which is around you? In the brightness which this week may have in store, let this question suggest itself: Am I hiding my face from the "Man of sorrows?"

2. Again, we hide our faces from the "Man of sorrows" when we forget that we are sent into this world to relieve misery. There is an evil which is done in this world by the "want of thought;" that is the sin of those who go through life, not suspecting, and not caring to inquire how much there is of human desolation. And there is an evil which is done in this world by "the want of heart;" that is the sin of those who are familiar with all that you can tell them of misery, and still go on feasting and dressing and amusing themselves, and doling out the driblets of their income with a grudge in the sacred cause of benevolence.

Brethren, there is a cause before us to-day about whose excellence there is no second opinion. A man may have objections to the system of collecting money for the able-bodied pauper; he may not see the stringency of the obligation to send missionaries to the heathen; he may call it a useless expense to endeavor to convert the Jews; but a hospital is a common ground on which all opinions meet—to heal the sick who cannot heal themselves; to soothe real anguish which is not brought on by fault—that is the universal sacred cause of the human race. Suffer, brethren, a personal testimony to the tenderness with which the Cheltenham Hospital is carried on. It is a minister's duty from time to time to visit those of his own district who may chance to be removed within those walls as in-patients—and he has opportunities of observing that the poor are treated with a gentleness, a human consideration, an attention as scrupulous as if costly rewards were theirs to give. "Had I been a prince," said one of these wretched ones to his minister a few days ago, after a confinement there of six weeks, "I could not have had my wishes more quickly obeyed." Oh, it does the heart good to go straight from the comfortless hovel to the clean, cheerful, sick-ward! There is human pain before you in abundance, but it is pain soothed; there is something like a resting-place for the burning temple; there is something like quiet for the racked and swimming brain.

You are reminded that you are in a world of sorrow; but you are reminded, too, that you are in a world into which the Cross and the love of Christ have brought a remedy, and taught men to minister to wretchedness. Brethren, the appeal is made to you to day on behalf of the man of sorrows, and the appeal is this: acquaint yourselves with his grief; hide not thy face away from him.

II.

DEGREES IN GLORY.

(FROM AUTOGRAPH MS.)

Christ Church, Cheltenham, May, 1846.

"And Jesus saith unto them, Ye shall drink indeed of my cup, and be baptized with the baptism that I am baptized with: but to sit on my right hand, and on my left, is not mine to give, but it shall be given to them for whom it is prepared of my Father."—Matt. xx. 23.

There are errors which belong to the first days of religious life which are to be reckoned in the list of mistakes rather than in the class of sins; and God seems to look upon them mercifully and to treat them leniently, as a father passes over the follies, and the wilfulness, and the outbursts of sullenness in his young children without severe remark. They are wrong, but still they are weaknesses, in a measure to be expected—things to be set right rather than to be punished.

Three such mistakes as these were exhibited by Christ's disciples in that conversation of which I have read a part. The first mistake was a misconception of what religious life is; the second was an entire miscalculation of their own capacities; and the third was a readiness to make a boastful profession of their religion. All these mark the outset of religious life.

First of all, they had very poor conceptions of what religion is: they reckoned it to be all enjoyment and blessedness and reward. Scarcely had their career begun. The hard part of it had not begun. Trial, opposition, persecution—of all this as yet they had known nothing; and yet, as if it were all over, as if the battle had been fought, and nothing remained except the partition of the conquered territory, James and John, or their mother in their name, came to Jesus with the request that they might sit one on His right hand and the other on the left in His kingdom. The reply that they received was in the first instance simply a charge of ignorance, "Ye know not what ye ask." We take that as the first mark of inexperienced Christians; ignorance of what awaits them. No marvel that it should be so. It is God's special mercy that hides it from His children, or who would have the heart to persevere? Christ had stood between His disciples and the world —the world's cold sneer and the world's sharp rebuke. He had borne all this, and they had stood as behind a shield. No wonder if they did not yet recognize what religious life means. Christian life, brethren, is not rest: "It is high time to awake out of sleep." Christian life is not making time pass away comfortably: "Woe unto them that are at ease in Zion." Christian life is not reward: "If in this life only we have hope in Christ," then "we are of all men most miserable." Christian life is work, trial, earnestness, victory. The disciples mistook all that. If they had mistaken it ten years later, they would have merited rebuke; as it was, they received affectionate but yet humiliating counsel: "Ye know not what ye ask."

There was a second mistake in their request—a misconception of their own capacities. It is so with all beginners. We require bitter, humbling experiences before we are persuaded that there are some situations infinitely above our powers. The disciples were ready at a moment's warning, without anxiety, to undertake the responsibility of the highest duty which God might have to lay on mortals' shoulders. They would have taken the right hand and the left without shrinking from the dangerous honor. In God's kingdom there is no such thing as high privilege without high responsibility. There is no sitting on God's right hand in the place of honor, without at the same time having a high and arduous trust to execute. James and John were ready for that; they never paused to ask, Are we qualified? There was a terrible preparatory education; they never stopped to ask, Can we go through it? Modesty is seldom the attribute of the untried. Modesty is a thing we learn generally by shame and failure. A young Christian is ambitious to distinguish himself as a saint at once.

It is the aged saint who counts it an honor if he be permitted "with shame to take the lowest place."

There was yet a third error, characteristic of early and not advanced religion, and that was the readiness with which they committed themselves, by boastful profession, to lead a life which they were then far from able to endure. Their Master replied to their questions by another. They asked, "Let us sit one on Thy right hand, and the other on the left, in Thy glory." He inquired, "Can ye drink of my cup, and be baptized with my baptism?" And then it was that these frail novices pledged themselves to bear a trial whose very name they scarcely understood. What knew they as yet of the cup of agony, and the baptism of blood; and yet — Can ye drink My cup? Can ye bear My baptism? We can. This was boasting. This was ostentation. But let us observe, Christ did not rebuke them. He did not even attempt to make them retract by explaining what it was to which they had committed themselves. He took them at their word: Ye shall drink indeed of My cup. They had erred; but it was an error, not a sin; and He quietly left it to time to teach its own sad, humbling, strengthening lesson. He knew well they would find out their mistake, and be ashamed of their confidence, soon enough.

In passing, we make one observation. In all this there is a lesson for us of condescension to inexperienced Christians. It is in the spiritual as it is in the natural life. There is a time when the child passes into the man. We call that period boyhood—the most unruly, the most selfish, the most ungovernable of all the epochs of human existence. But the wise parent is not disconcerted when he discovers all this beginning. There is much of the folly of the child, but there is also much of the strength and dignity of the man. And so he waits till this chaos time is past, till added years have brought added humility, and added experience has taught his boy to distrust himself. So, also, in religious life there is a time when the spiritual child passes into the spiritual man—a period marked almost always by error and numberless inconsistencies. But by the example of our Master, Christ, we are not to be disconcerted at all this. And if we find much of the old love of worldliness hanging about the young Christian still—a desire for the distinction of religion, a wish for the right hand and the left—we are to wait. Or if we see that, with much love, there is also little experience of weakness, and therefore much boasting, still we are to wait patiently. The Christian is in process of formation, and by-and-by the child will have disappeared, and the man be established in its place.

But now our present point is this: Christ did more than bear with these infirmities; He attempted to remove them. Infirmities are pardonable, graceful, in the child; they are contemptible in the man. He would be lenient to His disciples, passing as they were from spiritual childhood into spiritual manhood; but He did not intend them to be forever in a transition state. The corrective which our Master applied to these weaknesses was the doctrine of the Cross. Instead of ease, He told them of trial. When they spoke of enjoyment, He reminded them of the pain without which enjoyment is not safe. To shame them of their boasting, He warned them of endurance. "Can ye drink of My cup?"—"Ye shall drink indeed of My cup." This, brethren, is the subject we are to examine: the meaning and the results of suffering. An appropriate subject for this day on which the Redeemer expressed to the world the Divine significance of suffering. In preparing for the highest attainments, the Son of Man can be perfected only through suffering.

We shall pursue this subject in two branches:

I. The difference of degrees in glory;
II. The principle on which that difference is regulated.

I. There is contained in this passage a very distinct intimation that in the world of glory beyond the grave all saints will not stand in a position of exact equality. There will be degrees in glory. There will be differences of blessedness. There will be varying steps of dignity. We are not at liberty to infer that there will be degrees merely because the apostles took it for granted, for it might have been an unfounded fancy which made them dream of places of superior honor. But we do infer it from the Redeemer's answer. His reply was not, Ask not for high places, for all are equal there. Theirs was a serious misconception, if it were a misconception, and one which it was needful to remove without delay. But we look in vain for anything like correction. He gave countenance to their conception, He acknowledged that it was no blind fancy. His admission came to this, that in the kingdom of heaven there is a right hand and a left, which "shall be given to them for whom it is prepared of My Father."

This, brethren, is the doctrine we have to establish and examine—the doctrine of degrees in glory. And, first of all, it is most natural that it should be so. If in heaven there were anything like universal equality, it would stand out an exception in God's universe, it would not be like one of God's plans. Everything we know, everything man ever heard of in God's creation, goes by steps, gradually and beautifully smoothing off from the lowest to the highest. The vegetable world slides into the animal world, and you cannot tell where one ends and the other begins. Step by step, from lower organization on to higher, till you come to the division-line where instinct borders upon reason, and you cannot for certain draw the boundary. The animal which possesses highest instinct treads so close upon the man who is gifted with lowest reason that you hesitate whether the nobler beast has only instinct, and the animalized man has truly reason. This is God's chain, His beautiful chain, of unequal links. This is God's world, God's work. Every spot in which you can trace God at work, there has He made degrees. Each thing in this universe has its own destined place. The thing below it cannot occupy that place, nor can the thing above it. Make the experiment, and there is a link broken.

Trace next that principle in one of the single links—man himself. Men are not born equal. Say nothing of circumstantial differences, such as climate and education and property; there are differences between man and man quite distinct from these. Give two characters the same advantages, will any system of education insure that they shall be equal? Education can give habits of mind, information, memory, power of attention. Can education give the instinctive eagle glance of genius? Can conditions? Can circumstances? There are some men upon whose brow nature has impressed the diadem of intellectual royalty; and there are some men who are marked for intellectual inferiority. There are minds born to command; there are minds born to be feeble, except when supported and led by others. There is the first-rate, and there is the second-rate—born so, not made by human will; God created one man to differ from another. Again and again revolutions have tried to level all differences; but in the next generation God's insulted law has vindicated itself: the towering mind has risen into a new aristocracy; the feeble mind has sunk into a fresh lowest class. Men can make human distinctions to proceed on a new principle; break down, destroy, level as they will, equality they cannot get.

Brethren, these are only specimens of a universal law, and the law is found in the heaven as in the earth: "One star differeth from another star in glory." It is God's law of inequality. In earth, in matter, and in mind there will be, and there must be, thrones and dominions, with principalities and powers. Now this does not prove that there will be degrees in heaven, but it makes it exceedingly improbable that there will not. The beauty and the harmony of this creation consist in each thing having its own appointed niche in the magnificent fabric of the universe. The order of this universe is constructed upon the principle of degrees. Is it likely that God's heaven will be, not a series of steps ascending up to God, but a dead level? Is it probable that it will be a thing marring this glorious symmetry and this exquisite gradation by being dependent on a principle of equality?

So much, brethren, for likelihood. But we have much more than likelihood. Except that excellent men have denied it, it would seem impossible to read Scripture without perceiving that its assertions are distinct upon this point. First of all, there is a promise given to the apostles that in the regeneration they shall sit on twelve thrones, judging the twelve tribes of Israel. Thrones, and something like the sway of ancient judges—a royal jurisdiction over others. Here is superiority in one class, subordination in another. If we only grant thus much, that there is something peculiar reserved for Christ's apostles, you have introduced the principle of degrees in heaven. Is it conceivable that it should stop there? Once more, there is something in heaven which is represented by the figure of being ruler over ten cities, and there is another something which is equivalent to being ruler over five cities. What is that but gradation of some kind? Whatever it may mean, this is clear, that there is one position amounting to only half the other. Lastly, brethren, we take the passage before us, and we hold it to be decisive and full upon this point. There is a post of honor. There is an affliction working out "a far more exceeding and eternal weight of glory." There is a peculiar nearness to Christ. There is a right hand to the throne of God. And there are some for whom that transcendent blessedness is specially reserved: "it shall be given to them for whom it is prepared of My Father."

There is a difficulty in the way of all this which it behooves us to consider. The doctrine of diversities in glory has seemed to some men to interfere with the Redeemer's merits. It has appeared to them that if every Christian stands before God complete in the righteousness of Christ, there can be no difference in one above another, for the position of one is exactly the same as the inheritance of the other. And so, from a most affectionate and loyal zeal for the honor of Christ, they have refused to admit that there can be anything like a right hand of God's throne.

Brethren, the imputed righteousness of Christ gives every man exactly the same title, the same right, to enjoy heaven, but it does not give to every man the same soul for the enjoyment. Each man remains an individual self, not merged and lost in Christ—an individual still, with his powers, his character, exactly what his time of education upon earth made him. The thief who had but an hour or two of Christian life, and the aged saint who has been disciplined in Christ for seventy years, stand exactly on the same footing so far as title is concerned. The Redeemer's merits are the passport for the saint, just as entirely as they are the passport for the penitent. Each has the same heaven—so far they are equal; but unless each can enjoy that heaven with the same intensity, so far they are not equal. Let two men listen to the same swell of glorious music, and yet just because there is a difference in their internal nervous organization one shall be only moved and pleased, and the other shall be entranced and thrilled. Let two men gaze on the same masterpiece of sculpture or of glorious painting; one has the perception of the beautiful cultivated by an artist's education, and the other has only the duller associations of a peasant. The same admission has been granted to them both, the same colors are spread out before them; but is their heaven of enjoyment equal?

These, brethren, are inadequate illustrations, but they are enough to make this thing conceivable. There may be the same heaven for all God's redeemed. There may be the same glorious presence, shedding its blessedness upon all. There may be the same right to sit at the marriage supper of the Lamb. There may be the same strains of entrancing melody, carrying home the harmonious and the beautiful to the spirits of all who are there. And yet it is perfectly conceivable that there may be a right hand and a left. Just because here on earth there has been produced in some a more exquisite meetness for the enjoyments which are found there, and a more enlarged wisdom, and a stronger power of love, therefore one soul may be drawn, as it were, more closely to God, and, consequently, to blessedness, than another can.

II. We have now, in the second place, to look at the principle on which all this is carried on. There is a right hand of God's throne. On what principle is that dignity conferred?

Now, to this Scripture answers, first of all, that it is not on a principle of arbitrary selection. The two apostles seem to have thought that it was. They appear to have conceived that their Master had the glories of the other world lodged in His hands for the purpose of being distributed according to His own personal affections. The prime-minister of a country is intrusted by his sovereign with certain dignities which he is at liberty to confer. But friendship, family connection, favor, regulate all these. And the apostles seem to have looked upon heaven's honors as distributed in that way, and so, in their spirit of eager manœuvring, they came as the first applicants to forestall a promise: "Grant unto us that we may sit, one on Thy right hand, and the other on Thy left, in Thy glory."

Let us mark our Redeemer's answer, for it is full of instruction: "To sit on My right hand, and on My left, is not Mine to give." Did He mean to tell them that the office of dispensing those glories was not His, but another's? Surely not; for the Son of Man will dispense them as the Judge at the last day. Did He mean to say that He had no authority of His own to give away the glories of heaven? Surely not; for there is given to Him authority: "All judgment is committed to Him, because He is the Son of Man." But the plain meaning was this, that they were not His to give by absolute or arbitrary right. There were certain eternal principles in the bosom of the Deity which must guide Him in their distribution. John the beloved asked this favor of his Lord, but Christ's personal love to John could not place him one step above another. Personal favor had nothing to do with it, justice everything. Steps of glory are not won by favoritism, if such a word may be reverently used. Not by arbitrary selection: It is not mine to give except to those "for whom it is prepared of My Father."

The last question, then, we have to ask is, Who are they for whom the Father has prepared the special glories of the life to come? There seems to be in our Master's conversation a most clear reply to this. They who have borne the sharpest cross are prepared to wear the brightest crown. They who best and most steadily can drain the cup which God shall put into their hands to drink are the spirits destined to sit on His right hand and on His left. Our Master's question was significant. They asked for honor. He demanded if they were willing to pay the price of honor: Can ye drink of My cup? Here, brethren, is the everlasting principle which no dispensation of favor can set aside. There is no preparation for any son of man except through suffering. The grandest diadem which God has to bestow upon His selected children of this earth is the crown of thorns. For highest blessedness there is no preparation without unusual trial.

And now, first of all, Christ submitted to this eternal law Himself. He became "obedient unto death, even the death of the cross; *wherefore* God also hath highly exalted Him." Prophets spoke in the old days of the "sufferings of Christ, and the glory that should be revealed." One was impossible without the other. Christ, being man, became subject to the irreversible law which binds humanity. Victory over trial, that is man's only glory. Christ had to suffer before it was possible for Him to reign.

Let us understand what this cup was which Jesus drank. It was martyrdom. Has any man ever tried to realize what it is to be a martyr? There was the agony of a sharp death, of course, but that was only a part. In days of martyrdom men live with the possibility of death before them. False hearts are apostatizing on every side, friends are weakening resolution, life is smiling with its promises of peace, and in the midst of all that a martyr has to steel his soul, and quietly bear the sickening, harrowing uncertainty, and then, when the cup is put into his hand at last, he has to drink it calmly and cheerfully as his Master did. All that men have done for the love of Christ. That is in the most literal sense Christ's baptism of blood. And it would seem to be the language of the Bible that there is a peculiar coronet of glory for men who suffer for the truth. But now, is there anything like this in daily life? Brethren, *much*. To be a martyr is to witness for Christ's truth. To be a martyr is to take up Christ's cross. The worst part of martyrdom is not the last agonizing moment; it is the wearing, daily steadfastness. Men who can make up their minds to hold out against the torture of an hour have sunk under the weariness and the harass of small prolonged vexations. And there are many Christians who have the weight of some deep, incommunicable grief pressing, cold as ice, upon their hearts. To bear that cheerfully and manfully is to be a martyr. There are many Christians who know what doubt is, such doubt as Christ experienced on the cross, shutting out light and consolation, and making this world a wilderness: "My God, my God, why hast Thou forsaken me?" To tread that down, as if with an iron heel, upon the serpent's head is to be a victorious martyr. There is many a Christian bereaved and stricken in the best hopes of life. For such a one to say quietly, "Father, not as I will, but as Thou wilt," is to be a martyr. There is many a Christian who feels the irksomeness of the duties of life, and feels his spirit revolting from them. To get up every morning with the firm resolve to find pleasure in those duties, and do them well, and finish the work which God has given us to do, that is to drink Christ's cup. The commonest life, brethren, has its cross for him who has the heart to love the cross. We do not want back the days of martyrdom. The humblest occupation has in it materials of discipline for the highest heaven, and for the right hand and the left in Christ's kingdom.

The cup which Christ drank was self-humiliation. This was the peculiarity of His death, that He *humbled* Himself unto death. God has prepared the right hand in His kingdom for the humble: "Whosoever will be great among you, let him be your minister; and whosoever will be chief among you, let him be your servant." The longer a Christian lives, the more he feels this, that the only true greatness is to destroy our evil selves—that self which cleaves to us, that self which ruins and degrades everything we do.

To conclude this subject there are two remarks to be made:

First, let the cross of Christ teach us to look calmly on this suffering world. Life is full of trial, and it is a perplexing thing to look around us and see the race of men groaning under their burden. We know but one satisfactory explanation of that strange mystery—thoroughly satisfactory—which calms all doubts. The cross of Christ is the explanation. The cross is the distinct announcement to us of that wonderful law which fills all life, that "through much tribulation we must enter into the kingdom of heaven." Perfection through suffering, that is the doctrine of the cross. There is love in that law. Trial is not the mark of an angry God; it is the evidence of deepest parental love. This is ever true, that the humblest Christians are the holiest, the most subdued are they whom God has baptized in suffering. Let us learn to take that view of this strange existence, for it is the true and cheerful view.

Secondly, we learn to leave our own future destinies calmly and trustfully in God's hands. The apostles asked Christ about their place in heaven, and He gave them no information on the subject; He left them upon that point entirely in the dark. He told them that exaltation is won through humiliation; He warned them that the preparation for a high heaven is sharp trial. But, whether theirs should be a high heaven or not, He did not choose to tell them. Now there is a distinct lesson for us here. Present duties, brethren, are ours; future destinies are in God's hands. Be content to leave them there in trust. The Father hath prepared for them that love Him the right hand and the left. We are to ask no more. Each of us will have his destined place. Each will occupy in the life to come exactly that position in which he can best perform God's appointed work.

Moreover, we gather from this Scripture that there is a sense in which every man's destinies are in his own hands. It is not by an arbitrary decree that heaven's highest places are given away. Christ bestows them on those for whom they are prepared by the Father. Those things which "eye hath not seen, nor ear heard" He has prepared for those who love Him. He has prepared them for the meek and humble in heart. He has prepared them for those who have with the most scrupulous fidelity borne the cross. There is also a sense in which every man's future position depends upon himself. Each place is regulated according to the way in which each man has fitted himself for it. What you are here, that, by a most righteous regulation, you will be hereafter. Oh! let this be our motive to diligence, that our "labor is not in vain in the Lord." Let us not be content with sowing little; sow much, that you may reap much. Every evil feeling that a Christian crushes is so much increased power of being happy. Every self-denying act that gives him more of the spirit of love is a clear step in blessedness. The more you learn here to understand God, the more you will be able hereafter to enjoy God. Every light affliction, borne as a cross should be borne, worketh out for you a "far more exceeding and eternal weight of glory." Christian brethren, work done faithfully in Christ shall by no means lose its reward.

III.

THE PHARISEE AND THE PUBLICAN.

(FROM AUTOGRAPH NOTES.)

Oxford, June 18, 1847.

"And he spake this parable unto certain which trusted in themselves that they were righteous, and despised others."—Luke xviii. 9.

THE subject of this parable is the Beauty of Christian humbleness, and the Danger of self-satisfaction.

I. Beauty of Christian humbleness, "He that humbleth himself shall be exalted."

Humbleness is peculiar to Christianity. Goodness is admired and taught in all religions. But to be good, and feel that your good is nothing; to advance, and become more conscious of pollution; to ripen in all excellence, and like corn to bend the head when full of ripe bursting grain—that is Christianity.

Observe the subtle, insinuating character of pride. It creeps in everywhere. Worldly pride is natural. But religious pride! To stand aloof because better! The idea of merit in a thing that errs every hour! This is marvellous!

"He that exalteth himself shall be abased." This shows the falsity of worldly estimation: "He that experiences self-gratification, and he whom the world exalts, shall be abased."

Here is a Pharisee, counted by his nation as religious. But God looks in, holds him up as a beacon, and says, You are all mistaken. To see ourselves as others see us, but still more as God sees us—be this our prayer. For there is a fearful day of reversal: "He shall be abased."

A solemn expression occurs among repeated denunciations of the Pharisees: "Whited sepulchres"—painted with color of purity. There is a false inscription: "Not what he was, but what he seemed to be." Is there a whited sepulchre among us now?

This abasement may take place—

In life: first, by discovery. The man is found out, for he cannot always stand apart; he gets known in his family, in business, and in society.

Or, again, by a grievous fall: "Pride goeth before destruction." A thing wafted on high by the wind comes down. It was Peter's boast, "Though I should die with Thee, yet will I not deny Thee." It is our own experience; for after what periods did our chief falls occur? . . .

In the dying hour: man generally does not die an actor. The mask falls off. Man fronts reality. He is going to stand before God, not before an ignorant publican. Think of that, and be self-satisfied if you can!

In the judgment-day: sometimes strong delusion holds a man fast on the death-bed. Therefore abasement comes not till trial by fire. Nothing stands then but gold. Gilding will not pass.

II. Danger of self-satisfaction.

(I.) Spirit of self-satisfaction.
(II.) Spirit of Christian penitence.

(I.) *Spirit of self-satisfaction.* The Pharisees, like all sectarians, stood apart. This is the danger of party spirit. When a congregation marks itself off from another congregation, when people get names — Evangelicals, Tractarians, etc. — and make all this minister to self-complacency, this is Pharisaism.

And against this Christ's indignation was roused. Never did it seem to burst forth but when a hypocrite, an unreal person, stood before Him. It was like the quiet ocean stirred from its depths, and the roar of the surges telling out its might.

There are certain marks exhibited in this Pharisaism:

1. Satisfaction with negative goodness. The Pharisee in the parable enumerates the faults from which he was free: he was no extortioner, no adulterer, nor yet unjust. Like men now on their death-beds, he was free from glaring impiety. Wretched boast! Not so bad as you might have been. A highwayman glorying that he is not a murderer. Well—few stripes—less hot hell! Is that any consolation?

And, after all, extortion, injustice — what temptation had a Pharisee to commit them? It was a comprehensible ground of boast for a rare publican. Government penal colonies, prisons, hulks, are full of the poor. Of course, how could the rich be there? Will the rich boast of that? Or will the poor boast that they are not duellists? Shall we boast of the freedom which comes from circumstance?

Moreover, he was free from adultery. Well, there are those who are pure because phlegmatic, and virtuous because constitutionally cold; and they call that virtue which is only nature. They

"Compound for sins they are inclined to
By damning those they have no mind to."

2. Satisfaction with external ceremonial acts.

Let us do this Pharisee justice. He put in a claim for something done, as well as something left undone: "I fast twice in the week; I give tithes of all that I possess."

But this was ceremonial goodness.

We must distinguish: moral goodness is goodness always and everywhere. Justice, mercy, truth, are the same under the tropic and at the pole, in the year 4000 before Christ and 4000 after Christ. But ceremonies are only good at certain times and under certain circumstances. Fasting, if it make a man peevish, is no duty. Tithes are a way of supporting God's ministers; but the Church or the State may provide another way, and then tithes cease to be duties.

Now, observe why Pharisaical men find it easier to be content with ceremonial observances than with moral goodness. They are definite acts; they can be counted. Twice a week the ceremony is done. Go over my fields; not a tenth sheath or shock is left standing. Search my stalls; not a tenth colt or calf is kept back.

But moral goodness is more a state of heart than distinct acts. Take the law of love; you cannot at night count up, and say "It is all done," for love has no number of acts.

3. Satisfaction with self: tenderness to self coupled with severity to others.

The Pharisee judges from appearances—"even as this publican;" yet *his* heart was gushing out to God. We know nothing of motives, nothing of temptations: "Judge not, and ye shall not be judged." Let us learn to modify our opinions of others.

Moreover, contempt shows and produces littleness of mind.

> "He who feels contempt
> For any living thing hath faculties
> That he hath never used; and thought with him
> Is in its infancy."

He narrows his own heart. There is an enlarging, ennobling power in admiration of others, and in making allowance for them.

In that contempt the Pharisee was doing more injury to himself than to the publican.

4. This satisfaction led to cant: "God, I thank Thee that I am not as other men are."

Religious people have a way of speaking of their past evil life as compared with the present, and of referring all difficulties to God's mercy. This is a subtle form of pride. It is former self sacrificed at the shrine of present self. It says, Admire me *now*. And the glory given to God is but a false show of humility, or a mask to admit features of self-praise.

Consider what cant is. The Pharisee was not a hypocrite in our sense—a wilful deceiver. In the Bible sense, a hypocrite is a false character. How came that? Public admiration is given to religion. We see its beauty; we wish to be admired as we admire. Now there is a danger of imitating what is admired. Hence upturned eyes, demure looks, peculiar tone, slang phrases. This is cant.

Be natural; clear your mind of cant; avoid phrases of a party, even Bible phrases. Have no phylacteries, which show that a man is bidding for a character.

Be religious. Be not anxious to *seem* so.

5. This satisfaction led, moreover, to the fluency of his prayer.

It was preaching to God, not praying. Well divided, accurate, regular, fluent.

"God is in heaven, and thou upon earth; therefore let thy words be few." To men we use rhetoric, eloquence, because they are influenced by it. To God we use the simplest, shortest words we can find, because eloquence is only air and noise to Him.

What people call fluency and the gift of prayer is often delusive; it is mere excitement from the presence of others, and from the sound of our own voice. Spiritual emotion and external emotion are often hardly distinguishable.

What are our prayers—the language of a full heart or of a full lip?

(II.) Spirit of religious penitence: "The publican, standing afar off, would not lift up so much as his eyes to heaven, but smote upon his breast, saying, God be merciful to me a sinner."

The publicans were not tax-gatherers simply, but farmers of the imperial revenue. They paid a certain sum to government, and reimbursed themselves. Hence the opportunity to oppress, to threaten with action, and to extort by fear. Consequently the profession became disreputable; and its disrepute made the despised men worse. Call a child perpetually a dunce, he will become stupid. Destroy self-respect in a man, he will become what he is thought.

Moreover, it was a low standing, and men were satisfied where all was bad. We see this was almost inevitable when we consider the publican's temptations; his exclusion from common hope; his likelihood to make the most of what little goodness he had.

And yet we see a sense of guilt: "Me a sinner."

Remark, there is no specifying: not, last week I injured a man; yesterday I terrified by a threat; last night I was in riotous society. Conviction of sin cannot stop to enumerate acts. The whole state of heart seems radically diseased. Like a wound in battle, you sicken over it. Let the anatomist care to discuss what nerves are contused and what veins severed; you cover it up, and look away: "I am wounded." So with the over-sensitive conscience.

And a plea for mercy: "God be merciful to me a sinner."

Under the law recollection of sin makes men worse. We live under law when we merely remember condemnation, duty, and transgression; when remorse and shame are the sole feelings. Then we become degraded in our own eyes, and feel helpless; and remorse only prepares for fresh failure. No element of hope finds a place under law.

To live under the Gospel is to understand God's love in Christ; to trust, to know that bygone guilt is buried in blood; to believe in remission of the sins that are past. This, and only this, makes past guilt a stepping-stone to future strength. Humble, tender, broken feeling, and withal loving too.

And confession: "To me a sinner."

Confession is the appointed power to relieve the burden of sin.

Confession does this because it gives the feeling of sincerity. We abjure our fault, we say to God, "It is not mine, I disown it; it is not I, but sin that worketh in me." My whole nature casts it out with throes and convulsions, as my flesh expels a foreign substance lodged in it—a thorn, a needle, with swelling and inflammation.

There is ease when we are rid of it. Observe, moreover, the instantaneousness of relief: "*He went down to his house* justified."

Sinner! go and confess AT ONCE.

IV.

THE CHRISTIAN'S HOPE AND DESTINY HEREAFTER.

(FROM AUTOGRAPH NOTES.)

Oxford, June 20, 1847.

"Beloved, now are we the sons of God, and it doth not yet appear what we shall be: but we know that, when he shall appear, we shall be like him; for we shall see him as he is."—1 John iii. 2, 3.

THE peculiarity of John's character was love.

He was more familiar with Christ than the other disciples; he had lain in His bosom. Hence he was more like Christ. He had drunk in his Master's looks, tones, character, way of thought, and form of speech. In his writings he is short and sententious; not arguing, but glancing down into the very heart of truth.

More than any man he was capable of judging what is meant by two expressions here used—" We shall be like Him;" " We shall see Him as He is." For he was like Him; he had seen Him as He was;, to him He had been unbosomed without disguise.

John can tell us what heaven is, and what spiritual life is. For every word of his shows that he considered it a thing of unutterable blessedness to be a Christian, and that he was accustomed to look beyond the grave as to a thing not dark, to regard it as full of grandeur, beyond what the wildest imagination of man can picture.

We consider—the Christian's hope and destiny hereafter.

The Christian's hope and destiny hereafter is partly mysterious: "It doth not yet appear what we shall be." It is partly certain: " We know that when He shall appear we shall be like Him."

I. The mystery of future existence: "It doth not yet appear what we shall be."

The mystery of future existence arises from three causes.

1. Our ignorance of the mode of existence.

There are two states to come—a state without our bodies, and a state with what is called a "spiritual body."

Here all sensations are connected with organized form. The beauty of this world, and of music, give sensations which plunge us into the infinite. But try to imagine that which is called "I" disembodied, existing apart from form! You cannot. A strange, lonely sensation of awe steals over us even in the attempt to realize "what we shall be."

Then consider the "spiritual body." Powers existing now only in rudiment shall then be fully developed. How unlike the oak is to the acorn! Yet the oak was in the acorn. Who could look at the acorn and form the wildest fancy of what the oak will be? Who conceive how earthly bodies will develop into spiritual bodies?

2. It is inconceivable what our feelings shall be.

All life here is associated with persons, relatives, home; there they "neither marry nor are given in marriage." Relatives are for temporary purposes. There, husband, father, wife, and children meet not *as* relations.

That state we cannot conceive now; nay, we ought not to try. A union with God so close as to dissolve all other unions would be inconceivable to us.

Therefore "it doth not yet appear what we shall be."

3. The place of that existence is inconceivable.

What is heaven—a place or a state? Where—what? "Eye hath not seen, nor ear heard; neither hath it entered into the heart of man to conceive the things God hath prepared."

Glory: what is it? Not brilliant light; not the little drop which men call fame; not shouts, nor processions, nor the homage of the multitude.

Heaven must be a state—a state of internal happiness. But there will also be external objects; for we read of floods of melody from everlasting harps, of temples of gorgeous magnificence.

In describing all this, Scripture speaks of things appreciable by the senses; for imagination paints this in vain—we do not understand it. Let us take two illustrations. A seaman strains through the evening fog to catch a glimpse of land; just as he makes out the outline, dim and vague, his eyes water, and all is dark. Or you lie on your back on a summer's day, straining into that quivering, trembling mass of blue. . . . So with that "undiscovered country," we strain till the mind is lost and dizzy. Again, consider the infant unborn. Its future state is inconceivable. Even light, the life and expounder of all things, is unknown. Now *this* life is the state of human babyhood. Life here is infancy.

II. The certainty in future existence.

Consider that part of our future destiny which we do know: "We know that when He shall appear we shall be like Him, for we shall see Him as He is."

St. John gives two characteristics of our future destiny—resemblance to God: "We shall be like Him;" and a clearer vision of Him: "We shall see Him as He is."

1. Resemblance to God—what is it?

God is the Fountain of Light and Wisdom. To be like God is to become wise, to gain mastery of intellect, to become less material and more purely things of mind; to have our darkness rolled away—the darkness of superstition, of ignorance, of evil—and to "walk in the light, as He is in the light."

"God is Love." To be like God is to love goodness, purity, truth. "If we love one another, God dwelleth in us." And now understand what love is. Take no earthly notions of weak, foolish fondness. Love is unselfishness; it is the power of sympathy to "rejoice with them that do rejoice, and to weep with them that weep;" it is to have something of that spirit of self-sacrifice which led Christ to lay down His life for us; it is to feel that all powers are given us to make others happy, and to be contriving forever happiness for others—that is to be like God.

God is Serenity. Christ the "same yesterday, to-day, and forever." Often have I felt, when fevered by earthly excitement and ruffled by earthly difficulties, as I looked up to the expanse of heaven above in the pure, still moonshine, that it was an emblem of God's unchanging calmness, rebuking the tumult within, and saying to the storm, "Peace, be still." Beneath that sky nations have maddened; ages upon ages there have been war, misery, evil passions; but the sky is there, as calm as when it looked down on Adam in his innocence. There sits God, enthroned in His everlasting calmness, with no agitation of emotions in Him. To approach this state is to be like God. The more serene a man be

—the more incapable of being ruffled and agitated by outward circumstances, looking on the universe as God does—the more nearly does he resemble God. And what is heaven? "There remaineth a rest for the people of God."

But an objection arises: you will say, How can we be all that—like God? He is the Creator, we the created; He infinite, we finite. To this I answer, There is that within you, even now, which tells that you may be like Him. There is something infinite in man. There is a human grandeur in the meanest here to-day.

The infinite character of the soul of man is proved by—

The capacity of remorse, and the anguish of guilt.

There are two kinds of fear. There is the fear of pain, a base fear, shared with the lower animals. You can keep a dog in order by fear of the lash. But the fear of polluting one's own heart, of darkening a light brighter than the sun—to possess a mind which dreads to wrong and betray and destroy itself—only man feels that.

And, oh, the unutterable anguish of a soul that is conscious of having degraded itself! It is a foretaste of the worm that never dieth. A noble mind fears that; and the nobler the mind, the keener the suffering. That is a proof of infinite majesty still remaining. A spirit that is capable of infinite misery is capable of receiving the infinitude of goodness.

Let us take as another proof of man's infinitude the examples of noble character of which we read in history, and also our own feelings in our better moments.

It is no dream, such men have been as Moses, Isaiah, Paul. Patriots—men who, while on earth, proclaimed the grandeur of their origin, and showed the divinity within them, by their pure and incorruptible public spirit—men such as Fabricius. Martyrs—men the energy of whose indomitable will the universe could not subdue. There they stood, the world against them. The tyrant crushed and mangled the body of Anaxagoras; he could not disturb the deep rest of the hero's soul. The fire crackled in their limbs; but their last look upward, till the eye shrivelled in its socket, proclaimed the feeling that God was near and in them. Was this a boundless or a finite nature?

Is it in books only that I have read of goodness, generosity, unselfishness? Nay, in human common life, in loving looks, in gentle words!

Meanest here! Have you never felt the stirrings of the God within you? Only now and then? Yes, but one glimpse of blue sky is enough as proof. See one gleam of the celestial behind the clouds of selfishness, and the possibility of likeness to God is proved.

Let us take another proof: Man's love of the sublime.

The heavens, the ocean, the rush of wind, the tempest, all wake in our hearts a strange enjoyment, but make the cattle tremble. What is the source of that proud feeling of ecstasy which makes man's spirit rise with the storm? It answers to the Infinite within him.

Montgomery's child was discovered by his lying down in a splendid bed. The son hears the voice of his father's home, and it has sounds that his spirit understands.

Never say that the being who feels all this cannot become like God.

Now, Christ came to elevate all this. . . .

2. A clearer vision of God: "We shall see Him as He is."

What is meant by *seeing* God? You will never see God as form and color. God is the spirit of beauty in nature at this season of the year, the spirit which makes all glow and burst with life; the spirit which guides sailing clouds and far-glittering star. Never can you see that with eyesight.

To see a thing is to comprehend its nature. "As He is," not deceptively: in His real, not distorted, nature.

The ship in a fog, the fish in the water, are not seen as they are.

Remove all impediments of sin and selfishness; take off the film from your eye, then you shall see God when His character shines as it really is. For example, this world seems evil; goodness—wisdom—all seems wrong. The ship is hideous, spectral, through the fog. To feel it all right—to see wisdom and goodness—that is to see God. Or, again, God seems your enemy—all wrath. This is a distorted view, like a crooked stick. See Him as love in Christ, then you see God. John saw Christ as He was, the Gadarenes did not.

Now observe the connection between likeness to God and seeing God. Mark the apostle's argument: No man can see God as He really is unless he resemble Him in character.

So in earthly life, to understand a public character such as a prime-minister, for example, and his measures, you must be on his side at least, and hold his opinions. Would you ask one of his political opponents for his character? Tell of his eloquent speech —all for effect; his wise measures—oh, love of fame; his generous patriotism—all cant.

So also in common life. An evil man cannot appreciate, or even see, a good man. The spiritual man is discerned by no man. The world suspects a sinister motive; will not believe in disinterestedness. Mark their sneer; listen to their insinuations; observe their contemptuous scepticism about human goodness.

And so with God. To see God, you must first be like Him. You see Him, feel Him, believe in His existence, just in proportion as you resemble Him in goodness. You have the witness in yourself. "We shall be like Him, for we shall see Him as He is."

V.

NATIONAL EDUCATION.—CHARACTER OF MOSES.

(FROM AUTOGRAPH NOTES.)

Oxford, June 27, 1847.

"In which time Moses was born, and was exceeding fair, and nourished up in his father's house three months: and when he was cast out, Pharaoh's daughter took him up, and nourished him for her own son. And Moses was learned in all the wisdom of the Egyptians, and was mighty in words and in deeds."—Acts vii. 20-22.

THE subject of national education has of late years become familiar to us in pamphlets, newspapers, sermons, parliamentary speeches, conversation. "The people must be educated"—this is the echo. Yet, with all this popularity, it is uncertain whether we adequately understand what education means; and whether, with all this praise of knowledge, knowledge is loved for its own sake, or only for what it brings—loved because talent is admired, and knowledge helps in life.

It is my intention to put forward hints to be worked out by yourselves. My way of investigation is, to take the life of a man highly and completely educated; and so make the subject a real one. A chief personage in Scripture, Moses, stands at the head of a dispensation.

Our subject divides itself into two branches:

I. The education of the lawgiver of Israel.
II. The results of that education.

I. The education of Moses.
1. He was instructed by strangers.

Pharaoh's daughter found him in the Nile, and had him taught Egyptian learning at her own expense. So far this is a parallel to the education of children in schools by strangers. Instruction by parents is not always possible, because of their incapacity, ignorance, poverty, and labor. Moses' parents were crushed down by the laws of Egypt. Therefore education must partly be the work of strangers.

Observe, God appointed a princess to instruct Moses, as if to honor the teacher's office. There are great mistakes on this point. People say, Any man will do. But your watch-spring is broken—do you give it to a blacksmith? Its wheels are deranged—do you confide it to a wheelwright? No, it is too delicate. Can a common mind guide that delicate, ethereal, mysterious thing—a child's soul? We must understand human nature, read hearts. We want first-rate men.

Miserable economy in parents! The poor grudging one penny per week. Esau sold his birthright for a morsel of meat; you weigh your child's mind and soul against copper! The rich spending on accomplishments and grudging the teacher. Alas! we do not estimate the teacher. We measure his services grudgingly, and *we must* for want of funds.

Consider the influence of teachers. Thirty-five hundred years ago an Egyptian princess took a poor man's child and taught it. The result of that education is not over yet. A thousand thousand Jews reverence the laws that child made. The nation he formed and freed lives on. Compare the influence of Pharaoh's daughter with that of Pharaoh himself. He ruled an empire. Pyramids could rise at his bidding. His skeleton is in some pyramid. Nothing else remains! To rule in a single heart, to form and guide a child's mind, is greater than the grandest sway. I say it calmly, the teacher is greater than the king. The king rules without, the teacher within. It is the influence that is deep compared with the influence that is widely spread in glory, glitter, and noise. Whether is greater, to educate a child or to rule a state? Let it be tried by the test of blessing your fellow-creatures. Here is a man perched up on high, dressed in a little brief authority, with fingers pointing: That is he! And here is *Christ with children round Him:* "He took them up in His arms, put His hands upon them, and blessed them."

2. He was under home influences.

By a merciful arrangement, Moses' early years were not entirely superintended by Pharaoh's daughter. His mother nursed him. Pharaoh's daughter gave him instruction, his mother education.

There are mistaken notions on this point. People think education to be reading, writing, ciphering; loading the memory with information, and making preparation for a trade or profession. You may do all this to make your child an expert accountant or a good engineer; you may infuse knowledge, and useful knowledge, such as geography and literature, to enable him to earn his bread. Well, is that all? Nay, it is only the wisdom of Egypt.

We must distinguish between education and instruction. Education is to unfold nature; to strengthen good and conquer evil; to give self-help; to make a man. To draw out the affections, we must cultivate the heart. To awaken great ideas we must generate the spirit of freedom. To direct the soul to God. . . .

The teacher cannot do this. Books cannot infuse religion; the catechism cannot.

You want influence bearing on the heart.

Now, influence is given at home. It is God's plan. He gives the father to impart strength of will, and the mother tenderness of affection.

Moses owed his lawgiving, his politics, his wisdom, his power of governing, to the Egyptian princess; his religion he owed to Jochebed.

Jochebed — that woman of poverty and toil; her hands black with brickmaking; bred in ignorance and crushed down. Jochebed, that woman of faith, whom love to God enabled to disobey the laws of Egypt. Mothers, know your work! You stand at the fountain-head. God has given you the destinies of the world. All great men had mothers high-minded. Our schools fail for want of mothers and home influences. When your child leaves school he has got instruction; what he wants is education.

3. He was disciplined by circumstances.

Pharaoh's daughter had done something, and Moses' mother something, for the child. But to make him the man he was, other things beyond man's control contributed.

He belonged to an oppressed nation: hence his patriotism—that deep, long devotion to one vast cause which can only be felt in such circumstances.

He was a banished man: hence his sympathy with the crushed.

He was a long time in the solitary desert: hence his depth and solemnity of character.

He travelled much: hence his knowledge of the world and man, and his enlarged views.

But he needed some sudden impulse. It came in the burning bush, which at the age of eighty fixed his destiny, and spurred him on to a new life. The man of learning, the man of contemplation, became the man of public action.

Observe, therefore, in the first place, education goes on through life. After he left Egypt and home, his development continued. Parents and teachers alone do not educate a child. He is given to the universe. All life contributes. The aspects of nature—summer and winter, bright spring and sad autumn, day and night, with their thousand sensations.

The lot of many is poverty, with struggling, scrambling life: hence their hardness of character. It is often the lot of the orphan: hence may spring self-help; or, if the disposition be weak, bad habits. Riches may stunt the child's moral growth, and produce, in spite of expensive education, only indolence of character.

Again, we are disciplined by public circumstances. We live in time of war or of peace, during a revolution, or in an age of trade, science, and philosophy. All this disciplines the character. Therefore education does not end with the schoolroom. We talk of "finished education!" Education only ends when a man is in his winding-sheet. The best teacher is he who sends forth children not only with great attainments, but convinced that education is the work of life, and resolved to improve themselves. It may be said, "If circumstances thwart education, and form character, why educate at all? Great minds have risen without education." Yet observe; education is useful to call forth power to grapple with and modify circumstances. Trees on the sea-coast or in stony soil are thwarted, yet they may be pushed by agriculture. The best agriculture is in Scotland, which has but a poor soil.

Observe, in the second place, education is God's work, for circumstances come from God. Teaching cannot do all; we must look for fruit to God. We must wait for our best impulses, which come like a flash, unexpectedly: "The wind bloweth where it listeth, and thou hearest the sound thereof, but canst not tell whence it cometh, and whither it goeth: so is every one that is born of the Spirit." Look back upon our past lives; what governed our most remarkable moments and alterations in character? Not systematic education, but some impression like that of Moses in the wilderness, that looked like chance; an impression from some great kindled soul which expands hearts; or an old truth forcibly put. Our grand ideas and alterations of character come we know not how or why. They come as glimpses, or as suggestions. And for this the simple life like that of Moses in the wilderness is most favorable.

Teaching the catechism does not impart religion. You want God's voice. The flash from above; the bush in the wilderness set on fire without human agency.

Review what education is. Formation of character—Development of the entire man—To put man in possession of self.

II. Results of Moses' education.

(I.) On his own character.

(II.) On his nation and on the world.

(I.) The result on his own character was twofold, mental and moral.

1. Mentally, it gave him the habit of inquiry. He turns aside "to see this great sight *why* the bush is not burnt." Other men would have simply seen the bush on fire; Moses remarks the singular phenomenon.

The first thing in education is to encourage a habit of observation and inquiry. When your child asks, "What is the use of this? why is that?" don't call it troublesome. The best education is that which is the answer to our own inquiries. Cultivate the habit of asking "Why?" But, observe, not "why" in duty. "Why" in phenomena of nature and art is the acknowledgment of ignorance; "why" in practical duties is the boast of presumption.

2. Morally, it gave him boldness and tenderness. Many men are bold, yet tyrannical withal; many tender, yet effeminate and weak. The perfect character joins both.

Observe Moses when his fellow-countryman is injured—one moment more, and the Egyptian is in his own blood at Moses' feet. Wild, irregular justice was permissible in those wild times, when there was no legal redress to be had.

Again, observe him in defence of Jethro's daughters at the well. He is ever the champion of the oppressed. The shepherds drive the women away. Moses says, "Not so; this is God's well; you shall not have it. By the law of the Most High God might is not right. I stand one man against you all."

High and noble spirit!

But, now, was this tyranny? Nay. Moses was no quarrelsome person, no seeker-out of brawls. Witness his attempt at peace-making: "Sirs, ye are brethren; why do ye wrong one to another?"

This is a noble disposition; to be firm, daring, true, a man that can't be put down in the cause of right; yet, at the same time, tender, gentle, loving.

3. But Moses was more. He was mentally great, morally good; but, besides, Moses was religious.

This is shown in his reverence: he takes off his shoes in humble adoration.

In obedience: God says he is to go before Pharaoh, and God's will is law; he will brave the angry king.

In meekness: he was humble as a child; a deeply gifted man, but self-distrustful; "very meek above all men who were upon the face of the earth."

A beautiful thing it is to see all excellencies crowned by religion.

And now remember all this was the effect of education. This is what we mean by education: it is to produce mental power, moral worth, and religious character.

(II.) The public results of Moses' education; that is, its results on his nation and on the world.

The result on his own nation was chiefly the elevation of the laboring classes.

Let us describe the political degradation of Israel. There were two classes in society, a ruling and a ruled. In all ages there is something similar; but in this case it was not the question between rich and poor, but between superior and inferior nations, like that between the whites and the blacks in slave countries. The Egyptian policy was to keep the Israelites down, to refuse them educational and political privileges, to prevent their increase of population. And the task of Moses was the emancipation of his people.

So is that of every Christian. Let us define what we mean by the education and elevation of the laboring classes. It is not to exempt them from toil; this were no blessing. Labor is a blessing. The rich would be happier if they were forced to spend some hours each day in manual toil. Labor brings out strength of character. A world where all was rest would make the human race degraded. Neither is it to introduce them into society, for there is the misery of fashionable life. It is not to break down classes. Christianity levels; education levels; but they level up. Mistaken men would level down. Elevation of the poor is to give them moral and religious worth; to strengthen their minds; to raise them above the almost brute life they lead to the higher life of the spirit; to make them men; to make them like the Israelites, *free*. But observe, free from their own selves, the worst of all tyranny. "He is a freeman whom the truth makes free." Had Moses freed Israel and given them no education and no religion, it would have been but a poor boon.

And now observe. Egyptian policy prevented all this. The wisdom of Egypt would have been to say, "These Israelites are a great people; let us treat them as brothers. Let us so treat them that their inventions, their skill, their labor, shall be shared by us; so that when Egypt is invaded they, feeling it their home, may fight side by side with us, the Israelite and the Egyptian, for a common country." They did not do this; therefore, at last, by apparent chance, the Israelites got intelligence, they got numbers, and they learned their power. They said, "We will be free." Egypt might have raised them gradually. Raised suddenly, a revolution was the consequence. The hosts of Egypt were buried in the Red Sea as the result of their own infatuated policy; just because they would not give Israel's lower classes a national education.

There might have been a pyramid erected on the shore with this inscription: "Here lies a nation which perished because . . ."

Let us say a few words of application. Thank God, the time has passed when English policy was the policy of Egypt. Fifty years ago the insane cry was raised, "The people must not be educated because it will unfit them for their station, and teach them to cope with us." Thank God, the echo of that cry has died away.

Egypt's sovereign said, "The people shall be crushed down." A voice from England's throne has said, "My people shall be instructed." Egyptian aristocracy sided with their sovereign. The horsemen who perished with their chariots in the Red Sea were sided with their sovereign, and would have kept the Israelites slaves. And English aristocracy have also sided with their sovereign. I speak as the mouth-piece of a society composed of English clergy and English nobles when I say, "Let us raise our poor brethren to our own level." "Sirs, ye are brethren; why do ye wrong one to another?"

Thank God for this. The mighty chasm between rich and poor is filling up. That selfish, useless indolence, that savage, sullen hatred, are alike disappearing, and men are beginning to feel the very reverse of the Egyptian policy. If England is to be happy and great, we must be one nation, not two; rich and poor joined together in bands of unity and chains of love.

Yet there is a discouraging aspect also. History tells that the struggle between rank and numbers has sometimes ended in a satisfactory adjustment. But in the struggle between wealth and numbers we have had no example yet; there has been national ruin in every case.

Therefore, my first appeal to-day is to you as Englishmen. The only thing which stands between us and national revolution is to educate our poor, to make them feel that we do not monopolize wealth and education; that we are their friends, not their enemies.

My second appeal is to you as Christians. Egyptian instruction is not education. It must be joined with religion, and that on the basis of the Bible.

VI.

THE KINGDOM OF HEAVEN.

(FROM AUTOGRAPH NOTES.)

Oxford, July 11, 1847.

"And when he was demanded of the Pharisees when the kingdom of God should come, he answered them and said, The kingdom of God cometh not with observation: neither shall they say, Lo here! or, Lo there! for behold, the kingdom of God is within you."—Luke xvii. 20, 21.

THIS passage was occasioned by the sarcastic question of the Pharisees: "He was demanded of the Pharisees when the kingdom of God should come."

If we ask what was the expression most frequent on our Redeemer's lips, the answer is, "The kingdom of God." It was this which occasioned the fear in Herod, and the slaughter of the Innocents: "Where is He that is born King of the Jews?" It forms the subject of a petition in the Lord's Prayer: "Thy kingdom come." Again, in the parables, the kingdom of heaven is likened unto leaven, etc. A voice was heard in the wilderness: "Repent ye, for the kingdom of heaven is at hand." It was the definite announcement of a Church to be set up on earth.

A man who is filled with one idea, repeating it, is looked upon as a dreamer, an enthusiast. People smile when they hear his project, as a kind of monomania. So the repetition of "kingdom of heaven" became at last ludicrous in the ears of the Pharisees. The same words were repeated again and again. But months and years rolled by. Jesus continued teaching simply as usual, and there was nothing resulting. Then they would smile and sneer. At last they came to Him, and said: "Well, when is this kingdom, that we hear so much of, to come? We have heard of it long, we should like to see it."

Jesus then unfolded his own meaning, and explained why they had not seen it.

His answer divides our subject into two branches:

I. What is meant by the "kingdom of heaven?"
II. The false expectations of men concerning it.

I. What is meant by the kingdom of heaven? Let us define our notion of a kingdom. Literally, it is a place where a sovereign's influence rules; in this sense it is the reign of a person. Figuratively, it means the domain in which one principle predominates; in this sense it is the reign of a principle.

The vegetable kingdom is the place where vegetable life reigns. The animal kingdom where sentient, conscious, feeling life reigns. And this is not bounded by locality, by earth, air, or water; not "Lo here, lo there." Nor is it limited by form. We see it in the small green insect on the leaf, and in the whale tumbling in the seas. It presents no outward uniformity; it is a *kingdom within*.

Again, take the kingdom of England. Wherever the laws of the English sovereign are acknowledged, there is the kingdom. Not in this bounded isle alone, on land or water, in Europe or Asia, so that we can say, "Lo here." Nor can it be recognized by dress, language, color, for the kingdom is within—it "cometh not with observation." Wherever a foreign flag is lowered in token of admitted superiority, there is the English empire of the seas. Wherever the colonist's axe hews forests away under government protection; wherever the royal salute is fired, and the submission of the subject paid; and wherever the offended majesty of British law claims a victim—the hangman's rope drawn, and the hangman's bolt let fall—there is the kingdom.

Observe, there are four ideas connected with the notion of a kingdom—the expansion of the kingdom; the power; the glory; and the right of judging.

These four you find in the Scriptural notion of the kingdom of heaven. Wherever God rules, and God's character prevails, and God's laws are recognized.

We see the idea of expansion in the parable of the mustard-seed; here is colonization.

The idea of power: "He shall reign for ever and ever;" here the flag lowered.

The idea of glory on the Mount of Transfiguration, and in the archangel's trumpet; here the salute of the universe.

The idea of punishment: when the kingdom of God came in the destruction of Jerusalem; here the right of execution.

There is one idea in all this; the kingdom of heaven means the rule of God and Righteousness on this earth.

Three characteristics marked the entrance of this kingdom into the world.

The first is its silence: it "cometh not with observation;" it is secret and unostentatious. There is no parade, no display; but as a still small voice. There stood Christ: nothing wonderful in His look; and the Pharisees asked for the kingdom when the King stood before them!

And so in all God's great movements. The great revolutions in this world are brought about quietly. Look at a conqueror! His name goes through the world like a peal of thunder. Twenty years elapse, and what has he done? The destroyed towns are built up again, as if he had cut through the ocean. The battle is over, the slain are buried, the cannon silent.

Look, on the contrary, at the power of a truly holy thought. It *lives.* That still, small voice—the universe begins to hear it. Which is mightiest, the lightning glaring, or the genial gentle vegetation of this season making all nature burst out in beauty and in joy?

The second characteristic is that it was internal: "The kingdom is within you." A day is coming when God's rule shall be felt in crushing, outward power. It will be His execution; the expunging of evil from the earth. But His real truest kingdom is seen in voluntary submission.

Look at these two pictures—In the one, subjects kept down by force, tithes and taxes collected at the point of the bayonet, rebels marched off under armed escort. In the other, a king issuing beneficent laws from his cabinet: he himself is not seen, but his name revered; no armed police, but smiling corn-fields, health, towns stately, and commerce prosperous. Which is the truest picture of a kingdom, compulsion or grateful acquiescence? The kingdom is within you.

Christ did reign. When the Pharisees spoke, the King had already come. He reigned in the fishing-boat, etc. And this is God's kingdom. In one sense we are all subjects of God's kingdom, because within His power. In another sense, and that the truest, only those are in it who receive His laws—the laws of love and self-denial, with a pure heart and life. This is a simple truth, but a sublime one. God reigns in the heart; God's kingdom is a kingdom of goodness.

But men find substitutes for this "Lo here!" something tangible, visible, and localized—forms, creeds, priesthood, etc. Therefore a third characteristic is that it is not local.

II. False expectations of men concerning the kingdom of God.

1. The kingdom of God is not a Church kingdom. Ask men what they mean by extending Christ's kingdom, and we find that many mean extending their own form of Church government. So Rome compelled men to be baptized by thousands, and made subjects of the Pope. The Churchman thinks he extends the kingdom if he can get Episcopacy established over the world; the Presbyterian, if he can get Presbyterianism; the Dissenter, if he can get his own form. This is proselytizing, not to Christ and goodness, but to party.

Well, it is done. Here you have sacraments all regular, and consecrated buildings, and ministers apostolically ordained; but worldly men and women come—flaunting, gay, idle persons—to stare: is that the house of God? If men are here with hearts and lives straining after God, it matters little what the building is—"This is no other than the house of God."

Observe the feverish desire to find the true Church; the anxiety to know, Do I belong to the true Church? Let us inquire, first, Am I a true member of any Church? It is a matter of some importance to be in the right Church, but not of the first importance. Fénelon, Robert Hall, and other such like-minded men were in wrong churches. A Church is a society of men for putting down evil. The framework of a Church is a hothouse to ripen and mature. I believe that a hothouse will nurture grapes better than outdoor culture; yet if I find a Hampton Court vine, I do not say these are not grapes, but I say, I would not try the experiment again, though it has succeeded here. I say, his Church is a bad system for making Christians; but it has made a Christian of him.

Mark, you do not become a Christian by entering the true Church, but the Church is made by true Christians entering it. It is not the Church which makes Christians, but Christians which make the Church. This feverish desire to find the true Church, this anxiety to know do I belong to the true Church, arises from the Pharisaical error: the expectation that certain mysterious influences will act upon us from without, independently of our own activity and toil. Dreams! dreams! The framework of the Church is a help, not a force; mere outward culture to nurture the kingdom within you.

2. Nor is it a State kingdom. People expect the regeneration of society from political government and acquired rights. This is another dream. Witness the ardent expectation throughout Europe during the French Revolution.

Samuel's sons were exchanged for Saul—was it an improvement? In Chartism *we* have seen great hopes and great changes, yet society remains much the same. Life goes on as usual; there is the same struggle.

> "How small, of all that human hearts endure,
> That part which laws or kings can cause or cure!"

You get your darling measure, and then things settle down as before. Evil hearts are not subdued by State regulations. Contentment does not come. Poverty does not vanish. You get rid of the tyranny of an aristocracy, and get the tyranny of a mob.

Reform yourselves. Often I have thought of this when I have seen political placards in workshops, inscribed with some feverish cry of the day. When will the kingdom of God come? It is the same old cry doomed to disappointment. Brethren, the Pharisees asked that question. It never came, because they were for beginning outwardly. If they had got rid of the Roman yoke, what then? Christ was divinely wise, and He said, "Free yourselves; if the Son shall make you free, ye shall be free indeed." Not political oppression, but the slavery of sin, is your malady. Christ was quite content with existing forms; there were better, but there were also worse.

Do I speak to one who burns with the idea of doing good to his country by this measure or that measure? Well, I honor it! It is generous! A high yearning, but a dream. Do not expect more than political improvement is capable of giving. Prepare for disappointment. The sad page of history says that countries got free and civilized, and that human happiness was not increased because the kingdom was a State kingdom. There may be happiness in Austria or Russia; Paul, under the Roman government, was in prison, and was yet happy; and so are all who have the kingdom *within*. The natural man strives from things outward to things inward; and hence the Mohammedan kingdom and its failure; hence the failure of desolating pestilences, which only make the reckless more reckless still; and hence the failure of Rome.

3. Neither does it consist in outward forms. Some people think the kingdom of God will come when we all worship after the same pattern, and when forms are alike in liturgies, dresses, and hymns.

The best intentions in the world are at the bottom of this mistake. Laud tried it; he punished and pilloried, and nearly got it; but his sovereign lost his throne, and England was convulsed. A few years before, Elizabeth made Dissenters. A few years after, two thousand of the best ministers in England were driven from the Church.

Let us distinguish between Unity and Uniformity. Unity is inward resemblance; Uniformity, outward. The army is one; yet is different in arms, dress, and accoutrements. Uniformity would destroy its unity. It is complete unity ruled by one will.

In a garden with box and quickset clipped and squared, we have uniformity; in another garden with each tree growing in its own natural way, yet planned by a pervading mind which has placed them so as to harmonize, we have unity.

Artificial crushing forms are not life nor union. Love is the bond of perfectness. Let forms differ! Forms must be! But let each Church choose those which most naturally express its own feelings. Christ's kingdom is not in forms, but within you.

4. Nor is it found in locality. It is a common error to say "Lo here, or, Lo there," which binds religion and God to a certain place. It is the old controversy between the Jews and the Samaritans. It is the controversy as to the sacraments. There are people who fancy that regeneration is in the water, and Christ in some mystical way in the bread and wine after some magical words. Observe the localization of this "Lo here." Or, again, people say a Church is a holy place. So it is if holy people be in it—not else; the kingdom is within you, not in stones. Where is the holiest place on earth? Where souls breathe the holiest vows, and execute the most heroic purposes. Where is the Holy of Holies in this city? Perhaps in some small, dark, miserable room. Where does God reign, where are His splendors felt? Is it in the pealing organ, or in a good man's soul? Where music pours out its melody, or where human hands have collected all graceful and all lovely forms?

Again, if we speak of locality, people would say where Christ was, or where some pious minister is. But Christ was there to the Pharisees, and yet was no king to them. The kingdom of God is not a thing near you, but a thing *in* you.

And so people run about. Salvation is not got in a place, here or there. It does not depend on finding the best teacher or the best book. They are like a young boy running about from study to garden, from sunshine to shade, from shade to garret, from posture to posture, trying to fix his mind. He carries desultory feelings within him, go where he will. Attention is not got by change of place. Let him sit down where he is, and seek the kingdom of thought within him, and the power of will.

So in religion. People look to helps, they change from Church to Church. This is the secret of the recent secessions to Rome. Men who could not find sympathy and assistances. They become restless, and come back. Try the helps you have. Christ's own presence would not give you what you want. A Christian thrives anywhere.

VII.

THE SECRET GROWTH OF THE SEED.

(FROM AUTOGRAPH NOTES.)

Oxford, July 15, 1847.

"And he said, So is the kingdom of God, as if a man should cast seed into the ground."—Mark iv. 26.

LAST Thursday we examined the subject of the entrance of Divine life into the soul in the case of Jacob. Conversion consisted both in impressions and resolves. Jacob's impressions arose from his leaving home, from the direct voice of God, and from feeling the full earnestness of life. His resolves were the fastening upon him recollections, and the devoting self and substance to God.

To-day we take the subject of the sustentation of the Divine life.

The Divine life is real. Ask you what it is? There have been men to whom it was so real that no outward temptation could seduce them from its contemplation; no outward menace deter them.

Tyrants let loose the lion and the flame in vain. There are other men who see nothing beyond the present, and who live for it— men to whom goodness is a dream; they are of the earth, earthy.

And the Divine life is supported by discipline here. Seventy years are given for the education of the spirit. Life infused in the Infinite is one thing; life supported another.

Our subject divides itself into two branches:

I. Progress of the life of God in the soul of man.
II. Periods of its development.

I. 1. Real life is that which has in it a principle of expansion. It "springs and grows up." Moreover, it is not only growth, but tendency ever towards a higher life. Life has innate energy, and will unfold itself according to the law of its own being. Its law is progress towards its own possible completeness: such completeness as its nature admits of.

By this we distinguish real life from seeming life. As you cut the stone and carve it, so it remains. But cut a tree; lop off its branches, strip it; it will shoot and sprout. Only deadness remains unaltered. Trees in winter all seem alike. Spring detects life. Man can impart motion, and make automatons. Growth and power he cannot give.

This is the principle of all life. And in the higher life especially, there is not only expansion, but progress. The limpet on the rock only increases in volume. The plant develops into the flower. The insect develops from the egg into the caterpillar, grows, spins itself a coffin, and becomes hard and shelly. But the life goes on, and it emerges a brilliant butterfly. Look at a child sprawling on the floor, then think of railways, steamships, manufactures. The power of mind is developed out of the materialism of baby pulp.

Observe, therefore, the test of the real life of God is growth.

Amiability dies, grace grows, as life goes on.

2. Real life is that which has individual, independent energy: it "bears fruit of itself."

Observe its hardihood. It needs no petting. It is no hothouse plant. Let the wild winds of heaven blow upon it, with frost, scorching sun, and storms. Religion is not for a cloister, but for life, real hardy life. Observe Christ's religion, and compare it with the fanciful religion of cloistered men. Religious books which speak of fastidious, retiring, feeble delicacy. The best Christianity grows up in exposure. The life of Christ Himself is an illustration of this. So, too, that of the apostles in the world, and that of a Christian in the army.

Again, it can be left to itself safely. It will grow. Ministers need not torment themselves about the issue of their work, for God gives the increase. It can be left; for it is God in the soul. When once the farmer has sown, he can do little more except weed.

Moreover, it *is* apparently left to itself by God. There is no visible interference. God seems to sleep—sleep "night and day." God's work seems left. So was it in the progress of the Church. Christ withdrew, and the Church's history is a perpetual question whence came the tares? Evil men prosper. There are no lightning flashes!

And thus is it in the individual soul. The planting of life is often almost a visible interference of God. Afterwards all is silent; no interposition. Even prayer is left unreplied to.

Once more, we observe the sacredness of individual character—of Originality. It bears fruit *of itself* in its own individual development. The process is never exactly repeated. Life is no mechanical thing. It is everywhere alike, yet different. Count the leaves and grains, measure the height of the trees, notice the sheep, examine the leaves on an oak! So in the Christian life. No two men think the same, or believe the same. It is always so in the highest life, and in national character. There is ever a beautiful diversity.

3. Its growth is mysterious, secret: "He knoweth not how."

The law of development is hidden though real. After long years, work is visible. In agriculture you cannot see the growth. Pass that country two months after, and there is a difference. So in a clock. You cannot see it move. But the hand is altered when you look again. It has described a large revolution on the dial-plate.

So we grow. It is marvellous when and where we get our Christian knowledge. Not systematically, but here and there. A man whom you have known young, you meet again in middle age, and you ask, Where did he get all this knowledge, this character, this heavenliness?

There are Christians who are anxious to see growth. They scratch, and dig away at the root. Wait!

4. It manifests itself *incessantly* during daily occupations; while " rising night and day."

Go and stand by a field at night. Men are asleep. No light in you cottage. But growth and motion are in that field, and more rapidly by night than by day. We learn even when we are doing nothing—contemplating, suffering.

Our souls do not rest any more than our bodies. Hearts beat out their life-pulses while asleep.

There comes a solemn feeling at moonlight, and by the seaside, or by Schaffhausen. The Spirit of the Universe moving on! Mighty pulse!

So we acquire firmness and experience incessantly. Every action, every word, every meal is part of our trial and our discipline. We are assuredly ripening, or else blighting.

II. Periods of development—blade, ear, full corn in the ear.

Sometimes these periods correspond with periods of life; sometimes not. The blade may be in old age, the man born when he is old. Or in very youth there may be maturity of yellow corn.

1. The blade. Marked by tenderness and negativeness.

No distinct views—"blown about with every wind of doctrine." The only feeling of life is the desire to live to God. And better so. Men who begin with rigid views of Church, etc., and whose religion begins in opinion and controversy, are not so healthy as they who begin with feeling—Divine life rather than Divine creed—*Amanda* rather than *Credenda*. Young brethren, we are not anxious to give you views, but convictions—warm hearts rather than definite opinions.

Negativeness: no distinct character. What is it to be? Oats, barley, rye, wheat, tares? It is an anxious moment when a child is born; it is an anxious moment when first religious thoughts come. Blade—but what? Wheat, to be gathered into God's garner, or only a weed?

2. The ear. Marked by vigor and beauty.

Vigor: erect, with decision, fixed principles and views.

Beauty. Describe the flowering petals, etc. Solemn season. What promise! What thoughtfulness! Yet blight is more frequent now—prostration.

Deep solemn silence in Confirmation.

3. Full corn in the ear. Marked by maturity and ripeness. It

has no further stage of development on earth. It must die and sprout again. But its present work is done.

The few stalks that stand rot: they have not been ripened. The old man in his imbecility. He might have borne more grains, etc., but *his* ripeness is over.

What is ripeness? Completeness, all powers equally cultivated. It is the completion of the principles, feelings, and tempers.

This period is also marked by humility and by joy. By humility: the head hangs gracefully down in token of ripeness; always so with men of great attainments. "I am but a little child," said Newton, "picking up pebbles on the shore of the vast ocean of truth." By joy: the happy aspect of waving corn! But its beauty is chiefly felt by the thoughtful man. It is the calm deep joy of the harvest being safe, and famine impossible. The food of a nation waves before him.

Perhaps the green blade might be more beautiful if this association were not felt.

So is the joy of age. Deep, calm, nearness to God.

Sickle—harvest—well!

There is a truer, deeper happiness of age than of youth.

VIII.

THE LAW OUR SCHOOLMASTER.

(FROM AUTOGRAPH NOTES.)

Brighton, September 19, 1847.

"Wherefore the law was our schoolmaster to bring us unto Christ, that we might be justified by faith. But after that faith is come, we are no longer under a schoolmaster."—Gal. iii. 24, 25.

This verse contains the information that God's dealing with His world is a kind of education. The word "schoolmaster" implies this. God treats His world as schoolmasters should treat their children.

Therefore we contemplate the world's development as an education. And from the way in which God brought the world from infancy to manhood we learn the deep principle on which our own system of education should be conducted.

There was a time of the world's minority, and a time when the world came of age. These times were marked by two different stages of feeling—bondage and liberty; and by two different principles of action—acting from law and acting from faith. There was the time when Moses was the world's schoolmaster, and the time when Christ became the world's higher teacher.

This principle is an extended one.

It is true in national life. There is the period when laws which grow into a constitution are rigidly observed; and also the period when all these, like a scaffolding, are relaxed in rigor, because the nation has got that character, good or evil, which the constitution was capable of giving. The old forms have gone, the spirit lives on.

It is no less true in the single heart's life. In the heart history of every religious man there are two periods, longer or shorter, more or less definitely marked (for one passes into the other)—the state of pupilage and the state of faith. There is a time when he acts from law, and a time when he acts from a larger, more liberal, more noble principle—that of faith. A time when he is under law, and a time when he is without law.

Take these verses. Read them. Observe the broad general sentiment. These two stages must be kept separate and observed in their right order. One must go before the other. There was a time when God put His world under a schoolmaster, then it would have been preposterous to apply faith. There is a time when a larger spirit has come, and then it would be going back to use law: "After that faith is come, we are no longer under a schoolmaster."

Our subject, therefore, divides itself into two branches:

I. The uses of restraint in the heart's education.
II. The time when restraint may be laid aside.

I. The uses of restraint in the heart's education. "The law was our schoolmaster to bring us unto Christ, that we might be justified by faith." *How* was this? We use the word "restraint," and substitute it for the word "law," as more intelligible. Law to a Jew meant what we mean by a system of checks and restraints. And that whether by special laws or by the forms in which religious feeling was to be guided.

1. The first use of law is to restrain from open violence; to act

as a check: "The law is not made for a righteous man, but for the lawless and disobedient, for the ungodly and sinners, for unholy and profane." That is, it was made to check transgression, it was "added because of transgression."

As an example of this use, let us take the law against coiners. It was not made for us; we are not under it, because we are not restrained by it. Abrogate it to-morrow, we should not coin. The penalty does not prevent us from coining. But some would coin were they not restrained by that law. They know the penalty, and therefore they abstain. The law was made for them; it is a schoolmaster to them. The law hangs as a drag on the wheels of evil, not absolutely stopping, but checking it.

Observe, therefore, the law is a schoolmaster to rule those who cannot rule themselves. It is intended to lead to a state when men may be able to rule themselves without the restraint of law. Therefore we ask, For whom is law necessary, and how long is it necessary for them? It is necessary for those who feel the inclination to evil; and so long as the inclination remains, so far must a man be under law.

In this stage it would be madness to relax from restraint. Imagine a governor amidst a population of convicts trusting to high principle. Imagine a parent having no fixed hours, no rules, no *law* in his household, no punishment for evil! There is a morbid feeling against punishment; but it is God's system. Men have often false notions about personal liberty and personal dignity. They are trying the principle of faith when the stage has not yet come to have done with law.

2. The second use of restraint in heart-education is to show the inward force of evil.

This is best expressed by an illustration. A steam-engine at work in a manufactory is so quiet and gentle that a child might put it back. But interpose a bar of iron many inches thick, and it cuts through as if it were so much leather. Introduce a human limb—it whirls round, and the form of man is in one moment a bleeding, mangled, shapeless mass. Now, observe, it is *restraint* that manifests this unsuspected power. In the same way, law discovers the strength of evil in our hearts. Not till a man has felt something resisting that evil does he know its force. . . .

3. The third use is to form habits of obedience.

Let us thoughtfully try to realize Israelitish life. It was made up of numberless observances and duties which gradually formed in the mind a feeling of subjection to a higher Will. Hence was developed the old Hebrew character—that fine, heroic, stern race of chieftains, who had no speculations about right and wrong. Life was with them an action, not a thought.

In that profession which is specially one of obedience, the military profession, you cannot mistake the imparted type of character. Immediate, prompt obedience; no questioning "Why." Hence comes their decision of character. Hence, too, their happiness.

This is a principle of all education that deserves the name. Would you have your child happy, decided, manly? Teach him to obey. It is an error to teach a child to act on reason, or to expect reasons why a command is given. Never suffer a child to ask "why?" For, observe, from that moment you constitute him judge of your decision. All is well if you convince him now; but next time he may not be convinced. Then ensues wretchedness, distrust, and scepticism. The first thing a child has to learn is that there is a will above him. Better is it that he should obey a mistaken order than be taught to see that it is mistaken. A parent must be master in his own house.

4. The fourth use is to form habits of faith: "To bring us unto Christ, that we might be justified by faith." As Judaism was a system calculated to nurture habits of obedience, so was it one which nourished the temper of faith. Let us take, for example, the case of the Sabbath-day. Imagine how it was passed. It was somewhat as it was in Puritanical times, somewhat as it is in Scotland now. The Jew was forbidden to do any work, to speak his own words, to think his own thoughts. He might only walk a "Sabbath-day's journey." Yet consider how all this stern system was calculated to throw a man in on himself. It was a barrier thrown across the stream of his busy, working, noisy life, and forcing him to remember the unseen world.

This prepared the nation for Christ. Judaism was not Christianity, but it was a preparation for it. So God educated His young world.

If we would view education in a right point of view, we must remember that its use is to form faith. All education begins with faith. The child does not know the use of the alphabet, but he *trusts*. The boy beginning mathematics takes on trust what he sees no use in. In learning science, the first principles must be granted, or else there is no progress. Fancy the child, the boy, the tyro in science, stopping to comprehend the propriety of the use of scientific or algebraical symbols! The child has to take parental wisdom for granted. Happy the child that goes on long believing that nothing is wiser, better, greater than his father! Blessed spirit of confiding trust, which is to be transferred to God! Let not the parent infuse suspicion of his teacher in the child's mind. It is the "better part which shall not be taken away from him."

Now, let us understand what faith is. It is just this, the conviction "what I do thou knowest not now, but thou shalt know hereafter." Faith is trust—in the midst of the perplexities of evil to feel sure that all is right, to believe that partial evil is universal good; in spite of all hard thoughts, and suspicious thoughts of God's goodness and God's love, to dare to call Him Father. That is faith, and that is to be first begun in law and education.

II. The time when restraint may be laid aside: "After that faith is come, we are no longer under a schoolmaster."

1. Restraint may be laid aside, in the first place, when self-command is obtained. Then command from another is not needed. Law was, to bring us to Christ; after that we do not require law. Now, to be brought to Christ is, in other words, to have learned to act on principle; to have got self-command. Hear Christ describe such a one: "If any man will come after Me, let him deny himself."

Let me illustrate the principle that self-command needs no schoolmaster. Some of us surely there are who have got beyond childish meanness: we *could* not be mean; restraint is no longer needed; we are beyond the schoolmaster. Some of us there are who have no inclination to intemperance: childish excess in eating and drinking exists no longer. Some of us there are who no longer love indolence: we have advanced beyond it; we love labor. The law may be taken away, for we are free from law. Some of us there are who could not steal or cheat or overreach, who would rather suffer loss ourselves; therefore, we are not "under a schoolmaster."

Now, observe what that expression means—"Free from law." There is a great mistake about liberty from law. Some religious persons think it means free, so that, though you sin, law will not punish. This is the liberty of devils: free to do as much evil as you will, and yet not suffer. True Christian liberty is this, self-command; to have been brought to Christ; to do right and love right, without a law of compulsion to school you into doing it. If we have not got so far, the law has all its power hanging over us still; we *are* under a schoolmaster.

2. Again, restraint may be laid aside when the state of justification by faith has been attained: " The law was our schoolmaster to bring us unto Christ, that we might be justified by faith."

Let me explain that. Justification is a state of acceptance with God—admitted goodness. There are two states of justification: by the law and by faith. Justification by the law implies a scrupulous and accurate performance of minute acts of obedience in every particular; justification by faith is acceptance with God, not because a man is perfect, but because he does all in a trusting, large, generous spirit, actuated by a desire to please God.

In a state of faith man acts on principle, and he gets below enactments. For instance, David at Nob ate of the showbread, which was only lawful for the priests to eat. The disciples ate the ears of corn as they went through the fields on the Sabbath-day. And the apostle says, in that state it is not good to go back to the schoolmaster. It is higher far to act on grand principles than to act timorously on small rules. Let me illustrate this. The grown son, living in his father's house, may not hear a command for years. Yet he is in a state of acceptance—neither of commendation nor of punishment for every act. Treat him as a child and he will at once rebel. Again, observe, when a child returns to compulsory forms, it is not a good sign. There is a great distinction between Judaism and Christianity. In Christianity there are few or no definite laws; all men are left to themselves. It is an unhappy sign when a Church multiplies her laws and makes them stringent; when people get zealous for forms and small things, not as privileges, which they are, but as essentials, which they are not. Those are her days of dotage, not of childhood.

There are two periods when a tree needs propping—when very young, and when very old. In the first case, it is a prelude to strength. But in some old park you may have seen a gray, venerable oak, past its prime, but preserved as a relic of past nobleness; buttresses hold it to the ground, hoops and iron bands are round its giant limbs. It is the weakness not of youth, but of the decline for which there is no second youth.

We live in a day when it is exceedingly difficult to judge fairly whether men are returning to forms for order's sake, or whether from a want of faith to screen them from scepticism, and from a want of manliness which loves to cultivate romantic sensibility. Remember "we are no longer under a schoolmaster." "Stand fast, therefore, in the liberty wherewith Christ hath made us free, and be not entangled again with the yoke of bondage."

3. Lastly, restraint *must* be laid aside when the time of faith is come, whether faith itself hath come or not.

It is so in academical education. Childhood and youth are past, the young man is on the verge of manhood. If his heart be undisciplined, his mind unregulated, and his passions unsubdued, then more than a child does he want restraint. And yet he is no longer under a schoolmaster. So also in the religious life. We may have attained the full intellectual comprehension of the Gospel, but religious goodness has not kept pace with it; and the man wakes to conviction that the Gospel is a name and the powers of the world to come are not in him. You cannot put him to school again. Fear will not produce goodness. Forms will not give reverence. System will not confer freedom.

Therefore the work of childhood and youth must be done while we are young, when the education is not too late.

Let me now apply this to parents and teachers.

It is a sad fact that the children of religious parents so often turn out ill. And this because there has been either no restraint, or restraint used injudiciously. In other words, faith is used when it is the time for law, and law applied when it is the period for faith. There has been an absence of discipline. Now, discipline is not severity, but firmness; calm, quiet training, which has not necessitated one unkind word. There are some who expect God to do all the work of education as by a miracle.

I address parents and teachers. If there be a man for whom a heritage of misery is prepared, a man who has cause to look bitterly back on his instructors, it is he who grows up with an undisciplined mind and heart. Love is not the only principle in education, nor tenderness, nor faith. Parents make the error of appealing to principles before principles are there. Teachers preach to feelings, instead of issuing commands. Remark that Moses comes first, then Christ. The law is our schoolmaster to lead us to Christ.

Another error of parents and teachers is the application of restraint when there should be an appeal to principles and faith. So did Jeroboam, and lost ten tribes. So does a Church when, dealing with an enlightened, intellectual age, she tries severity. So does a parent when he treats the young man like a boy. The poor man says, "I know not how my boy turned out so ill: I corrected him again and again." Yes, it was that correction which lost you your child, and made him a rebel.

There is one work which is to be done on the character by restraint and law, and there is another work which is to be done on the heart by faith. Let us take care we do not mistake them.

IX.

ELIJAH ON MOUNT CARMEL.

(FROM AUTOGRAPH NOTES.)

Brighton, September 25, 1847.

"And Elijah came unto all the people, and said, How long halt ye between two opinions? If the LORD be God, follow him; but if Baal, then follow him. And the people answered him not a word."—1 Kings xviii. 21.

ELIJAH belongs to a class of men specially gifted for special purposes. Their weapon is not love, but truth. They are born not to win, but to coerce by will. Self-conquerors, and therefore subduers of men.

Hence they are qualified for reformers—they are stern, inflexible. Such men have few loves, and few private affections. Their life is public; their interests national, not private. Hence their characters are sad, for they are separated from sympathy: but hence, also, are they elevated. The less they have of a home here, the more they make themselves a home in the awful other world, and find sympathy in God. Such a man was the Baptist, and such was Elijah. The spirit of the old Jewish character had descended on them; that race of heroes, disciplined by law, iron—severe, like Jephthah and Joshua.

Elijah mourned over his degenerate countrymen; and blushed for the effeminacy, voluptuousness, and idolatry of his apostate countrymen.

He gave his challenge. The people came, the court, the nobles, and the priests. One man meets them, with no nobility but the nobility of earnestness, with no credentials but the priesthood of the truth and the power of the right.

The first salute—"How long halt ye between two opinions? If the Lord be God, follow Him; but if Baal, then follow him"—expresses two things:

I. Indecision of character: "How long halt ye between two opinions?"

II. Religious earnestness: "If the Lord be God, follow Him; if Baal, then follow him."

I. Indecision of character: "How long halt ye between two opinions?" "Halt," literally, to limp, go lame; implying pain and instability. *Pain*, the first idea that strikes one on seeing the injured limb come to the ground with a shock. The pitiable and cruel state of the man who cannot make up his mind. *Instability*, the awkward motion between higher and lower ground, with danger of a fall. So in indecision: one moment on the higher ground of principle, the next on the lower one of interest. You cannot calculate on such a man. St. James's comparison is, "wavering like waves of the sea;" unstable element, a mirror to-day reflecting the tints of heaven, to-morrow turbid, and the day after foaming in fury.

1. The first cause of this arose from the multiplicity of opinions. There had been a split between Judah and Israel. The question was one of antiquity as to which is the true Church. The appeal was to ancient documents. Men looked on, and said it was a priests' squabble. A new religion was now introduced by Jezebel from Sidon, and men asked themselves whether Jehovah's worship or Baal's differed much, after all.

There is, too, a multiplicity of opinion in our own time. Hence the halting; the appeal to antiquity as to which is the true Church. Sarcastic men and sad men look on. The sarcastic say, After all, is one creed better than another? Sad men doubt: they go to Rome or dissent; or they remain perplexed and doubting, and ask, "What is truth?"

2. The second cause arose from religious inconsistencies.

Men asked, Which religion produced the most godlike characters? They could arrive at no decision. Jezebel is the type of Baalism. But then there are Nadab and Baasha, Zimri and Omri, and now Ahab! not much to choose between them.

In our own day earnest men are kept by religious inconsistencies at a distance. When they see men standing apart, they watch, and they hear discussions about popular preachers. They observe that in honesty, self-government, punctuality, and such-like matters, such men are no better than others. Jezebel was the worldly woman exclusively on worldly principles; Ahab was the religious man, but worldly withal. The only difference between them is that Jezebel is the more honest of the two.

3. The third cause arose from a desire to please men. This in three forms produces indecision.

First, over-amiability. Nothing falsifies the character like softness; the want of power to say No, when it would give pain. Eli was not a bad man, but there was a softness and feebleness of character which left him powerless to say No to his sons.

Secondly, love of popularity. To be the universal favorite! Ordinarily, how dangerous!—"Woe unto you when all men shall speak well of you! for so did their fathers to the false prophets."

Let us paint a universal favorite who offends none. Pilate wished to save Jesus, so far as he could do it consistently with his own popularity. The Pharisees knew his weak point, "If thou let this Man go, thou art not Cæsar's friend." He did not dare to *be* Cæsar's friend without *seeming* it. He tried at the same time not to offend the other party. He washed his hands, and delivered Jesus to be crucified. Remark, this crime was committed not by a bad man, but by one who was made undecided by a love of popularity.

Thirdly, the wish to please our own party. Some can stand against the world if friends be with them; but the difficulty lies in acting on conscience against friends. We know the miserable indecision of the statesman who longs to vote against his own party, and will not; and of the religious man who fears suspicion when he dare not act against his friends.

4. The fourth cause arises from selfishness. If we appeal to our own experience, we find that when indecision was wretched, interest and self were the elements that made it so. We put one

pleasure over against another, like a child vacillating between grapes and glittering red cherries. Alas! men for things as wretched, hesitate; torture self because they fear to lose; and choose wrongly. Or, again, when interest is on one side and duty on the other. Never, indeed, does indecision last long where the question is truly about duty; then the way becomes clear: or if a man errs, there is no remorse. Balaam saw his duty clear at night; but the next day he looked again and he saw the glittering bribe. He could not be sure; at last he thought God's voice said, Go. Marvellous is it that thoroughly worldly men are more straightforward than men half-religious.

Now choose, and choose in earnest. Serve God; but don't regret. If the man of business will be honest, he will suffer. But what does he win? He wins a clear conscience, pure self-approval, God.

Or else choose the world; but do it *thoroughly*. Say to pleasure, Be thou my god; say to gain, I worship thee; say to ambition, I consecrate my energies to attain thee. And the world will give you pleasure. Baal has his rewards. Happy while life lasts; and then—ay—what then?

II. Religious earnestness. "If the Lord be God, follow Him; but if Baal, then follow him."

Religious earnestness was marked in Elijah—

1. By self-forgetfulness. Was Elijah whispering, "Now I am doing a brave thing; people's eyes are on me?" This is the finest scene in Scripture. Elijah was quite unconscious that he was making a scene. He had lost himself in his cause. Hence the people understood that it was no contest between Elijah and the priests, but between Baal and God. Hence they did not exclaim, "Elijah," but the "Lord," He is God.

All sincerity forgets egotism. Moses' skin shone, but he "*wist not* that the skin of his face shone."

2. By action instead of speculation. Remark, Elijah was in a schismatic Church. Speculative minds would have dreamed of outward unity, and thought that nothing could be done till that was got—or of a millennial state. Elijah acted as he was, and where he was. The work given him was not to restore unity, but to destroy unbelief in individual hearts. All earnestness does that, it *acts*. Do the duty next you, leave the rest to develop itself.

3. By sternness and unmeasured language. Elijah mocked the priests of Baal. He killed them. We are not concerned to defend this. The Jewish spirit differed from the Christian. Yet observe, it marked earnestness. It is a precedent to interpret character. Among the charges against Luther was this, that he was not so delicate in his language against opponents as modern softness requires. Were the prophets? Was Elijah? John the Baptist? Christ Himself? In matters of life and death, men cannot pick words. Let cavillers breathe for one hour the air which such men breathed, feel their zeal for God, their hatred of hypocrisy; feel their soul blazing up with earnestness—then they may judge of terms.

4. By resting on his own heart and conscience. Consider what might have been said. The world is against you, the wise, the court, the priesthood; this is presumption. What was Elijah's answer? Numbers are not the test of truth, but the voice within clear. The world against Elijah. Well, then, in the name of God and truth, Elijah against the world.

This opens the question of the Protestant right of private judgment. It has its use and its abuse. Its abuse is seen when young persons dare to say their Church is wrong; or when persons in the world of fashion and idleness, guiltless of thought, ignorant of the discipline required for investigating truth, venture to decide about opinions, as if it were just as easy as to decide about the last new fashion, and quietly say, The last sermon was not Gospel.

Young brethren, Elijah judged independently. But remark, Elijah was a grown man; he had fasted and prayed, he had lived alone, pondered; and when he did defy his Church and country's judgment, he was preparing for probable death. The next time you are inclined to be flippant, remember that Elijah's character alone can qualify for Elijah's judgment.

Let me say in application—

1. Remark the power of earnestness to produce a miracle. Who is he that brings down fire from heaven but he that believes? Its power to gain influence—but, observe, only by degrees. Its power to diffuse faith. It communicates itself, it works a reformation.

2. I address boys. Boy, standing alone in school, was not Elijah's a fine character? Yours may be just as fine.

X.

GROWTH INTO CHRIST IN LOVE AND TRUTH.

(FROM AUTOGRAPH NOTES.)

Brighton, October 3, 1847.

"But speaking the truth in love, may grow up into him in all things, which is the head, even Christ."—Eph. iv. 15.

THE previous verse describes Christian childhood, this verse Christian manhood. The characteristics of childhood are instability of character, unfixedness of opinion, and credulity. All of which, natural and even graceful in a child, are in a man weakness, unfitness for life, and folly. Manhood is truth, love, likeness to Christ.

We therefore consider:

I. The standard of Christian excellence: "the head, even Christ."

II. Christian progress towards that standard: "We grow up into him in all things."

I. Christ's Headship.

1. The prominent notion suggested is His rank in the universe. He rules as God in creation. But evidently the apostle does not mean this in the text. We are to grow into Him as Head. Growth into Christ's Godhead is impossible. Godlike we may, God we cannot even by truth and love, become.

2. He is the Head, as being the source of spiritual life.

This is implied in metaphor. The highest life-powers—sensation, feeling, thought—come from the brain.

To one who has read the history of those times, there is an emphatic truth in Christ's being the Life of the world. The world was dead when Christ came.

Look at the Roman world. There is no belief; all is hollow, all pretence. Diana is great; to make her image gives employment to a craft. The capital of the Roman Empire is a metropolis of abomination. Read what was going on at Rome and Baiæ. The heathen heart had every fibre rotted.

Turn to Judaism. The Pharisees were clinging to forms from which life had long since died out, and were hanging over them as you hang over a corpse whose features present the illusion of life. The Sadducees, too honest to believe this, said, "We are infidels." Others, with minds too honest to believe in forms, and hearts too affectionate to rest in infidelity, were gasping, languishing, sadly hoping for better times.

The world was like a raft becalmed in the tropics: some of its freight dead and baking in the sun, some sucking as if for moisture from dried casks, and some sadly, faintly looking for a sail. Christ's coming to that world was as life to the dead, imparting new impulse to human heart and human nature. It was like rain and wind coming to that bark—once more it cuts the sea, guided by a living hand.

So also with each man who drinks Christ's spirit. He becomes a living character. Not sustained on dogmas, or taken up with opinions, but alive with Christ. . . .

In this sense, to grow into Christ is to get fresh spiritual energy. The child and the man become equally alive; but in the man it is developed life: "I am come that they might have life, and that they might have it more abundantly."

3. He is Head, as chief of the human race.

Never had the world seen, never again will it see, such a character. Imagine exotics beneath our inclement sky. They grow indeed, but they cannot thrive. A foreigner would scarcely recognize them as intended for the plants of his own country. Imagine one such plant in peculiar circumstances lighting on a kindly soil, in a sheltered spot, and with its innate vigor reaching perfection. That would be the realized idea of the plant. Such was Christ among other men. Humanity found in Him a genial soil, and realized God's idea of what man was meant to be.

He is Chief. Nothing comes near Him.

Last Sunday we contemplated Elijah, and saw that he was no common man, but one unearthly, borne away in a flame chariot. Yet we feel that Elijah is measurable: we can conceive the daring of Carmel; his weakness in the desert brings him near to us. The passionate disappointment of a proud but high spirit we can understand. Now turn to THAT character! "The first man is of the earth, earthy: the second man is the Lord from heaven." Christ is firm, unconquerable, true to the cause of God and man; but also loving, tender, gentle. Choose that type. He is the one model, the one type. Have no other. Before that all earthly excellence fades. All dims before our glorious Head.

II. Progress towards the standard of Christian excellence: " We grow up into Him in all things."

Let us inquire what progress means; and the approved mode of progress.

i. Progress is made in likeness to Him, and in comprehension of His character.

1. Growth in likeness to Him. The human soul was formed for growth, and that growth is infinite. The acorn grows into the oak, the child into the philosopher. And at death the soul is not declining, it is as vigorous as ever. Hence, nothing but an infinite standard will measure the growth of the soul of man.

Observe, moreover, the universality in this growth; " in all things "—completeness of character. Completeness, however, is not perfection. Take a field in which in some parts the crop is abundant; in places thin, and low and yellow. Such are some characters. Where the natural soil favors, graces are cultivated; where it is adverse, the character is not grown into Christ. The man is generous, but, it may be, bad-tempered, etc.

Completeness is proportion: the field all grown equally. St. Paul says, " Grow in all things."

2. Growth in comprehension of Him. Christ is not comprehensible at first. He is not appreciated in our childhood. Elijah's character is more striking to a child. Christ's is too calm, too pure, too inwardly great for the child's mind. A mountain disappoints at first. You arrive at night full of expectation. You look out next morning and are disappointed. But after you have lived beside it for weeks, and seen it in all lights, it grows upon you. Go where you will, there is the old white peak, shooting up to heaven, serene and calm, looking down on the smaller peaks—the giant and the monarch of them all.

So the young man forms ideals of excellence for himself—only by degrees does he appreciate Christ. Dazzled by military life, he wishes to fall in a cavalry charge; he knows nothing higher till the time comes when he begins to feel that to save men's lives is better than to destroy life. His next ideal may be intellectual superiority. He dreams of eloquence, and thinks it dazzling to hold a senate still. To be an orator, retaining a thousand men as one, eyes speaking to eyes, heart to heart—the dominion of mind! But this is shared by base and bad men. Or, it may be, his ideal is the ascetic life. This is a temptation to ardent hearts. Many now go to Rome for this reason. But, after all, it is a useless life, and a refined form of selfishness.

Then the man turns to Christ. He finds in Him, not the warrior, but "Ye know not what manner of spirit ye are of." Not the man of intellect, but "Become as a little child." Not the ascetic, but a man found in common life, at the marriage-feast of Cana, in the loving family of Bethany. Words cannot express the awe with which a man contemplates that character when it is understood. This is the true heroic; this the only Godlike; this the real Divine. From all types of human excellence I have made my choice for life and death—Christ.

ii. The approved means of growth, the mode of progress: "Speaking the truth in love."

Truth and love—and these joined.

There are two forms of character: one distinguished by strong love for what is true, the other by vivid perception of what is beautiful; one forming the man of integrity, the other the man of tenderness.

Each has its peculiar faults, and each is corrected by the other.

Compare, for instance, Northern and Southern Europe. The Northern nations are honest and true; the Southern nations are tender. The South is the home of beauty—arts, music, refinement.

Compare Protestantism and Romanism. Truth by itself degenerates into sternness, as in the case of Puritanism. Hard, inflexible—no elegance, no tenderness—it pronounces the sentence of death unmoved. Then look at the Roman devotee, and we find much of superstition, falsehood, and voluptuousness. If we must choose, then heart and soul we are for the Puritan.

But to "grow into Christ" we must have both traits of character.

Would you be like Christ? Cultivate love of beauty and tenderness. His soul was alive to beauty. He noted the rising and the setting sun, the waving corn, the lily of the field. His was love which insult could not ruffle, nor ribaldry imbitter; and which only grew sweeter and sweeter.

Would you be like Christ? Be true. He never swerved. He was a martyr to truth. Would He soften down truth for the young man whom He loved, or make it palatable? No; not for friendship, not for love, nor for all the lovely things this world has to show: "One thing thou lackest: sell all that thou hast, and distribute unto the poor, and thou shalt have treasure in heaven: and come, follow Me." That was "speaking the truth in love."

I address the man of truth. You hate hypocrisy, cant, pretence. You are a man of business, of intellect; you have all the elements of a fine character, if they are Christianized. But join to them love. Your danger is sternness, wounding men with cutting words. Your character wants the polish of love.

I address the man of tenderness, of accomplishments and refinement. Your danger, if you look in upon yourself, is superstition. The sharp edge of truthfulness is lost. There is only one step between softness and impurity of feeling. Join that tenderness with truth, if you would grow into Christ.

In conclusion, let me add one word of application. There is no good to be got from Christ except by being made like Him. There is no pardon, no blessing, separate from inward improvement. Sanctity of character alone blesses. Each man is his own hell and his own heaven. God Himself cannot bless you unless He gives you His own character.

XI.

SPIRITUAL WORSHIP. (1.)

(FROM AUTOGRAPH NOTES.)

Brighton, October 10, 1847.

"Jesus saith unto her, Woman, believe me, the hour cometh when ye shall neither in this mountain, nor yet at Jerusalem, worship the Father. Ye worship ye know not what: we know what we worship, for salvation is of the Jews. But the hour cometh, and now is, when the true worshippers shall worship the Father in spirit and in truth: for the Father seeketh such to worship him. God is a Spirit: and they that worship him must worship him in spirit and in truth."—John iv. 21-24.

CHRIST rests on the narrow rocky road between Gerizim and Ebal, before entering Sychar, near a well. A Samaritan woman comes to draw water. He asks for a draught. There had been a long controversy between the Jews and Samaritans as to the whereabouts of worship; and this turned on an antiquarian point as to which was the correct reading in Deuteronomy xxvii. Hence arose theological rancor. The Jews had no dealings with the Samaritans except in traffic and business; no giving or asking kindness. The woman, brought up in this system of malignity, marvels at Christ putting Himself under an obligation to her, a Samaritan.

In the conversation that ensued, Christ's uncommon character appeared to her. Instantly, thinking the period was arrived for the solution of the controversy, she puts the question, partly to escape from a conversation which was becoming too personal, partly from that love of controversy which is so common in us all. But Christ had no intention that it should end so. Hence He takes the opportunity of defining spiritual worship.

Our subject divides itself into:

I. Errors which have interfered with purity of religious worship.

II. The nature of the worship which God accepts.

I. Errors which have interfered with purity of religious worship.

1. The first error arises from a tendency to localize God. Her question was, in fact, "Where?" Christ's reply was, "Nowhere in particular; everywhere."

This question lies at the root of all superstition. It is observable among the heathen, who confine the agency of a god to a certain district; among the uneducated poor of our own country, in their notions of a cemetery; and among the more refined, in the clinging mysterious idea which they attach to a church, an altar, and the elements of the sacrament.

Let us define what we mean by sanctity of place. It is a thing merely subjective, not objective; it is relative to us. It belongs to that law of association by which a train of ideas returns more easily by suggestion in some one place than in another. Worship in a festive room or over a shop would suggest notions uncongenial with devotion. Hence the use of *setting apart*, or consecrating, places for worship. There is no other sanctity of place. Transfer what is in you to the place, and you verge on superstition. Therefore, the church, the altar, etc., are not holy — God is not there.

We hear an objection to this. It is said to be dangerous to say this: it will unsettle people's minds; a little of this illusion is wholesome, especially for the poor. To this I reply, in the first place, Christ did not so reason. Consider how unsettling this was to the woman. The little religion she had clung to Gerizim. The shock of being told that it was not holy might have unsettled all her religion. Did Christ hesitate one moment? And, in the second place, we are only concerned with truth. Some people are afraid of truth. As if God's truth could be dangerous! The straight road is ever the nearest. People *must* bear, and shall, what an earnest mind dares to say. Is God there or not? If not, at our peril we say He is.

The holiest place! Is this church holy? Yes, if a holy congregation be in it; if not, it is brick and mortar. Which is the holiest place in it? The altar? Nay; the spirit of the holiest man present. Which is the holiest place on earth? Not where architecture, music, solemn aisles, or fretted roof yield their spell; but, perhaps, a wretched pallet on which one of Christ's humblest ones is dying, or a square foot of ground on which an heroic Christian stands.

2. A second error arises from the idea that forms are immutable. "Our fathers worshipped in this mountain," therefore we must.

Let me explain what a form is. It is the shape in which an age expresses a feeling. The spirit of religion remains, but the expression alters.

There is, for instance, the present love of antiquity. Let us do it justice. Enthusiasm is always lovely — it is far better than coolnesss; but is it right?

There is a wish to restore the observances and the rubrics of the early Church. I will try to show why it is now not necessary: the times are altered. Religion is domestic now, then it was social. . . . Public daily prayer would be a mistake now. . . .

3. A third error arises from ignorance: "Ye worship ye know not what."

There is a feeling of devoutness inherent in the human mind. We hear the solemn tones of a child when repeating his prayer or hymns. Before what is greater, wiser, better than himself man bows instinctively. But the question is, *what* will he worship? We distinguish, therefore, between instinctive devoutness and enlightened worship.

To many there are three deities — Power, Wisdom, Goodness.

The heathen bent before Power. The universe was alive with deity to him: he saw God in the whirlwind, in the lightning, and the thunder. This is ignorance.

The philosopher is above this. He bows before Wisdom. Science tells him of electricity, gravitation, force. He looks down on warm devoutness; for he sees only contrivance and mind in Nature. He admires all calmly, without enthusiasm. He calls it Rational religion. This, also, is ignorance.

The spiritual man bows before Goodness: "The true worshippers worship the Father;" "We know what we worship, for salvation is of the Jews" — that is, God is intelligible in Christ as Love, Goodness, Purity. None but this is intelligent worship.

4. A fourth error is a mistake about the nature of reverence.

To have no veneration is to have no religion. But let me explain what reverence is. This Samaritan woman had what they call reverence, veneration for antiquity, zeal for her Church, lingering recollections of the old mountain, respect for a prophet. But what was her life? He with whom she then lived was not her husband. In other words, reverence, veneration, awe, are a class of feelings which belong to the imagination, and are neither good nor bad: they may go along with religion, but also they may not. A man may kneel to sublime things, yet never have bent his heart to goodness and purity. A man may be reverential, and yet impure.

[Show this from Tyrolese chamois-hunter—and all the nonsense that travellers talk of the devoutness of mountain people.*]

Next examine a man who is called irreverent. Constitutionally so framed that he does not happen to thrill at painted windows, Gothic architecture, and solemn music: is he, therefore, without veneration? Take him out into God's grand universe, or put before him Christ's character: is there no adoration, no deep, intense love? Tell him of a self-denying action: is there no moisture in his eye? Tempt him to meanness: is there no indignant scorn? The man has bowed his soul before Justice, Mercy, Truth, and therefore stands erect before everything else which this world calls sublime.

II. True character of spiritual worship.

1. It consists in a right appreciation of God's character.

Here it is presented in a twofold aspect: "God is a *Spirit*;" and "The true worshippers shall worship the *Father*."

What is meant by spirit? There are false notions which regard it as attenuated gas, a wreath of air or vapor. Observe, this is only subtle materialism.

Consider the universe, with the sun and stars, the harmony of the planets. All this force, order, harmony—that is God. This spring season, with bursting vegetation—its life is God. Our own minds, their thought and feeling—that is spirit. God, therefore, is the *Mind* of the universe. Force, law, harmony—all this is God. And yet remark the coldness of this, for He is thus revealed only as a God for the intellect, not for the heart.

Therefore for the heart He is revealed as a *Father*. Consider the endearing meaning of this word—in it tenderness is united with reverence. Let us fasten on one meaning out of many. Let us take the work of a father in education. Consider the use of this rugged, stubborn, material world to invigorate the mind by

* See "Life and Letters." Letter dated Botzen, September 28, 1846. (Page 66, People's Edition.)

trying it against difficulties. Agriculture, steam navigation, are the result. Consider the use of suffering. The cross is the emblem of life. It is only through struggle, through difficulty, that the soul can be invigorated. All that is a fatherly work. Who would wish to have his child luxurious, rich, indolent, rather than see him in honest poverty, struggling with sorrow? This explains what would otherwise be this "unintelligible world." We can take the bitter draught thankfully. "The cup which my Father hath given me, shall I not drink it?"

2. Next, spiritual worship consists in spiritual character. The true worshippers are those who "worship the Father in spirit and in truth."

That is, holy character is a kind of worship. All true life is worship: "Worship the Lord in the beauty of holiness;" "Lo, I come to do Thy will, O Lord." Before a material God a material knee would have to bow. Before a spiritual God, nothing but the prostration of the spirit can be acceptable.

> "He prayeth well who loveth well
> Both man and bird and beast."

Love is a kind of prayer—the truest lifting-up of the soul.

One word of application.

1. Christ came to bring man's spirit into immediate contact with God's Spirit; to sweep away everything intermediate. In lonely union, face to face, man's spirit and God's Spirit must come together. It is a grand thought! Aspire to this! Aspire to greatness, goodness! So let your spirit mingle with the Spirit of the Everlasting.

2. Scripture insists on *truth* of character. God is made known as a real God. The worshipper is to be a real character. The Christian must be a true man—transparent, who can bear to be looked through and through. There must be no pretence; no gilded tinsel—TRUE GOLD ALL THROUGH.

XII.

TEARS OF JESUS.

(FROM AUTOGRAPH NOTES.)

Trinity Chapel, Brighton, March 5, 1848.

"Jesus wept."—John xi. 35.

CHRISTIANITY is God manifest in the flesh.

Christianity is contained in the life of Jesus Christ.

To adore Christ, love Christ, trust Christ—that is Christianity.

Not dogmas about Christ, but Christ. This is the Gospel. The spirit of the life with which Christ lived—His character.

Therefore we must understand Christ. And this as a whole made up of many particulars.

Imagine a spectator advancing towards the earth—pausing at ten thousand miles' distance—contemplating a glorious star. Then alighting on a mountain. Then arriving below, and finding it peopled; a history to every spot, a science in every stone, in every atom the study of a life. To understand this earth, which looked one bright mass, is to be in possession of every science and every history: to know it in its atoms, and to know it as a whole.

So with Christ. We by degrees master that character, till we find it boundless. Thought and depth in every sentence. Few men know much of Christ—none the whole. Christianity dwells entire only in one bosom.

Some comprehend His reformation of abuses; others His abhorrence of pretence in religion; others His assertion of man's equality; others His purity, His courage, His truth; others the merely human aspect of His character. But His character is a whole.

There are persons who write treatises on one country's history —others on the structure of a plant. Only a few, like Herschel and Humboldt, can comprehend with something like adequateness the cosmos, or order of the universe. There is no one who cannot read a page of it—but to be able to compose "Cosmos!"*

Bear this in mind. We contemplate now one feeling only: "Jesus wept."

Our subject divides itself into two branches:

I. Causes of Christ's sorrow.
II. Its peculiar character.

I. Causes of Christ's sorrow.
1. The possession of a soul.

When we speak of Deity joined to humanity, we do not mean joined to a body. Not a body inhabited by Deity, as our bodies are by soul. But we mean Deity joined to manhood—body *and* soul. With a body only, Jesus might have wept for hunger, but not wept for sorrow. That is neither the property of Deity nor of body, but of soul.

Humanity in Christ was perfect. The possession of a body enabled Him to weary; the possession of a soul capacitated Him to weep.

2. The spectacle of human sorrow. And this twofold:

Death of a friend: "Behold how He loved him."

Sorrow of two friends: "When Jesus therefore saw her weeping, . . . Jesus wept."

The death of His friend was a cause of the sorrow of Jesus.

Mysterious! Jesus knew that he could raise him. All-knowing wisdom: all-powerful strength. Yet "Jesus wept."

This is partly intelligible. Conceptions strongly presented produce effects like reality; *e. g.*, we wake dreaming, our eyes suffused with tears—know it is a dream, yet tears flow on.

Conception of a parent's death. . . .

Solemn impression produced by the mock funeral of Charles V. . . .

To say that Jesus wept is only to say that His humanity was perfect; that His mind moved by the same laws as ours.

Moreover, it was only delay. One day Lazarus would die, and the mourning be real.

Now, observe, the sadness of Jesus for His friend is what is repeated with us all. The news comes—"He whom thou lovest

* Extracted from Lecture II. on "Influence of Poetry." The MS. contains only "To be able to compose Cosmos."

is sick," and then, in two days—"Lazarus is dead." Startling! Somehow we twine our hearts round men we love as if forever. Death and they are not thought of in connection. He die! He die!

It is a shock to find the reality of this awful life: that we are swimming on a sea of appearances—floating on an eternity that gives way. These attachments, loves, etc., they don't hold; there is no firmness in them. We are, and then suddenly are not. Life and death, what are they?

Next, the sorrow of His two friends caused the tears of Jesus.

Look at this family. Three persons: a brother lost, two surviving sisters.

The sisters' characters were diverse. Martha found her life in the outer world of fact; Mary in the inner world of feeling. They are types of the practical and the contemplative.

Their way of manifesting feeling is different. Martha expressed herself outwardly in word, in action, in small acts of attention; she loved to discuss earnestly with the intellect the question of the resurrection—contended how things might have been otherwise. Mary did not express—felt herself inexpressible; reached truth by the heart, not by the mind; lived in contemplation. In manhood, one would have found life in the storm of the world; the other in retirement. As students, one would have studied the outward life of man in history; the other, philosophy, the causes of things, the world visible, and the stranger world within.

Two links bound these diverse characters together: love to Lazarus, attachment to the Redeemer. And this true union—similars in dissimilarity, worlds differing, spheres differing, yet no clashing—bound them together by one common pursuit.

Now one link was gone. Of him, Lazarus, we know little. Only he was one whom Jesus loved, and he had the strong attachment of such women as Martha and Mary.

His loss was not an isolated fact. The family was broken up; the sun of the system gone; the planets no longer revolving round a centre harmoniously. The keystone is removed from the arch, and the stones are losing their cohesion; for the two minds held together only at points of contact. Points of repulsion, too, there were, manifest even in life. They could not understand one another's different modes of feeling: Martha complains of Mary at the feast. Lazarus gave them a common tie. That removed, the points of repulsion would daily become more sharp and salient.

Over the breaking-up of a family Jesus wept.

And this is what makes death sad. Let him who calls death a trifle remember this—not that one man is gone, but that Bethany is no longer Bethany. A blight is there. You open a book, there is a name. A day comes, it is a birthday—the chair is vacant. In reverie you half rise up, but the name on your lips belongs to none on earth.

II. Character of Christ's sorrow:—Spirit in which Jesus saw this death.

Calmly: "Lazarus sleepeth." It is the world of repose where all is placid.

Struggling men have tried to forget this restless world, and slumber like a babe, tired—yea, tired at heart. Lazarus is stretched out to his Divine friend's imagination, but he lies calm. The long day's work is done—the hands are folded. Nothing to fret now but the "small cold" worm. Waves of shadow are flying over the long grass on his grave.

Friends are gathered to praise, enemies to slander. But praise and slander on his ear make no impression. Conscious he is, perhaps, elsewhere; but unconscious of earthly noise. Musketry over grave—requiem mass—minstrels making a noise. . . . All this is for the living; the dead hear not. But "he sleeps well." That is the tone of feeling with which to stand over the Christian's death-bed: "Our friend Lazarus sleepeth."

Next, *sadly.* Hence, observe, permitted sorrow.

Great Nature is wiser than we. We recommend weeping, or prate about submission, or say all must die; Nature, God, say, "Let nature rule, to weep or not."

Do you say tears imply selfishness—distrust? I answer: Weep. Let grief be law to herself. We infer that grief is no distrust of God—no selfishness. Sorrow is but love without its object.

Next, *hopefully.* "I go that I may awake him out of sleep; thy brother shall rise again." Not merely calmness, nor sadness, nor sorrow, nor despair, but hope.

Observe, the amount of hope depends on character and imaginative power.

Sanguine minds are elastic; it is very easy for them to blame deeper shadow, as if that which is natural spirits were all faith.

Allowance, too, must be made for imaginative power. That is the world of shadows; this the world of experience and recollection. Some persons live in the past more than in the future. Others there are who travel with the sun ever before them, keeping pace with the sun.

Hope will be small when imagination is scanty; but feebleness of hope is not feebleness of faith.

Lastly, *in reserve*—the reserve of sorrow.

On the first announcement, Jesus speaks not a word. When He met the mourners, He offered them no commonplace consolation. He is more anxious to exhibit feeling than to soothe. But Nature had her way at last. Yet even then by act more than by word the Jews inferred He loved him; "Jesus wept; *then* said the Jews, Behold how He loved him."

There is the reserve of nature and the reserve of grace.

We have our own English reserve: we do not give way to feeling. We respect grief when it does not make an exhibition. An Englishman is ashamed of his good feelings as much as of his bad. In sarcasm, sneer, and hummed tune, tears will be concealed. All this is neither good nor bad—it is nature.

But let it be sanctified; let reserve of nature pass into reserve of Christian delicacy.

Let us add a few words of application.

In this there is consolation for us. But consolation is not the privilege of all sorrow. Christ is at Lazarus's grave, because Christ had been at the sisters' home, sanctifying their joys and their very meals. They had anchored on the rock in sunshine, and in the storm the ship held to her moorings.

It is desolate, when the heart is cut away by force, to seek a Saviour. He who has lived with Christ will find Christ near in death.

If you choose duty—God—it is not so difficult to die.

XIII.

SPIRITUAL WORSHIP. (2.)

(FROM AUTOGRAPH NOTES.)

Brighton, April 7, 1850.

"But the hour cometh, and now is, when the true worshippers shall worship the Father in spirit and in truth: for the Father seeketh such to worship him. God is a spirit: and they that worship him must worship him in spirit and in truth."—John iv. 23, 24.

The conversation between Christ and the woman of Samaria began on common topics. By-and-by it became more deep and interesting. He, to whom all things here were types, could not converse without a Divine meaning in all He said. A draught of water connected itself with the mystery of life.

So soon as she discovered His spiritual character, she put the question of her day.

A miserable question had perplexed two nations lying near each other, of the same blood, interests, and hopes. They hated each other: "the Jew had no dealing with the Samaritan." They excommunicated each other. Just in proportion to their nearness of relationship was their bitterness. A Jew hated a Samaritan far more than a heathen. Scarcely anything in the present day will exactly illustrate this hatred. Protestant and Catholic antipathies are perhaps the nearest; or just as some orthodox Christians hate a heterodox Christian, and resolve, by the grace of God, to have no dealings with him. For the spirit of men is the same in every age. And the intensity of abhorrence between Jew and Samaritan was the measure of their zeal. The more they kept aloof from their "brother whom they had seen," the more they thought they showed their love to "God, whom they had *not* seen." As if they could with the same tongue bless the Father and anathematize men who are "made after the similitude of God."

Before we pass to the consideration of our subject, we have two remarks to make. Remark, first, the difference between interest in theology and interest in religion.

Here was a woman living in sin, and yet deeply interested in a religious controversy. She found, doubtless, a kind of safeguard to rest on in the perception of this keen interest. Her religion was almost nothing, her theology most orthodox.

Theological controversy sharpens our disputative faculties and wakes our speculative ones. Religion is love to God and man. People do not distinguish between theology and religion. They make skill in controversy a test of spirituality; yet it is but a poor test. However, this is the test we use. The way the woman questioned Christ is a specimen of a common feeling. The moment Christ appears, she examines His views. She does not ask whether the Man before her were pure and spotless — His life spent in doing good; but was He sound upon the vital question of the temple?

A man dies, and you ask what were his opinions. Consider which is worse — a mistake about baptism or a mistake about love to God and man? The *life* is the test of faith.

The second remark we make is, that all that was worth notice in the question had disappeared.

Formally the Jew was right, the Samaritan wrong: "Jerusalem was the place where men ought to worship."

But wrong as the Samaritan was, he was not half so wrong for praying on Mount Gerizim as the Jew was for excommunicating him and having no dealings with him; or half so wrong as he was himself for hating the Jew: "And they did not receive him, because his face was as though he would go to Jerusalem." Right as was the Jew in his theology, it was negatived by his hatred of the Samaritan. The duty of being liberal to the illiberal was forgotten. And thus worship had disappeared in disputes about the place "where men ought to worship."

This belongs to us; we, too, have our miserable questions of *where?* and *when?* Every age has its own special question. The question once was, whether a miracle was performed in the Communion. The questions now are whether a miracle is performed in the baptism of a baby; whether rule resides in the State or in the Church; whether the priest is above the law or beneath it.

The days are coming when these questions will be debated with vehemence; and in proportion to our controversial stanchness we shall estimate our spiritual excellence. And the days, perhaps, are coming when we shall test each other by these questions, and pronounce all who disagree with us bad men, and refuse communion with them.

Yet, observe, while we battle about baptism—how and in what sense it makes us children of God, literally or figuratively—we are losing all that baptism means. Instead of a symbol of unity, "one baptism," it becomes ingeniously converted into a symbol of strife.

Just as worship disappeared in the miserable controversy about "the place where men ought to worship," Mount Gerizim or Mount Moriah, so is Christianity going while we battle about baptism—when, and where, the Spirit of God comes down.

Now tell us which was worse—to worship on a wrong hill, or to mistake the very essence of worship? Which was worse—to err respecting the interpretation of records on which the question rested *where* God had placed his name, or to err respecting love? A blunder of intellect, or a lack of charity? Which is worse—to hold incorrect views respecting baptism, or to lose the whole of that which baptism was given for?—to sacrifice before a wrong altar, or to bring wrong sacrifice to a true altar?

Now, Christ speaks of a new worship essentially different from the old. He made religion spiritual, He pointed out the difference between religion and theology, and He revealed the foundation on which true worship must rest.

A new time was coming for a new worship: "The hour cometh, and now is, when the true worshippers shall worship the Father in spirit and in truth."

Let us consider:

I. The foundation or the revelation on which the new worship rests.

II. The nature of spiritual worship.

I. The foundation on which the new worship rests is a revelation made by Christ respecting the character of God, which contains three points: His paternity, "God is the Father;" His spiritual nature, "God is a Spirit;" and His personality, "He seeketh."

1. God is "the Father." This is evidently the emphatic word of the sentence: "The hour cometh, and now is, when the true worshippers shall worship the *Father*."

Christ revealed a name—the Father. Great stress is laid in

the Bible upon the significance of names. Moses asked, "What is thy name?"—"I am that I am; I appeared to the fathers by the name of God Almighty, but by my name Jehovah was I not known to them." This was of peculiar importance in Jewish theology. A name was identical with the person; Moses means drawn out of the water; Jacob, supplanter; Israel, Prince of God. So each step in revelation added something to the name: first God; then Jehovah, expressing His being; lastly Holy Father, revealing His character.

Not but what men had, in a sense, before worshipped a Father. The Greeks and the Romans spoke of the "father of gods and men." The Jewish prophets said, "Have we not all one Father?" But the universality in the Name was wanting. A Father—yes, but of Rome alone, or Athens alone, or the Jews alone.

Therefore the old question was all in all. *Where* is He to be worshipped? For the real question hidden under that was, *Who* are His children? for if God be localized to one place, then His children are those alone who worship there. Is it the Capitoline Jove, or the Zeus of Olympus, or Jehovah of Mount Zion, or the Father of the family of man who is to be worshipped?

The appearance of Christ was the manifestation of the answer: God is the Father of the family of man.

The incarnation declared that the Son of Man is the Son of God. One appeared who was not the Jew, nor the Greek, nor the Roman, but the Man; One in whose veins ran the blood of the human race; One in whose character was neither exclusively the woman nor the man, but all that was most manly, and all that was most womanly—One so tender to the publican and the sinner that He could say to Mary Magdalene, "My Father and your Father."

All are born sons of God into this world. Yet do not mistake. There is a distinction between a son of God by right and a son of God in fact. The last century beheld the son of a royal house taken from his family and compelled to descend into the lowest ranks of life. He was heir of the royal family; by right, heir to the throne, but in fact heir to degradation—vile in character, ignorant, and unregal. So is it with the son of man. By right, a child of God; by fact a child of wrath, ignorant of his privileges, not knowing who or what he is, or "that imperial palace whence he came."

2. The second foundation on which spiritual worship rests is that "God is a spirit."

We should greatly mistake the meaning of this if we took it as a theological definition of the being of God. It is not theological, but practical. It is chiefly negative. It says what God is not: He is not matter, He has not a form: "A spirit hath not flesh and bones." He is Mind. Mind, properly speaking, has no *place*. Of love, generosity, thought—can you say *when?*

This, then, was the great truth, that God is a Mind, not separated by conditions of space and time from His creatures.

3. The third foundation on which spiritual worship rests is the Personality of God: "The Father *seeketh*."

There are two erroneous notions, both compatible with the idea of Spirit, that God is an idea elaborated out of our own minds, and that God is the Soul of Nature. There is a prevalent notion that God is an idea elaborated out of our own minds; *e.g.*, we have an idea of justice, truth, mercy; and this idea or assemblage of ideas we insensibly invest with personality and call God. Notions of this sort more or less float in all our minds, haunting us so that we lose the idea of personality. And then spiritual worship would be only this, cultivating goodness, cultivating truth, cultivating justice.

The other prevalent notion is that God is the Soul of Nature, the Spirit of the Universe. But at once you feel this is not religion. Oh no! that utter loneliness of soul which comes from sin and despair needs some one near on whom to lean, some one who can feel and sympathize. One *is* near and feels. No Soul of Nature, no abstract goodness, no ideal of our own minds, no Spirit of the Universe. Not an unconscious mind becoming broken into a myriad consciousnesses; but a living Father who "seeketh."

This is Redemption. This is the doctrine of Holy Spirit: "God is a spirit—He seeketh."

Oh, if in this dreary life, when one is struggling for truth, and struggling to God alone, it is only that we are realizing the ideal of our own minds!

Here is the value of belief in a Person. Personality belongs to spirit; not less personal because spirit. And, therefore, our Redeemer tells us this truth, "the Father seeketh such to worship Him"—not that we seek God, but that He seeks us; not that we rise to God, but that He descends to us.

This it is upon which we base our conviction that there will be hereafter a spiritual worship. We hear much respecting the "advancement of humanity;" if it meant only this, that there is a law in us rising to perfection, the question would not be *worth doubting;* but when we are told that the Creator has interested Himself in His creation, we know that the day shall come when the "true worshippers shall worship the Father in spirit and in truth."

II. The nature of Spiritual worship. Now, what we mean by "worship" is the highest reverence of the soul; adoration, awe; it may be, even, vague devoutness: "Ye know not what."

There is a vast difference between a man's creed and his worship. It is not merely what a man *professes* to reverence that constitutes worship. Moreover, to be spiritual, worship must be intelligent. It must be higher than mere words. It is possible for a Trinitarian to call Christ God, and worship mammon. It is conceivable that a Unitarian theologian may in word—I say *conceivable*—deny even the Deity of Christ, and yet, like the son in the parable who said "I go," and went not, that he may have learned to give Him the whole reverence of his soul : "Not every one that saith unto Me, Lord, Lord, shall enter into the kingdom of heaven; but he that doeth the will of My Father which is in heaven."

Again, it is not a thing which a man can decide, whether he will be a worshipper or not; a worshipper he *must* be: the only question is *what* will he worship? Every man worships—is a born worshipper. It is nonsense to say he does not believe in a God. Before what is greater than himself man bows instinctively. The feeling of devoutness is instinctive. Look at the child when he first enters the Church of God, how his soul seems filled with the grandeur of the service, how he tries to join his voice with the praises that are being uttered. It is man's necessity that he must love. He may call himself an infidel if he will, but he must worship something—it may be perchance himself, or the Rights of Man, or even Reason.

1. Once more, the new worship of God is to be a universal worship : "Neither in this mountain nor yet at Jerusalem shall men worship the Father." Are we, then, to understand by this that the difference between the old and the new worship is merely that the

one is localized and the other not? [Observe there was a use of space and place before the Father was known. Zeus of Olympus and Jove of the Capitol compared in effects.] Nay, the distinction is not that; what is meant here is that it is not in Mount Moriah or Mount Gerizim only, but everywhere, that we are to worship the Father. The distinction is between exclusive and universal worship. The time was coming when the question *where* would be felt to be unimportant.

A mistake is sometimes made, and it is said that local worship is here forbidden, that worship in a place is not spiritual worship, and that we must go into the temple of Nature to worship the Father in spirit. We are told that the everlasting hills are pillars far more grand than the pillars of the Church, and that the sky above is far more glorious than the roof of the most splendid cathedral. This is certainly a truth to be insisted on; Nature is the temple of God, and he who refuses to worship there refuses to worship as our Redeemer did. There is in the worship in the temple of Nature something elevating and grand; we feel ourselves higher than the Nature we contemplate, and so our pride begins to rise; and when we come back from it to worship among men, we find that we had been forgetting humanity, and the family of spirits congenial to us. Therefore do not fly to Nature for spiritual worship. We must content ourselves with a worship far less grand, but quite as true, and more humble.

2. Again, the new worship of God must be worship "in spirit." This truth the better men among the Jews had gradually seen. The later prophets had clearer and higher notions of worship than their predecessors. This we see from their notion of sacrifice: "Lo, I come to do Thy will, O Lord;" and, again, "He hath showed thee, O man, what is good, . . . and what doth the Lord require of thee but to do justice, to love mercy, and to walk humbly with thy God?" They recognized that all true life is worship: "Worship the Lord in the beauty of holiness."

3. Lastly, this spiritual worship consists in the worship of truth. . . . When we are told to worship the Lord in truth, it means the correspondence between acts and laws. . . . In spiritual life there are certain laws, obedience to which is truest worship. God dwells in the humble and contrite heart; to fear God, to be humble, and to love God, that is the spiritual worship of God.

XIV.

THE CONVICTION OF SIN IN THE MIND OF PETER.

Brighton, November 10, 1850.

"When Simon Peter saw it, he fell down at Jesus' knees, saying, Depart from me, for I am a sinful man, O Lord."—Luke v. 8.

This is one of the earliest, if not the very earliest, interviews of the Apostle Peter with the Redeemer. It was rendered memorable by the miraculous draught of fishes which attended it. It is worthy of observation that the last recorded interview of our Lord with the same apostle was marked by a set of circumstances precisely similar. In both cases Peter had toiled all night, and had been unsuccessful, and at last was relieved by miracle. In this case evidently there was much that was symbolical and which prefigured—so that the heart might understand many things—the future spiritual success of Peter, and also the unstinted exuberance of the loving-kindness of God, and the utter powerlessness of unaided human effort.

We have, moreover, a specimen of the Redeemer's teaching. He taught by actions; He was Himself the Word, the expression of the mind of God; every action was itself a word. His miracles had a voice, and His life was, as it were, a magnificent monument sculptured over with hieroglyphics which can only be understood and interpreted by him who has the key, which is the spirit of God. Now the advantage of this symbolic teaching was twofold:

First, it was a living thing. Our Master came into this world, not to be merely a signpost on which the way was written, but to be "the way" itself; not to be the teacher, but "the truth." And similarly, for the same reason, there is a special power in symbolic teaching. Sacraments have in them, as they say, more of grace than sermons or mere words. It is possible for a minister to say, "You are all God's children," but it is not possible to say it with so much force as is expressed in the sacrament which represents that fact. It is possible for a minister to say, "Ye are all brethren," and yet it is impossible for him to state it thoroughly with all that eloquence which is found in this instituted fact of Christ. By this institution rich and poor, great and small, master and servant, kneel together at the same table as brethren. It is possible for the minister to say that everything here is sacred, but he cannot say this as powerfully as it is said in that same sacrament: it is impossible for him to tell out this truth as it is told in our Master's institution, according to which the commonest elements and actions are taken and consecrated to be the most sacred symbols of His religion.

In the next place, this symbolic teaching saves us from dead dogmas. The words of Christ are living words; they speak to the imagination and the heart rather than to the intellect. For example, our Master took bread and said, "This is my body;" let the imagination and the heart feed upon that, and then you will feel that these words were such that no others could have been substituted for them; but let the Romish commentator come with his intellect, and force it into literalism, and demand that you should receive only the external meaning of these words, and then a glorious figure is turned into mere logic, and the life of the thing is gone. Again, our Redeemer here, by a significant act, proclaims to Peter many things on which his heart may feed—the loving-kindness of God, the powerlessness of man, and the success of the Gospel; but let the commentator come and force upon it a literal meaning, and its true life is gone; the poetry of it has fled—for all the highest truth is poetry. The life of Christ is the noblest poetry, the actions and words of Christ are poetry; with that the mind intensely elevated labors, without power of expressing it in words adequate, and therefore must find for itself figures; just as God is obliged to speak to us by the symbols of this universe, and just as the universe tells us of the beauty of God; but try to express in words the beauty, majesty, and love, and it will all fail. So in the words of Christ there is a something forever beautiful, but it is a beauty too refined for the mind to grasp; therefore these acts of Christ remain forever full of a meaning which can never be exhausted; these words it is our privilege to find each time we look into them as fresh and new as if they had never been interpreted before.

Our thoughts to-day will branch off into these two divisions:

I. The meaning and object of this miracle.
II. The effects produced by it on Peter's mind.

I. This miracle, more than all others, taught God's personality.

Brethren, at the bottom of all things here there is a law. Now it is the tendency of habit to look upon law, and see nothing below it. We gaze upon this great world of God and see nothing below the vast mass of laws by which it is governed; then a miracle breaks the continuity of these laws by a higher law. For let it not be fancied that a miracle is a contradiction of these laws, it is simply an interruption. It may be the ordinary law that a man under certain circumstances of sickness shall die; but if the hand of God be placed beneath that man to save him, there is, if you will, an interruption, but no contradiction. For what is a law? A law is merely the expression of the will of God; a law is God in action: there must be a will before there can be a law. God is imminent in this world; He is the life of all that is. The birds move and migrate unerringly from place to place, guided, as we say popularly, by instinct; let us rather say guided by the law of God. Certain fishes are found in deep water, others in shallow, to each of which they are guided by an impulse, and that impulse is God. Had Peter let down his net as usual, and without a promise received success, doubtless the will of God would have been working just as much as in the other case; but when in obedience to a voice Peter let down the net, and in exact agreement with the prediction his net was filled with fishes, then Peter felt that the words he had formerly used were inadequate, and that the "laws of chance" were false, for from this he learned that there is a living will. And this is the meaning and intention of every miracle, to break through the tyranny of the words "law" and "nature."

II. We pass on now to consider the effects produced on Peter. These centre themselves in one sentence; the effect ended in the production of a sense of sin—"Depart from me, for I am a sinful man, O Lord." Now, this was not mere wonder, nor was it curiosity or surprise; it was the sense of personal sin. His heart was bursting with the feeling, "I am a sinful man, O Lord."

In this division of our subject we find these two branches: first, the cause of this impression; and, secondly, the nature of the sense of sin itself.

1. When we come to look at the cause, we see that the impression was partly owing to the apostle's Jewish education. The miracle falling on a Jewish mind produced a different effect from what it would have produced on a heathen mind. For the Jews always recognized the personality of God; therefore this only awoke what was acknowledged before. Had this happened to a heathen, it would have produced nothing but surprise and wonderment; but the feeling of a Jew in such a case was not merely that he had erred against his nature, but that he had transgressed the will of a living person. This recognition of God's personality formed the vast distinction between the heathen and the Jew. The Jew felt, "Thou, God, seest me;" and he was ever haunted by that awful relationship which cannot be put aside, the feeling of the debt and account yet to be gone through between "Thee and me."

And, partly, again, this was produced by the pure presence of Jesus Christ; He interpreted man, and revealed the thoughts of many hearts, not by instituting any system of painful self-scrutiny, but by placing earthly imperfection in opposition to His own Divine perfection. And, therefore, wherever the Redeemer went, He elicited a strange sense of sin—the conviction of sin came instantly on the soul of Zacchæus as soon as Jesus spake to him, and he stood forth and said, "If I have done wrong, I restore fourfold;" the poor sinful woman in His presence poured out her tears in abundance; and the righteous centurion felt, "I am not worthy that thou shouldst come under my roof." Even the thief upon the cross confessed that he justly merited his condemnation; and Peter, brought before his Master, says at once, "I am a sinful man, O Lord."

And this is not the case only in our Redeemer's personal ministry, but it is so wherever Christianity is preached: it ever produces a sense of imperfection not felt before; it is the more radiant light making more intense the shadow that had been almost invisible before; and this shadow has so rested upon the heart that man could not stand beneath it in his own strength; and then, from the anguish of a heart pressed down by sin, there rose up the Romish confessional. In such days as these, when men's minds are fevered, it is almost impossible to understand the real meaning of such an institution, but a meaning it must have; we have seen its infinite evil, but this is no proof that it was originally established without a real and true meaning. The worship of the Virgin, idolatrous though it be, yet tells us a truth that there has been a revolution in society which has made men reverence meekness and purity rather than strength. So does the confessional, even through its mass of evil, proclaim to us the truth that through the light of Christ there has come into the world the necessity for a pure conscience.

2. We pass on now once more to consider the nature of this conviction of sin in Peter's bosom. There is a remorse which is felt for crime, there is a sting, an anguish represented so well by the apostle's words, "The sting of death is sin;" but this was not Peter's case. There is something very significant here; it is not merely pain, but a sudden throbbing, making life itself death. Now, such as this was not the apostle's feeling, for his had been a life not of crime, but of uprightness; he was a man not only of external regularity, but of inward devotedness. He had lived anticipating the Redeemer's advent; and this is plain from the fact that when Andrew went to call his brother to Jesus, the words he used were these: "We have found the Messiah"—thus evidently showing that they had been waiting for the "consolation of Israel." But the language of holy men, when they speak of sin, is startling; the world cannot hear them speak of themselves as the "chief of sinners" without surmising that there must be some crime to produce all this contrition.

In order to understand this, and to comprehend Peter's conviction of guilt, we must look at the three principles which guide the life of three different classes of men. The first is that of obedience to the opinion of the world, the second is the standard of a man's own opinion, and the third is the light of the life of God. The first of these makes the man of honor, the second makes the man of virtue, and the third makes the man of saintliness.

Some men live entirely by the world, so that their very life seems to hang on the opinion of the world—these are the men of honor. Such as these was Saul, the first monarch of Israel; he lived by the world's opinion. When he had done wrong before God, he desired Samuel to honor him before the elders of his people. He did not feel, like Peter, that he was sinful, but said, "I have played the fool exceedingly;" and when his life drew to a close, when his popularity was gone and his authority remained no longer, there was nothing left for the mere man of honor but suicide.

There are other men who live on a principle, and are to themselves a law; they live by their own opinions. These are the men of virtue; they often stand as rocks in the midst of a corrupt age, men of firmness, integrity, and strength, and, moreover, of self-reliance. Such a man as this was the other Saul at that period when he felt respect for his past life, and looked upon that life as blameless. Such, also, was Peter in his earliest life; and this spirit broke out once again in after-life when he exclaimed, "Though all should deny Thee, yet will not I."

There is yet another class of men, those who walk by the standard of the will of God. It is from the knowledge of that will that men learn the infinite littleness of their own achievements: this makes them feel as nothing in the sight of God; and then those actions which before appeared meritorious turn out to be nothing but bare duties, the omission of which is great sin. And here lies the distinction between virtue and saintliness: the man of virtue walks in firmness, resting on the law which he has fulfilled; while the man of saintliness walks humbly, meekly, lowly, as beneath the infinite heaven of duty that arches overhead. And such was the case with Peter when this new revelation of the majesty and purity of Christ was made known to him. Up to this time he had lived an upright man, full of self-reliance; from this time he began to walk lowly and learned self-forgetfulness. Till a man learns that he never attains to saintliness.

This is the way in which Christ produces conviction of sin, not by giving us the confessional, not by demanding that we should be thrown back upon ourselves in painful self-scrutiny, as if from the charnel-house of corruption it were possible to extract life; but rather by placing before us infinite love, infinite loving-kindness, and a perfect humanity; we fall in the dust before this and say, "We are sinful men, O Lord."

And now, brethren, one word in conclusion. I have purposely abstained from that subject which is now occupying the mind of all England—the impotent assumption of a foreign prelate to claim spiritual authority over free-born Englishmen. It would have been easy for me to agitate your minds, easy to awake your indignation; for myself, I love not such work. At least let the Sabbath-day be free from that. Give the week, if you will, to the attitude of defiance; let us give one day in seven to the attitude of soul-humbleness.

I have brought before you a personal subject. We are sinners, we have erred exceedingly, and we have seen the infinite charity of God stream forth in the majesty of Jesus Christ. It is possible for us to bear the splendor of that presence only when love has taken the place of fear, and we feel that we need fear nothing, neither death nor hell nor men. When others are in anguish and bitterness of spirit, what have we to fear, resting on the name of Christ? "For," says the apostle, "I am persuaded that neither death, nor life, nor angels, nor principalities, nor powers, nor things present, nor things to come, nor height, nor depth, nor any other creature, shall be able to separate us from the love of God which is in Jesus Christ our Lord."

XV.

GUILT OF JUDGING.—CONTEMPTUOUSNESS.

(FROM AUTOGRAPH NOTES.)

Brighton, November 24, 1850.

"But why dost thou judge thy brother? or why dost thou set at nought thy brother? for we shall all stand before the judgment-seat of Christ."— Rom. xiv. 10.

By the way in which these words are read the apostle's meaning may be preserved or lost. If you read, "Why dost thou judge thy brother? or why dost thou set at nought thy brother? for we shall all stand before the judgment-seat of Christ," it simply implies that the apostle, speaking to the same person, blames two things which he might do: why dost thou judge? or why dost thou set at nought?

Whereas if we read it thus: Why dost *thou* judge? why dost *thou* set at nought?—then the real sense is kept; and the apostle speaks to two classes of persons. To the first he says, Why judge? then, turning to the second, Why dost *thou* set at nought?

In the commencement of the chapter it appears that there were in Rome two sets of Christians, the weak and the strong.

The weak were those weak in the principles of Christianity, who had lingering scruples, the remnants of Judaism, for instance, respecting days and things. They believed in the inherent sanctity of Sabbath-days and new moons, and in the inherent pollution of certain things, such as tainted meats. Consequently they observed all the days, and ate herbs instead of meat. The other Christians were the strong—strong in the principles of Christianity. They understood the largeness and breadth of Christianity, and had grasped the truth that it is Christ in the heart, the Spirit of God within the soul. They understood that it is the spirit of man which sanctifies or pollutes what it touches; that no day has any inherent holiness in itself, and no meat any inherent pollution. Hence they esteemed all days alike; and they believed that they might eat all things.

So far there was no great harm. On the one side a little narrowness which would wear away; on the other a little more enlightenment was needed; and the apostle was content to say, "Let every man be fully persuaded in his own mind."

But then these Roman Christians went further. The narrow-minded, scrupulous Christians judged—that is, condemned, their freer brethren for doing those things from which they themselves abstained. Because they looked upon all days as alike, and ate all meats, they pronounced them unchristian. To these, therefore, the apostle said, "Why dost thou judge thy brother?"

On the other hand, the enlightened, strong-minded Christians—not necessarily better men, but only more clear in their views—heartily despised the bigotry and narrowness of those who were so particular about days; nay, apparently even went so far as to insult their feelings by a wanton indulgence in those things which they condemned. They openly profaned the sacred days; they publicly ate in the heathen temples meat which had been sacrificed to idols. To them, therefore, the apostle said, "Why dost thou set at nought thy brother?"

Our thoughts will therefore best divide themselves into these two branches:

I. The Supremacy of Conscience.
II. The Infringement of the sacred Rights of Conscience.

I. The Supremacy of Conscience. The principle on which Paul forbade uncharitable judgment and contemptuousness was the supremacy of the individual conscience. It is throughout the chapter the key-note, the master-thought, of all: "Let every man be fully persuaded in his own mind," "We shall all stand before the judgment-seat of Christ," "So then every one of us shall give account of himself to God," "Let us not *therefore* judge one another any more; but judge this rather, that no man put a stumbling-block or an occasion to fall in his brother's way," "Who art thou that judgest another man's servant? to his own master he standeth or falleth. Yea, he shall be holden up; for God is able to make him stand."

According to Paul, nothing is to supersede personal conviction. Conscience is the supreme tribunal erected within a man's own soul. There is no appeal to the opinion of privileged persons. The apostle would not allow them to condemn for conscientious acts: "Let no man judge you." Be indifferent to man's judgment. Brethren, for views and opinions and things which belong to our own consciences, and do not interfere with the happiness of others, do not mind the denial of your Christian character by fallible men. Be in no anxiety. Human passions cannot bar your Christian rights. Let them judge or despise. Feel that you owe allegiance to Christ, and in that sacred, solitary feeling remain calm.

There is no appeal to public authority. They who are zealous for uniformity would have thought this a great occasion for the Church or the legislator to step in—rule the question, decide it once for all, and so put an end to this variety. What could be worse than that one should keep the day and another not keep it? Now, therefore, if ever, was the time for an apostle to interfere. But there is a great lesson to be learned from the fact that Paul did not interfere. He did not rule that the weak must give up their scruples or that the strong must yield to them. His own opinion was undoubted; he would have held with the larger, freer view; but he would not enforce this his own opinion upon the weaker brethren. And if the inspired apostle would not decide, no Church has a right to enforce rules in these matters; no legislature has a right to step in to compel such uniformity. No private Christian has a right to ask a legislature to compel others to observe days as he does.

Let us guard ourselves from a possible misconception of these words. Let us not mistake supremacy of personal conscience for supremacy of individual will. "Let every man be fully persuaded in his own mind." We draw a distinction between the conviction, or full persuasion, which has become part of a man's self—that which he believes as the result of much inquiry—and opinion, which is but half-conviction. The apostle asserted the sanctity of convictions; they are the solemn solitary positions in which a man stands before God; but we must not exalt our opinions to the rank of convictions. Some people take up opinions in the lightest way, and expect for them all the deference due to Christian conviction. They say, Think what you like, it does not matter; your own opinion is just as likely to be true as that of another. The result would be universal anarchy and license.

St. Paul is very far from saying that; he does not say, You are not accountable for your opinion; he simply says, You are not accountable to fallible man. To God you are. "We must stand before the judgment-seat of Christ." He does not say, You may observe these things or not, as you like; he says, "He that observeth the day, observeth it to the Lord; and he that observeth not the day, to the Lord he doth not observe it; he that eateth, eateth to the Lord, for he giveth God thanks; and he that eateth not, to the Lord he eateth not, and giveth God thanks"—provided it is done conscientiously to the Lord. He does not say private judgment is right; he only says there is a right of private judgment, irresponsible except to God.

II. We pass on now to consider the violation of the rights of conscience, and this in two ways:

First, by unchristian judging: "Why dost thou judge thy brother?"

Let us explain what judging is. Judging is persecuting; it was the procedure of the Dark Ages: men were persecuted for their conscientious views. Rome assumed infallibility, and the secular law burned or tortured all whose minds were not shaped to the approved standard.

But let us come home to ourselves, and consider the judgment, persecution, condemnation, which is not peculiar to Rome, but belongs to human nature. We make the measure of our own conceptions the measure and limit of the thoughts and feelings of others. Let us take these very cases cited by the apostle—the observance of the Sabbath-day, and the abstaining from certain things pronounced worldly. What do we with such as do not coincide in our views on these matters? You hear insinuations and surmises, that the man is lax, or a Sabbath-breaker, or a worldly man. If he be a minister or a bishop, he is scarcely allowed to be called a Christian; they say he is a Socinian or an infidel. Further off, his morals are assailed, and a vicious life is charged against him.

Now this is judging. It is not life or personal liberty that is assailed, but character, which is as precious as life. If you spare a man's life and destroy his fair fame, you cripple his influence, and you make him a pariah and an outcast, till he feels alone. Have you not judged him?

Now let us look at the guilt and wrong of this. In the first place, there is its arrogance. Such judging can only be defended on the claim of infallibility. Rome makes that claim, and is consistent in persecuting; but Protestants, who do not make it, are inconsistent.

Are those who judge others wiser than their brethren? Are they free from human frailty? Are they the meek, the learned, the holy, and the wise? or are they not generally the self-instructed, the weakest of both sexes, the impetuous, the talkative, who presume to judge on the authority, perhaps, of some minister, who is to them as a pope? "*Who* art thou that judgest another man's servant? to his own master he standeth or falleth."

And, secondly, it utterly fails in procuring what it aims at, which is uniformity of opinion.

Uniformity of opinion is the ideal good which men have tried for ages to attain, by judgment, by denunciation, by exclusion. Rome tried it for at least one thousand years; England tried it for three centuries in Ireland. Have we got uniformity there? Is Christendom more united than it was in the time of the apostle? The airy dream is further off than ever!

And, in the third place, it destroys free inquiry.

We boast of our Protestant freedom; we say that Romanists shut up the Bible, but that we give it without note or comment, and bid men judge for themselves. Now think, do we not really say, "Here is the Bible: read it for yourself; but these doctrines, and no other, you must find in it; inquire freely, but at your peril arrive at any other conclusion than this; here is the truth, and here is the Bible to prove it by?" Is it not manifest that this is a bitter mockery, and that it only gives the name of liberty!

Hence it comes to pass that men will not bear to hear the truth. They think that they have it already, in the small compass of a single mind, and they come to church to hear it repeated to them in a sermon; not to get fresh gleams of infinite truth, but, holding all the infinite in their minds, to criticise any departure from it. The multitude dare not think, and they who think dare not speak. And this we call free inquiry! This is the present case of Christian society, to my mind an awful and appalling one. What is there to prevent the spirit of the old times being applied to us?—"The prophets prophesy falsely, and the priests bear rule by their means, and my people love to have it so; and what will be the end thereof?"

The other way in which these rights are violated is by contemptuousness: "Why dost thou set at nought thy brother?"

The sin of judging is the sin of the narrow-minded. But there is a sin into which the liberal-minded are apt to fall—the sin of contempt for narrowness, and scorn for scruples.

Now draw a distinction between largeness of view and largeness of heart. A narrow mind is not always a narrow heart. To be strong is not necessarily to be strong in goodness, only strong in power of grasping a principle.

There are worse things than narrow views. Nay, often formalism and superstition go along with great earnestness of life. The missionaries often hold views infinitely narrow, and yet these men give their lives and energies to turn men to God, and thus shame those of larger views. Doctor Johnson believed in apparitions, Pascal in modern miracles, Xavier in papal supremacy, Fénelon, one of the saintliest of men, in transubstantiation. Many a good English Christian is as scrupulous about the Sabbath as if he were a Jew. Many of another class are as particular about fasting as if it were a moral duty.

What, then? Shall we say that they are very narrow, and feel contempt for them? Oh, but take heed how you despise any of God's little ones, if they acted and believed thus to the Lord. For what is largeness of view compared with devotedness of life?

> "There is some soul of goodness in things evil,
> Would men observingly distil it out."

I have learned to perceive that where good men have clung to a superstition or a form, or a narrow miserable view, it is for the sake of some deep truth with which it seems to stand connected, and which I believe as well as they. So in the speculations so common in these days, our sin is likely to be contempt.

In conclusion, observe the great principle on which the apostle forbade contemptuousness, that there is a soul of goodness even in things evil. By things evil, I mean not things morally evil, but intellectually wrong. Hear what the apostle saith of these, that although those men were wrong in their conceptions, yet they did all things to the glory of God. Therefore we ever love to penetrate below the surface, for we are certain of this, that the Spirit of God in the hearts of His believing people is one and the same Spirit. Here were two cases: the one man thought that he might eat all things, the other felt that he was forbidden everything but herbs. These men, though they thought the opposite, yet in the depth of their hearts were the same, for the object of both was to give God glory. Now, this is the only principle on which to found Christian charity, not on that contemptuous indolence which holds that all opinions are equally right, nor, on the other hand, on that which looks on all as equally wrong; but on that love which looks to the good at the bottom of all false views, that love which looks to the heart rather than to the view; that love which, retaining its own convictions, penetrates and seeks to trace the faith, and holiness, and love which lie beneath the different forms of error. It is only when we have learned this that we can cease from judging and love all men as Christ loved us.

XVI.

"THE CHRISTIAN MINISTRY."

Brighton, December 15, 1850.

"What went ye out for to see? A prophet? yea, I say unto you, and more than a prophet. For this is he of whom it is written, Behold, I send my messenger before thy face, which shall prepare thy way before thee."—Matt. xi. 9, 10.

THE Church services for the first Sunday in Advent fix our attention chiefly on the coming of the Redeemer to judgment; and, accordingly, our subject was the principle of the judgment-coming of the Son of Man. On the second Sunday they rather fasten our attention on the Scriptures as the preparation for His coming; and accordingly our subject then was the principle of Scripture interpretation. No one can have read attentively the services of this day without perceiving that the main subject is the Christian ministry. The Epistle is that remarkable portion of Scripture in which St. Paul, after protesting against the exaggerated way in which the Corinthians had exalted their ministry, takes for the Christian ministry far lower ground: "Let a man so account of us as of the ministers of Christ and stewards of the mysteries of God." Ministers and stewards, that is, servants and dependents; "the mysteries of God" mean, not things hidden, but things once hidden and now revealed. In the Collect a parallel is drawn between the career of John the Baptist and the Christian ministry; and, turning to the gospel appointed for the day, we find the character of John the Baptist given by lips infallible: "What went ye out for to see? A prophet? yea, I say unto you, and more than a prophet." The Church of England has therefore selected as her pattern for the Christian ministry—not a priest, but a prophet; not Aaron, but John the Baptist—telling us distinctly that the Church regards her ministers as typified by prophets, not by priests. This, then, is our subject for to-day, the Christian ministry, what it is not, and what it is: it is not a line of priests, it is a succession of prophets.

I. In the first place, it is not a line of priests. Let us understand what a priesthood is. A priesthood is based upon the assumption of a spiritual inherent superiority of one class over another, so that the inferior class is incapable of offering any worship or sacrifice to God. Now, this system may be founded upon three supposed grounds—first, on the basis of superiority of race; secondly, on that of superior character; and, thirdly, on the basis of the superiority of inward knowledge. Almost all the priesthoods of the East are based on the superiority of race; they regard themselves as the mediators between God and man, the expounders of the will of God, through whom alone man can offer sacrifice acceptable to God. It is plain that a priesthood such as this can only be kept up by the priority of race. Another principle is that of personal superiority of character; but it is evident that such a priesthood is not hereditary, it ends with the man himself; such a priesthood we find typically in Melchisedek. The third basis on which such a priesthood may rest is the ground of superiority of knowledge both naturally and supernaturally acquired. In either case the only way to keep up a priesthood is by the exclusion of all others from knowledge. Such, brethren, is, will be, and ever has been the mode by which a priesthood has endeavored to maintain its superiority. Thus it was among the Jews; the prophets declared that the people perished for lack of knowledge. Our Redeemer Himself protested against them, saying that they had taken away the key of knowledge. That which has been done recently by the priesthood in Ireland is by the instinct of self-preservation, because the moment that there is equality in knowledge, the priesthood falls forever.

Now let us observe that the principle of the priesthood, after all, rests upon a truth, otherwise it could not so long have held sway over men's minds. There is in a certain sense a mediatorial power which man exercises over man; it is possible that the superior mind ever must be the medium of communication between God and the inferior character. It is possible that there must *ever* be a medium through which the idea of God is presented. But the difference between a priesthood and a ministry is this, that the object of the priesthood is to keep up that distinction, while the object of the ministry is to obliterate it. The parent is the medium of communication between God and the child; but that, in process of years, becomes obliterated when the child knows as much as the father. In ancient times Moses was in knowledge, both temporal and spiritual, immeasurably above the nation of Israel, and he is therefore called a mediator; but it was the object of Moses not to keep up that distinction, but to break it through, and therefore when one of his followers was indignant because others were prophesying in the camp, the noble expression of the prophet was, "Enviest thou for my sake? would God that all the Lord's people were prophets, and that the Lord would put His spirit upon them." There was an immeasurable distinction between John the Baptist and the nation he taught, but the life of John was intended to do away with that distinction. The apostles were in this respect mediators, and so far priests. But was it their intention to remain so forever? Listen to the Apostle Paul in those words of glorious irony: after having grounded his right to the apostleship, he says to those claiming knowledge equal to his own, "Now ye are full, now ye are rich; ye have reigned as kings without us;" and then, dropping the tone of irony, "I would to God ye did reign, that we might reign with you." In other words, he wished that their claim was true. And therefore it was that the prophecy of old was taken up joyfully by the apostles as the richest time in the mediatorial kingdom, when the last offices of the priesthood should be taken away; the time, saith the Lord, "When they shall no more teach every man his brother saying, Know the Lord, for all shall know Me from the least to the greatest." This, then, is the spiritual priesthood.

Now, let us understand what a priesthood so called is. It is the office of the priest to be the representative of man before God; he takes the mourning and the lamentation of the people for sin, bearing it upon his breast before God, and through his lips that remorse becomes acceptable to God. Now, by this intervention the spirit of man is cut off from God, and by the mysterious means of propitiation God is represented as far off; for you will observe that the office of the priesthood is not to reconcile man to God, but to reconcile God to man. To reconcile man to God, that is human, and is done by superior faith and love; but you do not thereby change the disposition of God: that is what the priesthood pretends to do. Let us observe the effects of this system: first it removes God far from the soul, whereas God is ever near; nearer when man prays, when he repents, when he loves, than when he is receiving any ecclesiastical ordinance; but the spirit of the priestly system is to remove God far off from man, to represent Him to us as a far distant sovereign, seated on a throne of splendor. Secondly, it degrades humanity, for its language tells us not of the affinity of man to God, but of the immense distance between the two; giving also an exaggerated expression of the weakness of man, and of the nothingness of the power of God within the soul. And then the tone and spirit of such a system becomes either depressed and melancholy, or else encourages a vicarious reliance on its ordinances. Once more, its tendency is to produce a slavish worship; for is it not true that under such a system men come into the presence of God rather to throw off guilt than to pour out the soul in adoration and thanksgiving? Theirs is but the trembling of a condemned criminal before his judge. Lastly, it is all retrospective—a retrospective holiness from which we have fallen, a retrospective purity in which we were once, retrospective sin to be obliterated; retrospective all, there is nothing of the ennobling of life, telling of times beyond. This, then, is the system of the priesthood: first, a distant God; secondly, a mean humanity; thirdly, a servile worship; and, lastly, a retrospective reverence.

II. We pass on now to consider what the ministry is. We say it is prophetical, not priestly.

Let us understand what the prophet's office was; John was a "prophet, yea, and much more than a prophet," and the Church of England has compared her ministers to him. We greatly mistake if we think that the office of the prophet was simply to predict future events; predictors, no doubt, the prophets were, but this formed a very small portion of their ministrations. Take, for instance, John; his sole prediction was, "The kingdom of heaven is at hand." Even their prophecies were far rather great eternal principles, which must fulfil themselves forever, than a reference to any one particular event. It is far grander to state eternal truths like these than to state facts which take place but once. This, then, was the office of the prophet, to teach eternal truths. We observe that this prophetic office was far higher than the priesthood; for we find that Moses, the lawgiver and prophet, creates Aaron the priest. This is a thing worthy the consideration of those who are shocked at the supremacy of the sovereign; the lawgiver and the prophet here made the priest; the king was above the priest, the priest beneath the prophet.

Secondly, we observe, respecting the prophetic office, that all the most sublime passages in the Bible are from the writings of the prophets. The priestly writings were but temporary. Take, for instance, the ritual of Judaism in the books of Leviticus and of Chronicles; the first we rarely read in our Church services, the second never. Ask you what the passages are that make our hearts burn and make the Bible *the* book? Are they not the Psalms and prophetic writings? The outpourings of a devout soul to God in all its ways, in humbleness, in trust, in aspiration, are the passages in the prophetic writings which make the Bible *the* book of all the world.

Lastly, we observe this difference between the prophet and the priest, that it was the office of the prophet to counteract the priestly office. Thus saith the Lord by the mouth of the Prophet Isaiah, "Bring no more vain oblations; incense is an abomination to me; your new moons and your appointed feasts my soul hateth; they are a trouble unto me, I am weary to bear them." And then He goes on to say, "Wash you, make you clean; cease to do evil, learn to do well." In the New Testament we find the priests demanding ritual sanctity and the performance of all the appointed services; while the voice of the prophet is heard saying, "Repent, for the kingdom of heaven is at hand." This was prophetic teaching, and consequently the priest was ever against the prophet. The priesthood stoned Stephen, put John in prison, and it was by sacerdotal orders that the great Prophet of the world was crucified and slain; for they knew that if the prophets were allowed to remain, the priesthood was at an end forever.

We say, then, that the Christian ministry is prophetical, not priestly. And let us observe that the ministry of our Blessed Lord Himself here on earth was prophetical, and not priestly. I lay a stress on that expression "*here on earth*," because unquestionably He is a priest in heaven above. The high-priesthood of the Son of Man is, I believe, spoken of in only one passage of Scripture, in the Hebrews; there His priesthood is denied here on earth, but asserted to be in heaven: "For if He were on earth, He should not be a priest;" in other words, there is a priesthood now, but no earthly priesthood. He is the eternal Word in the bosom of the Father, the medium of communication between God and man, the ladder that reaches from earth to heaven, and that which reconciles God to man, and man to God. The Christian ministry is preparatory, and accordingly the Church of England caught the spirit of that ministry and represented it by the ministry of John the Baptist; the minister of Christ is but a herald to prepare His coming; and then, and only then, has he done his work when he has endeavored to detach trust and admiration from himself and to fasten them upon Jesus Christ; and when he feels that he is becoming every day less and less necessary to those whom he has taught because he has imparted to them all he knows, and led them to the everlasting fountain which shall never be exhausted. The very spirit of the Christian ministry consists in these blessed words, "He must increase, but I must decrease." I fulfil my course; it will soon be done; I point to Christ.

Brethren, in conclusion, I notice two points which seem to favor the notion of a priesthood.

First, I say a few words on the matter of absolution. Unquestionably there is a power of absolution in the ministry of the Church of Christ; but I say again, it is the power of the prophet, and not of the priest. In the case of John the Baptist, men came to him confessing their sins; they were baptized by him in the river, and rose from that water doubtless absolved, and feeling their justification. Remember, I pray you, what absolution is: forgiveness is the act of God, absolution is the act of man. Nathan conveyed absolution to David: "The Lord hath put away thy sin;" this is absolution, the voice of man echoing here on earth the voice of God in heaven—"the Son of Man hath power on earth to forgive sins." Observe, however, that this is prophetical, not priestly; it is not the ministerial act of the priest, but the prophetic power of one representing God, speaking in His name, and so conveying the feeling of God's pardon. Tell us, brethren, if a man has taken from another superstitious feeling; if he has told him that the only one thing to be dreaded is doing wrong; and if, having thereby broken the shackles of superstition, he has enabled him to stand erect in the spirit of a son, has not that man absolved his brother?

Once more, that in which the ministry would seem to be a priestly power is the apostolical succession. This doctrine, as stated usually, is this: that by the imposition of hands, through physical contact, the power of God is conveyed and a Divine right given to the priests. A doctrine such as this rests upon a truth like most other errors. There is an apostolical succession; but it is a succession of prophets, and not of priests; it is a succession never extinct or broken; it is a race of prophets, not a race of priests, the spirit of those on whom God is breathing out the breath of life and love. This is the apostolical succession. The Son of God was Himself a prophet; the apostles were prophets, and their spirit has not died out; and so far as we imbibe their spirit, we are their successors. John the Baptist was endued with the same spirit as Elias, and therefore was his successor in a long line; and the great mind of the leader of the Reformation was the offspring of the mind of the Apostle Paul. And so far as we evince the spirit of the apostles and prophets shall we keep unbroken the line of the apostolical succession. . . .

XVII.

THE THREE CROSSES ON CALVARY.

Brighton, December 22, 1850.

"When they were come to the place which is called Calvary, there they crucified him, and the malefactors; one on the right hand, and the other on the left."—Luke xxiii. 33.

THERE is a twofold solemnity which belongs to the dying hour. It is the winding-up of life, and it is the commencement of eternity.

It is the winding-up of life; life then becomes intelligible. Most of us go through this life scarcely seeming what we are. One wraps himself up in coldness, another in half-hypocrisy; but when it comes to the last, the whole is wound up, and death lays a hand so violent upon the frame that the mask falls suddenly off.

Again, it is the commencement of eternity, for in a short time the body of the dying man will pass away, and his soul will be in possession of that secret which we are toiling all our lives to find. And the solemnity of the thought that he will soon be in possession of that secret communicates itself in a degree to those around him. It is this which gives importance and solemnity to the dying hour even of the meanest. Around his bed the great and powerful will come as if to read in his countenance the secrets of their own mortality. It is this which gives even to the dying hour of the suicide something of importance. The veriest trifler that ever fluttered through this awful world of God's commands for one hour at least the world's attention.

It is these two thoughts which make the dying hour so solemn; and a threefold portion of this interest belongs to the scene of Calvary. Upon this Mount three crosses stood; generally our attention is fixed only upon one, but it becomes us to remember that there were three, and that upon each a human soul was breathed away. From each there is its own peculiar lesson to be gathered.

Here, then, there is opened for us a subject for contemplation, dividing itself into three branches: first, the dying hour of devotedness; secondly, the dying hour of impenitence and hardness; and, thirdly, the dying hour of penitence.

I. First we look at the central cross; on that cross of Christ there was that transacted which never can be exhibited in any dying hour of ours. There was exhibited the grandest expression of that greatest law of ours; that law according to which life cannot be, except through death. But it is not on this, the atonement, that we dwell now; we look upon Jesus now simply as a dying man, and the first lesson that we learn is the conquest of suffering.

He was as much bound to perform the law of God as the meanest creature upon earth. He was as much subject to the law of suffering as we are; there was a work to be done upon His own soul; and of Him in His private, and not in His public, capacity was it said that "the captain of our salvation was made perfect through suffering." This it is which throws so much force on those inspired words, "He became obedient even to the death of the cross." It was not death alone, but death through the cross. The work of the Saviour's soul would have been left imperfect if one single drop of agony had been left untasted; and this seems to be shown by His refusing the mixture of gall and myrrh offered to Him in order to dull His sufferings: for it is written that "after He had tasted thereof He would not drink." He knew the strength and blessedness of suffering, and would not meet His death without intensely feeling it; He would bear all; He would suffer all; the Father had put into His hand the cup to drink, and He had, as it were, carried that cup, though brimful of agony, to His lips, with a hand so steady that not one drop of all its suffering trickled down.

Here is a lesson for us. Part of our obedience and work here on earth is to be done in vigor and in health; part when laid aside in suffering. Much of this must be unintelligible to us here. There is not one present who will not some day exchange the vigor of life for a broken constitution and a suffering frame; no one can know what suffering is till he has known mental torture; and no one can know the extremity of corporeal suffering till, like his Master, he has counted the long hours of torture one by one, and through night after night has heard the clock strike in protracted anguish. This is what we are called upon to endure, and then often it is that fretfulness and impatience break across our souls, and we wish that the whole of our future could be concentrated into one sharp hour. Brethren, a man's work is not done upon earth, so long as God has anything for him to suffer; the greatest of our victories is to be won in passive endurance; in humbleness, in reliance, and in trust, we are to learn to be still, and know that He is God.

In the next place, we learn from that dying hour the influence of personal holiness. The Son of Man came not to the cross to preach, but to suffer; yet in that hour two at least were added to the Church, two at least were enrolled in the number of those that shall be saved hereafter.

When God threw Christianity down upon the world to win her way through almost insuperable impediments, the weapon which He put into her hand, the only weapon, was the talent and eloquence of a life of holiness. Brethren, let the distinction be drawn between the life of holiness and the life of mere blamelessness. Blamelessness and accuracy are beautiful to look upon, but they do not save the soul. The world has enlisted into her service the power of talent and eloquence, but these are not the things that lead to God; men listen to your talent and your eloquence, and recognize the power of your influence; but they know that all you say may be unreal and unfelt; and, therefore, they come merely as looking upon a picture, and admire, but nothing further. It is not this, it is the divine, mysterious power of holiness that tells upon the world.

What these two men saw upon the cross was different from what they had ever seen before. And in the one case contempt was softened into adoration, "Truly this man was the Son of God;" in the other case, hardness was changed into adoring love, "This man hath done nothing amiss." Now, what was it that produced this change? It was not the courage, for thousands had died upon the cross before. And if they wanted recklessness, they had but to turn to the other cross where was one dying bravely enough, but where was none of the marvellous meekness that was seen on the centre cross, none of those words of infinite tenderness, "Father, forgive them, they know not what they do;" there was a recklessness there which enabled him to meet pain with defiance, but none of those words of meekness and trust, "Father, into thy hands I commend my spirit."

Brethren, it is not talent, nor power, nor gifts, that do the work of God, but it is that which lies within the power of the humblest: it is the simple, earnest life led with Christ in God.

II. We are now, secondly, to consider the lesson which comes from the dying hour of impenitence.

Round the cross of the dying thief were accumulated such means as never before met together to bring a man to God. He had felt the power of pain, that power which is often exerted in the soul to soften it. He had heard the truth preached by one recently converted, and we all know the intensity and earnestness of fresh love; preached also by a dying man, whose words are generally received with a kind of veneration, or, at least, attention. There was one beside that cross, moreover, a teacher such as no other man had ever had in his dying hour. And yet, with all these means and advantages, there was nothing but a soul steeled against the truth.

Brethren, the lesson we learn from this is the improbability of a late repentance. There are some men not looking for anything of the kind, but desperately looking forward to certain ruin hereafter, who can receive the announcement of approaching misery even with calmness. But this is not the feeling of most men towards death. The oldest among us here thinks there is yet space enough between him and death for a work still to be done; the day is to come when his present pursuits will be given up, and the things of this world exchanged for the care of his immortal soul; that which he loves now, he thinks he shall hate then, forgetting that what is pleasant now will be pleasant to the last. And this is what, more or less, we are all doing; there is not one of us who can lay his hand upon his heart and say, "I have given up all; I am living now as I should wish to die."

Now, let us endeavor to remember some of the arguments which make a future change improbable. The first argument is this, that there comes a dulness and rigidity of the intellect as life goes on; in the old man's mind channels cut themselves — channels through which thoughts flow; the opinions of the man become fixed; rarely does a man change his opinions after forty years of age. And then add to this the feeling of insecurity which comes from trembling between life and death, the agitation which comes with the dying hour. The probability of repentance is thus removed to a distance almost infinite. For either delirium comes, or else sharp, acute pain which dissipates the faculties.

Even looking at it intellectually, it becomes improbable. The dying thief had lived for years with the prejudice that Jesus was an impostor; and then, when racked in torture, was not in a state in which to change his opinions. As he had lived, so he died.

Again, the improbability of this change arises from the fixing of the affections. All life long this man had lived with his affections fixed on earth; this is the secret of that expression with which he taunted his Redeemer, "If thou be Christ, *save* thyself and us." Life is all he asks; if he could not save his life, all other salvation to him seemed useless. Brethren, grant it for one moment that reason should remain at the last steady to judge of the question then before us, yet this were not enough; even if a man could hear the spade hollowing out his grave, and could look upon the coffin-lid with his own name engraved thereon, with the date of birth and the date of death, there might be much in this to disengage his heart from earth, but would there be in it one element to fasten his soul on holiness?

Lastly, there is an improbability of change in the deadening of the conscience. There was an appeal made to the conscience of the dying thief, but made in vain: "Dost thou not fear God, seeing thou art in the same condemnation?" It was made in vain, because his conscience was in a state of deadness. We find it written that God hardened Pharaoh's heart. It is the greatest evil, and worst penalty of doing wrong, that at last a man ceases to distinguish right from wrong. This was the state in which this man was; and oh! I pray you to remember that towards this state we all are hastening who are hardening our hearts. If there be one among us doing that, putting off the time of repentance to a more convenient season, let him remember that there are two questions to be asked: whether it is likely that the change would come? and whether there is anything in pain that will make holiness more lovely and more dear? And if, in defiance of all experience, he answer in the affirmative, then there is another question—whether God will be trifled with so long, and whether He will suffer a man to go on enjoying life until he has no fresh emotion left, and then will be permitted to give the dregs of a polluted life and a worn-out heart to the God whom he has despised all life long. The ancient prophets spoke emphatically against offering God services which cost us nothing. The meaning they intended to convey is clearly that God will have our best; Christ gave the best, Himself.

My young brethren, now, while emotion is fresh and your affections are worth the having, before the time comes when you are worn and weary, "remember your Creator in the days of your youth!"

III. We turn now to consider the dying hour of penitence. We have said that repentance at the last is a thing *improbable*. Blessed be God, it is not a thing impossible. It has been well said that there has been one instance of a late repentance given us in order that none may despair, and but one that none may presume. The penitent thief expressed his sense of guilt in these words: "We suffer justly the due reward of our deeds." We can lay down no rules for the amount of grief and sorrow; to do so would be as absurd and futile as to lay down laws as to how often a forgiving spirit might pardon an offending brother. There can be no law here, for it is decided by many things—by age, by sex, and by constitution.

We believe that the Church of Rome has erred in substituting penance for penitence; and yet here Rome has in her way expressed a truth, that the natural result of great sin will be the expression of great grief. Perhaps we in our Protestantism have erred in making the way to holiness after sin unnaturally easy. We present a few doctrines to the soul, and then, on the acceptance of a few intellectual truths, it is expected that the great sinner will become the great saint without a tear of agony for the past. Great nature refuses to be thus trifled with. In God's dealing with the soul, there is something analogous with the cure of wounds. When the cut is deep and the blood flows freely, its first effect is to close the wound by its coagulation. So it is with grief: if it is allowed to flow freely, the wound may soon be healed; but if, instead of grief and sorrow, we expect a few doctrines to do the work alone, then we shall soon see the blood break forth afresh.

We also remark here the penitent's zeal for Christ; he spoke as if he himself had been offended, "Dost thou not fear God?" We talk much of toleration; if we mean by that a generous sympathy with the different forms of opinion, then it is Christian; if toleration mean compassion for frailty, and a willingness ever to make a distinction between tempted weakness and deliberate evil, then toleration is nothing more than another name for the mind of Christ. But if it mean that we are to reckon one form of opinion as good as another, and look upon sin merely as a disease against which we cannot feel indignation, then most unquestionably Christianity has in it no toleration. And I remark that zeal, even though it exceed the bounds of righteousness, is a more hopeful thing than lukewarmness; better far to be like the Apostle Paul before he was an apostle, better to be like the Sons of Thunder, better to be like the ancient prophets using the stern language of denunciation, than like Pilate, unconcerned as to the fate of his prisoner so long as he himself was absolved from blame. In the former case, the persecuting Saul became the large-minded Paul, the most liberal and the noblest of all the spirits that have been given to man; and the Son of Thunder became the Apostle of Love. Years and experience will by degrees soften zeal into love, but there is no remedy for lukewarmness.

Moreover, we observe, in the dying hour of the penitent thief, the missionary spirit of doing good. One opportunity only of doing good was given him, and he used it with all his heart.

If we were asked what mark distinguishes Christianity from the world, our reply would be, charity. It is not faith, for the religion of Jesus has faith in common with other religions, but it is charity. "By this," says our Master, "shall all men know that ye are my disciples, if ye have love one to another." The man of love may be guilty of many blunders of doctrine, while cold-hearted men may always be intellectually right; but in the last great day love will be recognized as the one thing needful. The faults of the men of love shall soon disappear in the Redeemer's blood, and leave nothing there, save the love of One who loveth much because much has been forgiven.

In conclusion, we have two remarks to make:

First, that the intermediate state is not a state of unconsciousness. It may be replied, "What signifies this?" this is interfering with things unseen; we can be calm in only knowing that the soul is with God. Our answer is, that if God has revealed it, it is our duty to receive it; and it is by no means unimportant, for though there may be those among men who can leave that matter undecided, feeling certain of the love of God, and can throw themselves into the arms of God, knowing that they will be with Him; yet there are others who cannot so think, and who feel "all their lifetime subject to bondage" in the thoughts of the long last sleep. Therefore it is that we point to this, and show how far Christianity thus differs from Judaism; for Judaism spake of the grave as dark, the place where the dead praise not God; while the New Testament speaks distinctly of a state of consciousness, for in the parable of Dives and Lazarus the rich man is represented as fully conscious in the world beyond of the condition of his sinful brethren. The Apostle Paul, too, longs to depart that he may be with Christ—another proof that the grave is not unconsciousness. And, in addition, we have the example of the dying thief now before us, to whom our Blessed Lord says, "To-day shalt thou be with me in Paradise."

And, secondly, we learn from this the completeness of the sacrifice of Christ. Some have so mistaken the meaning of their Master's death as to believe that, when the soul has departed from the body, there is still a penal fire to finish the Saviour's work. But look at the dying thief forgiven by his Lord; up to that time he had done nothing to make himself meet for glory, after his conversion he could do nothing; and yet, forgiven and redeemed upon the cross, he passed straight to Paradise.

My Christian brethren, we set this truth before you: "Ye are complete in Christ." He reconciled God to man; our work is therefore to become reconciled to God. To him that is in Christ there remains neither speck nor spot to be imputed.

XVIII.

THE STATE OF NATURE AND THE STATE OF GRACE.

Brighton, January 26, 1851.

"Among whom also we all had our conversation in times past in the lusts of our flesh, fulfilling the desires of the flesh and of the mind; and were by nature the children of wrath, even as others. But God, who is rich in mercy, for his great love wherewith he loved us, even when we were dead in sins, hath quickened us together with Christ. By grace ye are saved."—Eph. ii. 3–5.

The prominent point in these verses, manifestly, is the contrast between nature and grace. "By nature," says the apostle, "ye are the children of wrath, by grace ye are saved." Every one of us knows that these words are cardinal points in Christian theology; they have been the cause of bitterest controversies—controversies in which men understanding each other have differed, controversies also in which men really meaning the same thing have expressed it in different words. For example, if one man speaks of the majesty of human nature, it may be that another feels shocked at such an expression; and yet it is more than possible that a man may speak of the majesty of the humanity that God has given us, and still be deeply, intensely, convinced of the reality of his fallen nature. Therefore, in all teaching, more especially in public teaching, in which it is impossible to ask for an explanation, it is important that from time to time terms should be accurately defined. For want of such definition there may seem to be confusion where none really exists. As a proof of this we look to our Redeemer's teaching; let us take the memorable occasion on which He said, "I am the living bread which came down from heaven; if any man eat of this bread, he shall live forever: and the bread which I will give is my flesh, which I will give for the life of the world. The Jews therefore strove among themselves, saying, How can this man give us his flesh to eat?"—they understood in one sense what was spoken in another. And thus often it may seem that the teaching of the minister of God is self-contradictory.

Therefore, brethren, what we shall do to-day will be to define the meaning of two terms: the state of nature and the state of grace.

I. The state of nature.

In the first place, we observe that there is a twofold sense in which we use the expression "nature." When we speak of "nature," we may mean either what it is by right or what it is by fact, what it is meant to be or what it is. Let us take as an illustration of this the fig-tree whereof our Redeemer spoke; in one sense it was its nature to bring forth fruit, but in another sense it was the nature of that tree to bring forth no fruit. Because it was the nature of the fig-tree to bring forth fruit, therefore was the demand made—a demand which, if such had not been its nature, would have been most unjust. Take as another instance the case of the soil which God has made: the nature of the soil is to bring forth weeds; they spring up *naturally*, and yet no one would say that it was created for that purpose—the weeds are rather its perversion. Precisely in the same way, the evil tendencies in the soul of man are there, yet they are not the nature of the soul.

It is on this principle that we find passages in Scripture respecting nature which seem to contradict each other. There is one class of passages in which the right is called natural, and the unnatural is reckoned wrong. To live according to nature is to live according to the will of God; for example, in the First Epistle to the Corinthians, respecting a matter of mere propriety in dress, the apostle refers himself to first principles—"Doth not even nature itself teach you that if a man have long hair it is a shame unto him?" Again, in the Epistle to the Romans, that which is against nature is spoken of as the worst of crimes. Nor is there any way in which we ourselves can speak with more reprobation of a human being than to say, for instance, that he is an "unnatural" son or an "unnatural" father. Similarly, in the Second Epistle to Timothy, St. Paul speaks of it as one of the worst sins of the last times that men should be "without natural affection;" and when we refer to the teaching of our Redeemer Himself, we read, "Why do ye not of yourselves judge that which is right?"

So that, according to Christ's idea of human nature, to judge wrongly was not natural. Now, turning to another class of Scripture passages, we find human nature spoken of in a different way: that which is natural is called evil, and to live according to it is to tend to certain ruin. Accordingly, the Apostle Paul says, "The natural man discerneth not the things of the Spirit of God;" and here, again, in the verses I have selected for the text, "By nature" we are the children of wrath. The great question, therefore, is this: in what sense do we use the term "human nature?" If by human nature you mean nature as seen in this man or in that, then unquestionably nature is evil—individual nature, personal nature, is contrary to God's will; but if by human nature you mean nature as God made it, as it has been once, in one man of our species and only one, and as by God's grace it shall be again; if you mean nature as it is according to the idea of the Creator as shown in Jesus Christ, as it is in the eyes of God imputed, not as it is, but as it shall be, then that nature is a noble thing, a thing divine: for the life of the Redeemer Himself, what was it but the one true exhibition of our human nature?

Having premised so far, we now remark the two things that Paul says respecting this human nature. He says that by nature we fulfil the desires of the flesh and of the mind. I pray you to observe that it is in the second, and not in the first, sense that he here speaks of nature. The "desires of the flesh" mean the appetites; those "of the mind" mean the passions: to fulfil the desires of the flesh is to live the life of the swine; to fulfil those of the mind is to live the life of the devil. Imaginations given to ennoble the spirit degraded to the sensualizing of the spirit till they become the agents of the lowest vices, that is to fulfil the desires of the mind. But let it be observed that this is the partiality, not the entireness, of human nature. Where is the conscience, where the spirit, by which we have communion with God? To live to the flesh and to the mind is not to live to the nature that God gave us: we can no more call that living to our nature than we can say that a watch going by the mere force of the mainspring, without a regulator, is fulfilling the nature of a watch. To fulfil the desires of the flesh and of the mind is no more to fulfil the nature which God has given us than the soil fulfils its nature when it brings forth thorns and briers. This distinction is strongly drawn by the apostle in the Epistle to the Romans. He there speaks of himself in his unregenerate state, and reckons that it is not his nature; he draws a distinction between himself and his false nature, and says it is "not I that do it, but sin that dwelleth in me;" sin is the dominion of a false nature, it is a usurped dominion. The second thing that Paul tells us in connection with this subject is that by nature we are children of wrath. Some commentators have tried to explain that expression away, and have said that when he uses the words "children of wrath," he means men prone to anger. We cannot adopt this view; we take the popular idea, which in this case I believe to be the true one; it is the wrath of God which is here spoken of. And a great truth is thus laid down; that in the state of nature we are in the way to bear the wrath of God. Doubtless the expression used is a popular one, God is spoken of as He is felt by us, not as He is in Himself. Just as when we see the sun gleaming through the mists of evening it seems to us a red mass, and we say "the sun is red," so God, seen through the mists of our prejudices and passions, appears to be a God of wrath. And yet, brethren, God is not wrath, He is infinite love; the eternal serenity of His nature does not feel our passions, He remains forever calm, yet such is *our* nature that we must think of Him as wrath as well as love, to us love itself becomes wrath when we are in a state of sin. To say that the sun is red may not be philosophically true, but it is red to us; to say that God is wrath may not be metaphysically true, but for all practical purposes it is so.

Here is an eternal truth with which we would not part: God must hate sin and be forever sin's enemy. Because He is the Lord of love, therefore must He be a consuming fire to evil; God is against evil, but for us. If, then, we sin, He must be against us; in sinning we identify ourselves with evil, therefore we must endure the consuming fire. Oh! brethren, in this soft age in which we live, it is good to fall back on the first principles of everlasting truth. We have come to think that education may be maintained by mere laws of love instead of discipline, and that public punishment may be abolished. We say that these things are contrary to the Gospel; and here, doubtless, there is an underlying truth; it is true that there may be a severity in education which defeats itself, it is true that love and tenderness may do more than severity; but yet under a system of mere love and tenderness no character can acquire manliness or firmness. When you have once got rid of the idea of public punishment, then, by degrees, you will also get rid of the idea of sin: where is it written in the Word of God that the sword of His minister is to be borne in vain? In this world of groaning and of anguish, tell us where it is that the law which links suffering to sin has ceased to act? Nay, so long as there is evil, so long will there be penalty; and woe to that man who attempts to contradict the eternal system of God; so long as the spirit of evil is in the world, so long must human punishment remain to bear its testimony that the God of the universe is a righteous God. This is what we have to feel: sin, live according to the lusts of the flesh, and you will become the children of God's wrath; live after the Spirit, the higher nature that is in you, and then the law hath hold on you no longer.

Pass we on now to our second subject:

II. The state of grace. "By grace ye are saved."

As in the former case we had one word to explain, so now we have two; the first is "saved," the second "grace."

And, first, we observe that salvation according to the apostle originates in the love of God—"God, who is rich in mercy." It is not that we loved God, but that He loved us; not that we merited the love of God—for when we were yet in sin He loved us; not that the sacrifice of Christ has bought off the wrath of God, but that it was His love that designed the sacrifice of Christ, as it is written, "God so loved the world that He gave His only begotten Son, to the end that all that believe in Him should not perish, but have everlasting life." This, then, is the first principle from which we start, salvation originates in the love of God; and if we ask the reason, there is but one—the love itself, "For His great love wherewith He loved us." The second thing Paul tells us respecting salvation is that it consists in emancipation from evil. "Quickened us together with Christ"—that is, gave life. Remark, the apostle says not "saved from suffering," he says "quickened." Salvation and the love and mercy of God seem to us often no more than rescue from personal suffering. Such a notion entered not into the apostle's mind; according to him, the love and mercy of God were shown in this, not that He saved from penalty, but from sin. If love be merely the prevention of pain, how is this world governed by the love of God? It may be that it is God's intention hereafter to produce a state of painlessness: we know not, but this we know—that God's best and dearest servants have had the cup of suffering placed in their hands and been made to drain it deep. His beloved Son's reward was the cross; "the captain of our salvation was made perfect through suffering." . . . And that, O my Christian brethren, is what we want—life, more life, spiritual life, within us; to know in all things the truth of God and to speak it, to feel in all things the will of God and do it; and to give us that, to impart that Spirit to us, is the mercy and the love of God.

The next word to explain is "grace." It stands opposed to two things—to "nature" and to "law:" to nature in the text, and to law in this, "we are not under law, but under grace." Whenever "nature" means the dominion of our lower appetites, that state in which we feel left to ourselves, then nature stands opposed to grace. In the second place, grace stands opposed to law. Now, let us remember what Paul says respecting law: its language is, "thou shalt and must;" right words and glorious, but words incapable of arresting sin; and, according to Paul, what the law does is to exasperate sin into greater vitality: "I had not known sin but by the law." All that the law can do is to manifest sin, just as the dam thrown against the river shows its strength; law can arrest sometimes the commission of sin, but never the inward principle. Therefore God has provided another remedy—" Sin shall not have dominion over you." Is it because ye are hemmed round with greater penalties? Nay, but because "ye are not under law, but under *grace*."

And now, in conclusion, the application we make of this is contained in one remark—Paul states salvation here as a fact: "By grace ye *are* saved." These Ephesians were, many of them, most imperfect Christians; of none of them could the apostle be sure that they would reach the kingdom of God; and yet there is no word hinting the possibility of their non-election, but, broadly, of all he says, "Ye are saved." Now, there are two systems. The one begins with nature, the other with grace; the one treats all Christians as if they were the children of the devil, and tells them that they may perhaps become the children of God; the other declares that the incarnation of Christ is a fact, a universal fact, proclaiming that all the world are called to be the children of the Most High. I need not say that the system I have last described is that of the Baptismal Service of the Church of England, that precious service which we hold so dear, and through which we are taught to say, "I was made by baptism (that is, not magically created, but declared by the voice of God to be) the child of God, a member of Christ, and an heir of everlasting salvation."

It is thus that the Church of England speaks, but it is of more importance to observe that thus also the Bible speaks. The apostle here speaks of the baptized Ephesians, not hypothetically, but actually, as God's redeemed children. It makes an immense difference in education and in later life which of these views you may adopt. In the one case—if the first be true—we work with a faithless heart: that child of mine may be the child of God, or he may not; he may be elected, or he may not. I tell him to call God his Father, when perhaps He is not so. We thus go working on as if we had to work against nature, instead of with God; as if our work were merely to eradicate something from the soil, instead of seeking to bring forth fruit. Brethren, from such a system as this, what can come? Let us rather believe in grace, instead of beginning with nature; let us believe that we are God's children, that God is our Father, and that Christ has redeemed the world; and then let us seek His grace to keep us steadfast in our faith, that we lose not these inestimable privileges. Let us remember that it is said, "Work out your own salvation with fear and trembling," not because we dread damnation, but because "it is God that worketh in us both to will and to do of His good pleasure."

XIX.

THE CHURCH OF EPHESUS.

Brighton, February 23, 1851.

"Unto the angel of the church of Ephesus write: These things saith he that holdeth the seven stars in his right hand, who walketh in the midst of the seven golden candlesticks; I know thy works, and thy labor, and thy patience, and how thou canst not bear them which are evil; and thou hast tried them which say they are apostles, and are not; and hast found them liars: and hast borne, and hast patience, and for my name's sake hast labored, and hast not fainted. Nevertheless, I have somewhat against thee, because thou hast left thy first love."—Rev. ii. 1–4.

In the Bible high value is placed on the religious affections; in the world and in ordinary life almost none. In matters ecclesiastical and political we are satisfied with results; we care little for the principle, spirit, or feeling which has led to it. And even among religious people a very inadequate view is entertained of these aspirations, as is evident from the tone in which declension in religious feeling is spoken of. We hear it said that it is a matter of regret that these feelings will not last; but that it is inevitable, the thing is unavoidable, and, therefore, not to be greatly lamented. Sometimes a tone more philosophical is adopted: they tell us that the flower must pass away, in order that the fruit may come. Emotion and religious feeling, they say, are intended merely to bridge over the distance between duty and performance, and to make that easy which would have been difficult at first; so that when the flower has passed, we have the fruit; and when the feeling is gone, we have got the habit of duty, and the feeling may then be dispensed with.

Brethren, a sentiment like this stands in diametrical opposition to the language of the Bible. Beneath it, however, there lies a truth; for, by degrees, as love becomes more deep it will become less emotional; but to say that in proportion as wisdom and faith increase, in that proportion will love and tenderness abate, is to proclaim ruin to the Christian character. In the first place, we find it written in the Epistle to the Philippians: "This I pray, that your love may abound more in knowledge and in all judgment." Simultaneous with the growth in knowledge was to be the growth of the affections. Again, in the Epistle to the Thessalonians: "We are bound to thank God, as it is meet, because that your faith groweth exceedingly, and the charity of every one of you all toward each other aboundeth." And in the Second of Peter we find these religious affections made the ground of Christian grace: "Add to your faith virtue; and to virtue, knowledge; and to knowledge, temperance; and to temperance, patience; and to patience, godliness; and to godliness, brotherly kindness; and to brotherly kindness, charity." Where we remark at first the mere externals of religion; then, by degrees, the growth of particular and active habits; then the emotions; and, finally, the grand consummation of all, Christian charity. If it were not true that religious emotion was dear to God, how should we be able to explain that rebuke of the ascended Saviour to His Church of Laodicea, that it was "lukewarm, neither hot nor cold?"

And in the text you will observe that the Church of Ephesus had many marks which outwardly establish the claim to be a Church of God. She had orthodoxy, for she had tried those that said they were apostles, and, having found them liars, had put them from her; she had the spirit of martyrdom; she had activity and zeal, and much of outward earnestness. Her patience and labor are acknowledged; yet there was one thing wanting: her emotions towards God had lost their strength and vividness, and therefore her Lord declared that He would not have the outward husk without the inward kernel. From which it is manifest that the flower is not merely valuable from being the precursor of the fruit; it has an inherent worth in itself. And thus love has an inward grace and beauty, preciousness and value, in itself; the act is dear to God simply because of the affection that has prompted it. This, then, being the value of religious emotions, and this the danger of their decline, the passage which I have chosen for the text marks out for us these two branches into which our thought may flow.

I. The origin and marks of declension in religious feeling; and,

II. The apostolic remedy.

I. We must begin by understanding what is meant by this "first love to God." When we speak of love to God, we mean not an emotion different from what we call love to man; affection towards God is precisely the same feeling as affection towards man, but it is purified, exalted, concentrated. We are here for the very purpose of learning how to love God; without this we could not see the meaning of the manifold affection given us in this world. The love of parents and children, brothers and sisters, varies almost to infinity. Those on whom our affections have been lavished pass away; they die, but behind them is left the unburied power of love; and we find at last that we have been here in training for the love that knows neither age nor sex nor individuality. Our powers of loving are all concentrated and thrown on One; this infinite power of the educated soul we call the love of God. Therefore this love to God is marked by universality. God is truth, and the soul that loves God loves all that is true. God is goodness and purity, and in love to God we rest on all that is lovely, pure, and good as images of the infinite splendor of this love. God is the life of all that is; and when we love God, that love is felt in the delight that the Christian spirit takes in the blessedness and happiness of all that is; that feeling which makes the Christian merciful to his beast, and which forbids him to find his joy in the pain of the meanest thing that lives; love to universal being, love to the great All, that is love to God. Now, there are moments in our existence when this feeling dawns with a fresh power on the soul. "Our mortal nature doth tremble like a guilty thing surprised." It is a lovely thing to see the love of the young Christian, the startling warmth in the bosom of one whose heart is throbbing with first fresh love to God; there has come down upon his soul a flood of light so fresh, so pure, so new, that in the radiance of that light all seems fresh—the very world seems to be created over again; so that in him is fulfilled that which shall be hereafter; in the renewed love of that soul is produced a "new heaven and a new earth wherein dwelleth righteousness." And a man in such a state feels as the apostle did on the transfiguration mount—it seems as if it were almost impossible for him to descend from his high ground; we are ready to exclaim, "It is good for us to be here; let us make for ourselves resting-places." In that feeling there is not a shadow of a shade of selfishness; let theologians say what they will, in that first love to God there is no selfishness. Immortality, heaven itself, all that belongs to personal enjoyment, is lost in one burning desire to educate the soul and live afresh to God; to go, like Elijah, on the strength of sacred feast and staff, through the wilderness, asking only for God. We feel that God is our portion, our everlasting and all-sufficient portion, in this world and in the world to come. That is first love to God.

And this is the feeling, it may be, that the Ephesian Christians enjoyed to an extent which it is almost impossible for us to realize now; for in that day the iron hand of Rome was compressing the whole human race into one military empire; all domestic feelings were giving way, and even patriotism could scarcely subsist, for how is supreme love to be shown for a man's own country when none other exists to divide his affections? Then there burst upon the world a fresh feeling, a new love; and words such as these were heard, "He is our peace who hath made both, that is, Jew and Gentile, one." To us it is a thrice-told tale; but conceive it as a new truth—one God, one Father, one Mediator, one family, giving room for the heart's best affections—and then you may conceive the intensity of the first love of the Ephesian Church.

We will now consider the origin and progress of this declension.

1. The first cause and mark of it is the spirit of the world. Ephesus was at that time the metropolitan city of Proconsular Asia; it grew and flourished long after the cities that had surrounded it had decayed; it is known to us now as having contained one of the seven wonders of the world—the temple of the great goddess Diana. And there all that was refined in Asia and in Europe met. To this brilliant and dazzling influence was it that the young converts were exposed; and that which persecution could not do, refinement and ease soon effected; the iron of the Christian spirit was softened, the soul was robbed of its manlier part; they could no longer love their God with the strength they had formerly devoted to His service.

In that which we call the world we will now confine ourselves to one branch, of which Ephesus was an example, the love of worldly society and enjoyment. And, first, let us listen to what the Bible says on this subject, "He that liveth in pleasure is dead while he liveth," "Lovers of pleasure more than lovers of God,"

"If any man love the world, the love of the Father is not in him." The explanation of this is plain: in the life of pleasure we lead the life of excitement, and thus it soon follows that emotions will not rise at the call and bidding of excitement; the history being inevitably this: first sensibility of feeling, then excitement, then callousness, then apathy, and lastly hardness.

In the parable that we read to-day we are told that the seed which sprang up rapidly was sown on rocky ground; deep, profound is the knowledge of human nature expressed there; the superficial heart is the stony heart; where there is easily roused capacity for excitement there is often little real depth; frivolize the heart by pleasure, and thus you make it cold and hard towards God. There is nothing more remarkable in early religion than the scrupulous avoidance with which the young convert shrinks from the world. It is, however, often carried to extremes; then comes the reaction; and the recoil is strong just in proportion to the strength and exclusiveness with which the world has been avoided. And a history such as this has doubtless been the lot of more than one here present, either of himself, or of those whom he has loved. At first there was warmth of religious zeal; and then by degrees have appeared the symptoms of decline—frivolity, lightness of tone or dress or demeanor; little by little loss of zeal, and then a deadening of religious sensibility. It is a change which is at first imperceptible except to the eye of earnest, zealous friendship; for such a man is by no means less orthodox than before, no less regular in his outward duties, perhaps much more so, till by degrees the film and the veil become so thin that they can be worn no longer. The man ceases to profess—why should he encourage the spirit and habit of hypocrisy?—and then comes a cold, deadly, creeping despondency; and then the void of that soul is filled up with the extremes of sin, it may be with the extremes of crime.

2. The second cause we assign for religious declension is the neglect of devotional habits. Sometimes the history is what I have already stated, that religious acts survive religious feeling; in other cases it is the reverse—the decay of religious habits precedes the loss of religious feeling. In some unguarded moment the Christian man gives up his devotional habit; and then, once the habit is broken in upon, it is not renewed, and the result is a loss of zeal and a loss of love. Let us understand what is meant by

this expression, devotional habits. Let us not narrow it in to mean one thing only. By devotional habits we do not mean that a man must have the habit of attending daily prayers or the like; devotional habits depend upon all the varieties of age, sex, and temperament. To one man the devotional habit of every day is to consider a chapter in the Bible; to another man, according to the necessities of his temperament, it may be the attendance on public daily prayer; to another it may be wandering by the seashore, calming there his agitated spirit, and throwing open his mind to all the influences which God has shed so abundantly on the world. Sometimes it is a habit like that of Isaac, the wandering alone and meditating in the field at eventide; sometimes it is the voiceless lifting of the solitary soul to God in the chamber, in the crowd, and in society; but unless that habit, whatever it be, is kept up in some way or other, the life will inevitably decay.

And this seems to be the peculiar danger of this age. A few centuries ago the danger was a different one; it might be that in the hermitage the solitary, leading a life of contemplation, forgot that of action. Our danger is the opposite one: it is to substitute religious benevolence and the excitement of the public meeting and of the sermon for that for which they never can be substituted—the secret prayer, and the broken spirit, and the laying the soul before its Maker, imploring Him to search it thoroughly, "to see if there be any wicked way in it."

3. The last cause we assign for religious decline is the indulgence of the intellectual spirit. Ephesus was the seat of that form of corrupted Christianity which we find so often alluded to in the Acts of the Apostles as "science falsely so called," "vain philosophy," etc. Here let us make a distinction: confuse not the philosophy of those days with that of the present day; they are alike in name alone. The science of these days is a reverent investigation of the laws of God, and it is marvellous how men can fail to gain from it something of the love of God; but the philosophy of those days was simply the craving of the intellect for amusement and enjoyment in the things of God. And let it be remembered that religion's self may become a mere matter intellectual, and men may examine the evidences respecting the being of a God, or the proofs of immortality, with the same apathy and coldness with which we consider the evidences of the existence of some volcanic crater or of some distant nebula. But let

us beware; I say not that an intellectual religion is therefore no religion, for the intellectual man must have an intellectual religion, since he will give his energies to that which he most loves; but remember, I pray you, that intellect is one thing, heart is another. Religion is a thing of the heart, and not of the intellect; as the Bible so strongly tells us, "the world by wisdom knew not God." Religion is the banquet of the spirit, not the feast of the mind; and therefore the danger is ever present when men begin to listen to the sermon as a manifestation of intellectual force, and not for its spiritual power.

II. We pass on to consider the remedy suggested by the apostle; it was this, "Remember from whence thou art fallen, and repent, and do the first works."

In this we observe that the centre of it all is "repent." But that is precisely what man cannot do; it is alone the gift of the grace of God. The soul is powerless when it acts upon itself; the heart cannot produce one emotion simply by volition; therefore the apostle wisely gives us the means by which repentance may be produced: the first is, "Remember from whence thou art fallen;" the next is, "Do the first works."

You may go back in thought to the moments in which you were more loving, more holy; you may compare the sums you then spent on charity with those you now lavish on some selfish enjoyment; you may compare also the different way in which you spend your time now with what you did then; you cannot force the feeling, but by degrees, in such a way as this, the feeling will come—first remorse, and then bitterness; and then, gradually, it will perhaps pass into something gentler and more holy, till at last to "remember from whence thou art fallen" will be almost equivalent to this: "Repent."

The other remedy is to "do the first works." The wisdom of this advice is profound. It is not such as would have been given by us. We should, perhaps, have said, Think on the sufferings of Christ; or, Think on the reality of your adoption, remember that you are the child of God. The apostle knew far better; he knew that to refer a man in sin to the fact of his adoption is to tell him to look at what is to him invisible; therefore he says, "Do the first works;" for just as feeling will bring about action, so, when feeling is become cold, acting, by God's blessing, will bring back the feeling. It is not by meddling with the emotions or by considering our adoption, but by acting in earnest under the grace of God, that we get back the warm feeling we had lost, and return to the duties we had left, with such words as these, "Father, I have sinned against heaven and before Thee, and am no more worthy to be called Thy son."

Brother men, if there be any among us now who has "left his first love," know you what that is which is dragging down your soul? Be honest in your Father's sight. Be it business or pleasure or intolerance, be it what it may, that stands between your soul and Christ, there shall neither be peace to your spirit nor joy of love within your heart till you sternly tear it out.

XX.

WISDOM JUSTIFIED OF HER CHILDREN.

(1.)

(FROM AUTOGRAPH NOTES.)

Brighton, March 9, 1851.

"But wisdom is justified of her children."—Matt. xi. 19.

"JUSTIFIED" means acquitted, recognized, or acknowledged. "Of" means "by." And Christ says, "Wisdom is recognized by her children."

The wisdom of a Divine life had appeared in two forms: ascetic in John the Baptist, social in Christ. The world recognized it in neither. In John they said it was insanity: "He hath a devil;" in Christ worldliness and irreligion: "Behold a man gluttonous, and a wine-bibber, a friend of publicans and sinners."

To the world Christ replied, in simple and deep words, that they were incompetent judges of the question. None could recognize the Divine life but those who lived it; none justify wisdom except her children. The Divine life was always the same, but it expressed itself outwardly in no special single form of life. Wisdom, under whatever form she might appear—the life of asceticism or the life social—would be justified or recognized by her children.

On last Sunday * I expounded the principle that the judgment of doctrine is made possible by an obedient life. In every department of life there is an organ for judging. In the world of sense, the empiric intellect. In the world of spirit another organ altogether is needed; not the understanding, but the heart: "with the heart man believeth." Neither astronomy nor mathematics nor scientific analysis will enable you to reach God. You must *feel* Him: "Eye hath not seen, nor ear heard, neither have entered into the heart of man, the things which God hath prepared for them that love Him." Obedience is the organ by which you judge of things not seen or heard. One act of charity will teach you more of God, "of moral evil, and of good, than all the sages can." "My judgment is just: because I seek not My own will, but the will of the Father which hath sent Me. If any man will do His will, he shall know of the doctrine, whether it be of God, or whether I speak of Myself."

This is the only ground on which we can stand against Rationalism. Rationalism says, By evidence of the understanding, by historical investigation, by scientific research. We say, By the evidence of the heart. The mightiest chemist knows nothing about immortality or about God.

I then applied this principle to three cases—speculative truth, morals, and the understanding of character. A pure heart and a self-surrendered will clarify the heart to judge rightly. When all selfish motives for choosing one view rather than another are destroyed, speculative truths, such as those of Calvinism, become clearer. So also in moral truths, such as slavery, or the Epicurean "Let us eat and drink, to-morrow we die."

I omitted one case—"I judge no man; and yet if I judge, My judgment is true, for I am not alone, but I and the Father that sent Me"—which omission I now supply.

The humble desire to know and do the will of God is the condition on which we gain insight into human character. "If any man will do His will, he shall know" of the Teacher as well as the doctrine. The life Divine can only be recognized by the children of that life. You must be a child of wisdom before you can justly judge of the Teacher. You cannot otherwise say, broadly, asceticism is right, or social life right.

Therefore we consider—

* Second Series, Sermon viii.

I. The tone of mind which capacitates for judging character; and
II. The tone of mind which incapacitates for judging.

I. The tone of mind which capacitates for judging human character.

The children of wisdom possess an unerring judgment of doctrine, and an unerring insight into human character, gained by a childlike spirit of obedience, and not by intellect: "I thank Thee, O Father, Lord of heaven and earth, because Thou hast hid these things from the wise and prudent, and hast revealed them unto babes." The children of wisdom are here called "babes."

By sympathy alone can you judge of character. Children are those who are like children. By pure sympathy and by pure character you discern what is pure. Delighting in good, you discern it not as a rival, but as a friend, recognizing its characteristics. This is the doctrine of the metaphor. A mother, changing her garb, may be mistaken by strangers; but under every metamorphosis she is recognized by her children, who know her voice by the secret tact of sympathy.

And this is the universal doctrine of Christ. He never taught on personal authority: "Yet if I judge, My judgment is true, for I am not alone, but I and the Father that sent Me;" but on the authority of truth, evident to *true* minds; and on the authority of a pure life, evident to *pure* minds; "Which of you convinceth Me of sin? and if I say the truth, why do ye not believe Me?" You cannot separate the teacher from the doctrine; they are believed together. Therefore we believe Christianity because we believe Christ, feeling that He was true by intuitive perception. And we believe it, because we feel it true that God is love, and that we are immortal: "He that believeth on the Son of God hath the witness in himself." Thus, then, He taught the doctrines of Christianity: eternal life, the dignity and spirituality of the soul, the relation of humanity to God, the laws of self-sacrifice, and the paternal character of God. His was no long-drawn scheme of evidences, for "He hath the witness in Himself." They that were of God would hear Him, they that were not of God would not hear Him. "He that is of God heareth God's words; ye therefore hear them not, because ye are not of God."

"Wisdom is justified of her children." Sympathy is a test and example of this. Our judgment of Christ's actions depends on our sympathy with His mind. We must share His indignation against the Pharisees, and the strong expressions of His anger against the sticklers for the Sabbath, and against those who neglected justice, judgment, and truth. We must get into His atmosphere if we would breathe His spirit. By no other organ but that of sympathy can you judge of the character of Christ. Wisdom is justified by her children, *i. e.* by those who have the childlike spirit of obedience, and by none else; the things of wisdom are revealed to babes, but they are hidden from the wise and prudent: "I thank Thee, O Father, Lord of heaven and earth, because Thou hast hid these things from the wise and prudent, and hast revealed them unto babes." Clear intelligence fails here. It is common to say that the mind must be like a sheet of white paper in order to judge of truth. This is true in matters of sense and mere understanding, such as whether this world's duration has been ten thousand or ten million years; but in matters moral and spiritual this same white-paper tone of mind is not the best for arriving at truth. I cannot investigate whether there be a God, or whether God is love or not, in the same way as respecting a sea-serpent. Just fancy the evidence nicely balanced: "Nature red in tooth and claw," shrieking against the creed; while a strong, mighty throb of the heart, kindred with God, declares itself in defiance, and is indifferent to all evidence. Evidence comes after, not before.

Much more is this the case in judging of human character. I feel that a man is pure by sympathy. I must judge the action from the man, almost more than the man from the action. For example, there was such a man. before whom the evidence of Christ's character was placed — Simon the Pharisee. It is a touching incident. A sinful woman, weeping, shedding costly ointment; Jesus throwing Himself in mighty trust on the new sympathy of a regenerate heart; "Thy sins are forgiven Thee." Upon this the Pharisee looked with a clear intelligent eye, as cold and tearless as if he were summing up the evidence on some question of accounts. What was wanting in this man? Intellect? There never was argument more logical: "This man, if he were a prophet, would have known who and what manner of woman this is that toucheth him." Moral character? He would not touch a sinner. No! what he wanted was heart, living sympathy. Can you estimate music by mathematics? The child would have judged unerringly where the man failed. Generous impulses overleap a thousand steps of argument. It was hidden from the wise and prudent. It was revealed unto babes. "Therefore the publicans and the harlots go into the kingdom of God before you."

"What think ye of Christ?" Some said, "He is a good man;" some, "He is more than man, a prophet;" but Simon Peter said, "Thou art the Christ, the Son of the living God." The candid Pharisee Simon said, "This man is not a prophet."

You judge of Christ! Feel Christ. "Learn to love one living man." "Flesh and blood cannot reveal it unto you, but My Father which is in heaven."

II. The tone of mind which incapacitates, and the hindrances to right judgment of human character. "Wisdom is justified of her children" implies that they who are not wise will not recognize wisdom.

1. The habit of insincere praise incapacitates for forming a right judgment of character. During the life of Jesus the Pharisees and Sadducees alike flattered Him: "We know that Thou art true, and teachest the way of God in truth; neither carest Thou for any man, for Thou regardest not the person of men"— "Good Master"—"Blessed is the womb that bare Thee, and the paps which Thou hast sucked." To these unreal flatteries He returned indignant replies: "Why tempt ye me, ye hypocrites?"— "Why callest thou me good? There is none good but one, that is God."—"Yea, rather blessed are they that hear the word of God, and keep it." By these unfelt praises men were unfitting themselves from the power of estimating Him.

This is a habit which grows upon us, for it is easily acquired. We use courtly phrases, well-turned sentences, we write notes and letters which mean nothing. The temptation is great because we know it pleases; until at last, finding that these delicate insincerities succeed, writing and language become voluble. The worst injury is done, not to others, but to ourselves. We despise the man we praise too much; our genuine reverence for him is gone, and a secret contempt takes its place. We indulge in a language of admiration which means nothing; we praise that which does not merit it, until we believe that there is nothing deserving of praise. Goodness becomes a thing of fiction—a fiction in our praise, a fiction in itself. Accordingly, these unwise and unreal children of the world, on whose lips the unfailing phrases of politeness sit, are precisely those who are most sceptical of human goodness. And they who went out to be baptized by John, and gave lip-reverence to Christ, were saying in their hearts that John was mad, and that the Redeemer was a common worldly man.

2. A light, satirical, and irreverent spirit also incapacitates. The irreverent said, "He hath a devil"—"He is a common worldly man"—"How can this man give us His flesh to eat?"—"Ah, Thou that destroyest the temple, and buildest it in three days, save Thyself, and come down from the cross"—"He saved others, Himself He cannot save." See how ribaldry unfitted them for judging, and how even a Divine character could be made to seem ridiculous! That such cannot judge of character is intelligible. One reason is because excellence of character is not shown them. Who would give utterance to a generous emotion when he knows that it will be heard with a sneer, or pour out his heart when he knows that patriotism is reckoned pretence, religion cant, or man's honor and woman's purity childish fables?

Another reason, moreover, is because this spirit withers all that it touches. Hence wisdom of heart is necessary, moral earnestness, reverence, and belief in goodness are indispensable elements in a child of wisdom. You cannot judge rightly unless you feel that the heart of man is holy ground, and his emotions sacred. "Hollow smile and frozen sneer, come not near." Except in this spirit, *dare* not to judge your brother.

3. Jealousy incapacitates for forming a right judgment. The Scribes were jealous of Christ because His teaching was on a principle different from theirs; the Pharisees, because His righteousness was of a different stamp. It is melancholy to see how this jealousy blinds. The excellences which we are most capable of appreciating because they are kindred with our own are the very ones which we cannot see. It is melancholy to think of Joseph's brethren jealous of their father's love, and seeing in him only a dreamer of dreams; or of Haman unable to enjoy life because of Mordecai.

It is more melancholy still to see a high and good mind poisoned by some mean and ungenerous rivalry.

* * * * * *

XXI.

WISDOM JUSTIFIED OF HER CHILDREN.

(2.)

(FROM AUTOGRAPH NOTES.)

Brighton, March 16, 1851.

"And they said unto him, Why do the disciples of John fast often, and make prayers, and likewise the disciples of the Pharisees; but thine eat and drink?"—Luke v. 33.

THE outward religious life of Christ differed from that of John. One was social, the other ascetic. To the astonishment created by this difference among worldly people and Pharisees He vouchsafed no reply. When they said, "Behold a gluttonous man, and a wine-bibber, a friend of publicans and sinners!" He merely replied, "Wisdom is justified of her children"—by her children, and by them only. You must have sympathy with a life before you can understand it. You must do the will of God before you can judge the doctrine of God. You must have the spirit of the life of Christ in you before you can recognize the Divine character of the life.

This was our subject last Sunday. For judgment of character, sympathy is necessary. He only can understand who resembles: "For what man knoweth the things of a man, save the spirit of man which is in him? even so the things of God knoweth no man, but the Spirit of God."

Once, however, Jesus condescended to explain the difference between His life and the life of John. On the present occasion the question was asked by John's disciples,* not captiously, but for the sake of information, "Why do the disciples of John fast often, and make prayers, and likewise the disciples of the Pharisees; but thine eat and drink?" Therefore He replies, "Can ye make the children of the bridechamber fast while the bridegroom

---

* Matt. ix. 14.

is with them? But the days will come when the bridegroom shall be taken away from them, and then shall they fast in those days." And that reply goes deep into the grounds of a religious life.

Our business is with the question and the reply.

I. The reasons for the astonishment which caused the question.
II. The reasons for the form of life adopted.

I. The Divine life was social. He came eating and drinking. He lived the common life of men—outwardly nothing remarkable. There was nothing in His habits of dress, living, or worship to distinguish Him from those of His own rank, or to manifest eminent religiousness.

Therefore the world was astonished, because the popular vulgar conceptions of religious life are drawn naturally from those evidences which are most visible, fasting and prayers.

Now the two main elements of religious life are self-denial and love. The highest form of self-denial is self-sacrifice. Both meet in the cross—self-surrender in love. The highest form of love is communion with God: "He that dwelleth in love dwelleth in God, and God in him." Where these are, religion is; where these are not, religion is not.

Hence these two acts, fasting and prayer, express the whole of religious life—fasting, self-denial; prayer, communion with God. These are expressions level to every apprehension, translations into popular language.

All can understand the self-denial of fasting, because hunger is a low want, known to all. But all cannot understand the self-denial of hard mental work, or that of associating with uncongenial minds, or that of honestly pursuing a disagreeable occupation or profession.

Hence in rude ages this told. John's ascetic life was a power with the vulgar. Had Bernard been less emaciated by fasting, he had never led Europe to the Crusades.

All can comprehend that a man is praying when he kneels down, when he repeats Church prayers, or is at his place during the service. But not all can understand that the highest prayer or communion with God is a life of love; that

> "He prayeth well who loveth well
> All things, both great and small."

The self-denial of Christ was not abstinence from food, but the putting aside every soft temptation which turned Him from the cross. His prayer was a life of love. Accordingly, when these forms were missed, which were the best known because the most visible expressions of religious life, to the coarse popular mind religion itself was gone.

Here, however, a distinction must be drawn between the conceptions of spirituality which were false and those which were merely limited. The disciples both of the Pharisees and of John led the life ascetic. In the first case there was a false conception of spirituality, in the second a limited one. We must distinguish between those who are zealous for a definite form because it is all, and those who are zealous because of their affection to the Truth Divine which is linked with it. Oh, sacred be the form to which such affections are linked, and through which such truths are received, be it bread, or wine, or colored glass, or a crucifix, or a priest's white robe!

Beware, therefore. Nothing can be more uncharitable than that coarse, rude, indiscriminate, vulgar tone in which all that is formal in religion is treated as Jesuitry, Puseyism, or unspiritual feeling. Before we dare to use such language, if we have a faith which has "centre everywhere, nor cares to fix itself to form," let us be sure that we are opposing ourselves to Pharisees, and not to the disciples of a Baptist. For it is just as narrow to be blind to the spirituality which exists in a formal life as to think that it cannot exist separate from form. They were Pharisees who called Christ's life worldly; but, remark, they too were Pharisees who said of John Baptist, "He hath a devil." The children of wisdom only were able to recognize the spirituality of the Baptist's life.

Again, there is a tendency in disciples to copy and idolize the peculiarities of a master. You may know the school to which a man belongs by a single conversation, by his tone, phraseology, and manner. That great religious teacher who led the Romanizing section of the Church, and who for years wielded a wondrous influence over the most intelligent young minds of England, impressed his manner on his followers. Even now, in churches where his influence survives, you may recall the master's tones, gestures, silver voice, and the few faults of his exquisite, pure English. So, also, the Puritan manners still survive. Now in this it is easy to copy, it is hard to imitate. In the noble life of John, the disciples might copy the food, dress, indifference to comfort, of the Baptist; but they did not thereby get his zeal, his lofty love of justice and of truth. The peculiarities are missed sooner than the spirit. Hence when the breath is not bated, nor the usual cant expressions heard, nor the accustomed whine, nor the forced unction, a man is counted irreverent. But by using the brush and colors of a painter, you do not get his power.

Again, the indifference of Christ to ascetic forms astonished, because there is a real influence in asceticism.

The principle of Christianity is from within outwards: "The kingdom of God is within you," "Except a man be born again, he cannot see the kingdom of God."

The sacramental principle, the ascetic principle, the patristic principle, reverse this. They proceed from things outward to things inward. Hence, they say the sacraments are to pour God's Spirit into you; fasting is to make you pure; the habit of saying prayers is to give you the spirit of prayer. Now, there is a truth in this. The outward world does tell upon the spirit within us. Prayer persevered in will bring a calm, passion-subdued feeling. Fasting will not suggest one high motive, but it will produce lowness of animal energy, and keep down strong feeling for a time. It will give a sense of hardness, and make a man independent of comfort.

The passions distort the countenance. And when the actor distorts the features a simulation of the feeling of anger ensues, and real tears flow. So, no wonder that men habituated to an ascetic system, and feeling by experience its power to a certain extent, should have been sceptical of any good without it, or should have doubted the power of elevated feeling to do that which asceticism could not do. Accustomed to believe in the power of the flesh, no wonder they doubted the power of the spirit. "This I say, then, Walk in the spirit, and ye shall not fulfil the lust of the flesh." "Bodily exercise profiteth little: but godliness is profitable unto all things, having promise of the life that now is, and of that which is to come."

II. The reasons for which Jesus did not impose the life ascetic on His disciples.

1. Because it is unnatural: "Can the children of the bridechamber mourn as long as the bridegroom is with them." Fast-

ing was the mark of grief. The usual accompaniment of fasting was " to afflict the soul, and to bow down the head as a bulrush, and to spread sackcloth and ashes under him." The time might and would come when sorrow and dismay would be their portion. Then the forms of religious woe would be natural, and correspond. But now, while buoyed up with hopes of the Messianic kingdom, it would be unnatural and incongruous. There is grief enough in store for them. But to force grief, to pretend grief which they did not feel, would be like mourning at a bridal.

Here, then, is a principle laid down. Let the manifestation of religious life be natural. Christ imposed no form, and ordained no ritual. He simply left a place for future feeling to expand and express itself. He provided no hard unelastic case for the soul's affections.

Let us never use words or forms for ourselves merely because they have suited other men. John's locust food and camel's-hair garment were graceful in him because natural, but in a copyist simply falsehood. The dropped voice of reverence, so real in one, in an imitator becomes a sanctimonious whine. Be natural, be yourself, be real! David's sling was better for David than Saul's armor.

There will come a time when the sad experience of life will surround the soul with sombreness and mystery; a time when the insoluble riddle of this unintelligible world will press heavily on the spirit, and the soul must keep its solitary fast with God. But do not anticipate that time.

In the education of children, let this principle be borne in mind. The religion of the man is different from the religion of the child. The matin-hymn of early life is full of joy and praise, like the disciples. If you put into the child's mouth the language of penitence, and force him to acknowledge himself a miserable sinner, whose crime has been the murder of a butterfly, and whose omission the over-enjoyment of a holiday, all becomes unnatural. The penitential strains of after-life, the sorrow, and the sense of failure and perpetually foiled effort—let them come, but not yet.

2. His second reason was because of the results. These are given in two parables: the new wine put into old bottles, and new cloth put upon the old. Wonderful how the plain meaning of these parables has been missed by commentators. They have

thought of new doctrine and old, of Christianity and Judaism. And the doctrine taught seemed to be to avoid mixing new and old. Whereas the old cloth and the old bottles represent young novice disciples—the resemblance lying in the weakness, not in the age. New wine, new cloth, represent austere duties and doctrines. The lesson is not the avoidance of mixture of old and new doctrine, but the necessity of not *forcing* severe duties and forms on those unprepared to receive them.

Now, the result of that forcing system is twofold.

First, the destruction of religion. The weak old wine skin-bottles, the weak old cloth, are rent. Therefore avoid dropped tones and over-spiritual expressions. They are bad symptoms of the present day; they are the forcing of high doctrines and expressions of high spirituality. Force nothing; let us be true and simple—what we are, and nothing else. Content, if need be, like Christ, to be reckoned worldly.

A second result is hypocrisy. The piece "agreeth not." There is want of harmony; no agreement between the form and the life.

Hence result such startling incongruities as daily prayer with austere judgment of others; religious missionary meetings with gossip and scandal; fasting with pride.

At last the discordance becomes too plain even for the man himself. Then we say this must be for example's sake; and so we sham and sham till we become hypocrites. Example! Do we think that men take example from one form or from one spirit?

Now, understand from this the life of Christ. His was the life of God under the limitations of humanity. To that life we return at last. Understand that, and you understand Christianity. Misunderstand that, and you misunderstand Christianity.

The life of Christ differs in nothing outwardly from ours. He ate and drank. The difference was within, in the central deeps.

Christianity is love to God and man. To love the Lord our God with all thy heart and soul and mind, and to love thy neighbor as thyself. This is the life that is hidden with Christ in God.

The shape in which that life will show itself varies with age and sex and circumstance. It manifests itself in the stern Reformer or in the daily Friend.

You are not religious because your life is encompassed with form, or because it is enlarged and liberal and indifferent to form.

The life of God is in the soul of man.

XXII.

THE WISDOM OF CHRIST AND THE WISDOM OF SOLOMON.

Brighton, March 23, 1851.

"The queen of the south shall rise up in the judgment with the men of this generation, and condemn them: for she came from the utmost parts of the earth to hear the wisdom of Solomon; and, behold, a greater than Solomon is here."—Luke xi. 31.

THAT which lies at the root of many of the controversies of the present day is this, whether for the production of national greatness we are to rely on the illumination of the understanding, or on the training of the heart and the discipline of the affections. This question in the matter of education has divided the people of this country into two great sections. The first are those who, to borrow a Continental phrase, may be called the friends of light. With them light is equivalent for all that is good, darkness the equivalent for all that is evil; with them light is knowledge, and darkness ignorance. Let there be, they say, an expulsion of intellectual darkness, and with it you will banish every form of moral ill. The second class are those who are disposed to undervalue this secular education. According to them, to instruct the children of the poor, to give to the working classes a taste for the beautiful, is to do positive and actual harm. Extensive information they regard with jealousy. The inspired judgment contained in the text coincides with neither of these views. It does not agree with the view of those who would neglect or undervalue this secular education, for it declares that the wisdom of Solomon was great, and that the Queen of Sheba, who came to listen to it, was to be commended. Neither does it agree with the view of those who make secular illumination everything, for it says that there is something far higher than this. It says to intellectual illumination that she is to know her place, that she is second, not first; that Christ is greater than Solomon; it says that apathy with respect to spiritual knowledge is just as much more criminal than apathy with respect to intellectual illumination, as the wisdom of Christ transcends that of Solomon.

I am to appeal to you to-day on behalf of the Diocesan Training-school in this town; I therefore choose this as the most suitable subject for our contemplation. We shall have two things to consider:

I. The value of secular knowledge.
II. The transcending value of spiritual wisdom.

I. First, then, the value of secular knowledge.

1. The Queen of Sheba was commended for having come to hear the wisdom of Solomon; this commendation is manifestly implied, for it is said that she shall rise up in judgment with the men of this generation. Now, the wisdom of Solomon was chiefly secular—the knowledge of the objects of this world, and the materials whereof composed. We have a description of his wisdom, "He spake three thousand proverbs; his songs were a thousand and five." Here the first branch of his knowledge is a store of practical wisdom; but that wisdom is chiefly prudential, by no means the highest; it fits a man only to live in this world. We pass to the next verse, where we find that "he spake of trees, from the cedar that is in Lebanon, even unto the hyssop that springeth out of the wall: he spake also of beasts and of fowl, of creeping things and of fishes." All that is contained in the encyclopædic range of knowledge, all that is useful, and all that belongs to this world and its objects, with respect to their beauty—all this Solomon possessed abundantly.

Again, we are told that God gave him an understanding heart, to enable him to guide the people; here was the branch of political knowledge. To this he added a knowledge of the arts and sciences, and of all the means whereby he could extend the commerce of his nation, sending out his ships to Tarshish to trade there, and uniting by the same means Tyre and Jerusalem.

Once more, the reign of Solomon is chiefly remarkable for the building of the Temple—an edifice that proclaims to us that then the arts and sciences had grown to an extent scarcely known before or since. So that all that could adorn the metropolis, all that could gratify taste the most sublime and the most refined, met in Jerusalem; this era was forever celebrated in Jerusalem's annals.

It was not the age in which Israel was noblest or bravest, nor was it remarkable for the pureness of Jehovah's worship; neither was it the age in which the people were the most happy, but it was the age in which intellect had attained its acme, it was the age in which civilization was complete, and in which wisdom had shown all that she could do here.

2. We pass on to consider that this knowledge is good in and for itself. The Queen of Sheba came, not to see the wealth of Solomon, but to hear his wisdom. True it is they showed her the wonders of his reign; but it was not for these that she came; neither did she come to hear his wisdom that she might turn it to her own purposes; it was not for the utilitarian application of his wisdom, but to hear the wisdom itself. From this, therefore, we infer that this wisdom is good in and for itself, worthy of a sovereign to gaze upon.

We draw a distinction between the gifts of wisdom and wisdom itself. Knowledge is power; but if you worship knowledge for the sake of power, it is power you love, not knowledge. Therefore, if we are to be followers of the Queen of Sheba, we must seek truth for its own sake, and not for the sake of the power that it gives to make this life happy. Remarkable as this age is for the spread of knowledge that is useful, it may be doubted, and must be, whether knowledge—that mere secular knowledge which men worship now—is worshipped with a worship as disinterested and as pure as that of the Queen of Sheba. The ancient architects and artists built and painted for the sake of the pure idea of beauty they loved to realize; modern ones do it merely for the sake of aggrandizing their names. The result is that, degraded by mammon worship, their works have lost their position in the scale of arts. Therefore we say that to worship knowledge for itself has in it its own blessing. They only who thus seek wisdom can understand the flash of surprise and the beating and heaving of the heart, and the sense of joy with which such minds can rest in the contemplation of pure truth, unpolluted by any selfish consideration as to how that eternal truth can be made to promote their own interest.

3. In the third place, we remark, respecting this secular wisdom, that it is utterly insufficient. In the interpretation of the writings of Solomon it is common to force upon them a spiritual meaning, knowing that he was inspired. We take it for granted

that he must have been inspired with spiritual wisdom. But in so doing we lose the lesson he was designed to teach—we lose the infinite difference between the wisdom of Christ and the wisdom of Solomon. We gain most instructive lessons from seeing what Solomon could not reach; we see the frightful want in all that Solomon ever wrote or taught.

Now, to descend to particulars. The first thing that we observe here is the utter insufficiency of mere secular knowledge. Solomon was the earthly wisest of mankind; yet, when he comes to the close of life, we find him saying, " Vanity of vanities, all is vanity;" or, in other words, " Emptiness of emptiness, all is emptiness." It became a question to him whether that gift which God had given was worthy of being called a gift at all—" Of making many books there is no end, and much study is weariness of the flesh."

The second thing we notice is the tendency that there is in mere knowledge to end in scepticism. There is an appalling darkness in the old age of Solomon. That dark, mysterious Book of Ecclesiastes was inspired by God to show us the fearful end of wisdom. If you take the concluding verse of that book, you would say that faith had triumphed: " Fear God, and keep His commandments." But if we take the entire book, the conclusion we come to is that wisdom ended in scepticism; for you find the deepest truths and the most Epicurean untruths side by side together; and had we been without the exposition of the New Testament, we should have been left in uncertainty as to which was right and which was wrong: " Be not righteous overmuch, neither be overmuch wicked "—mere Epicurean prudence, the quenching of every noble feeling. In another place we read, " There is nothing better for a man than that he should eat and drink." That is the history of Solomon's wisdom, to that end he came at last. So may science set out at first with God, and end at last with dark, deplorable, miserable, desolate atheism.

The last thing we observe of this earthly wisdom is its tendency to surround life with luxury and sensuality. When wisdom has left its centre, God, it has no centre left but self; more especially is this the case when commercial enterprises and manufacturing activity have taken hold of a nation's heart. This was the case in Solomon's reign; the end of that worship of the beautiful in arts and science is the soft, enervating, feeble unmanliness that degraded the last years of Solomon. Ask you the danger of this age? Some will say, Popery; nay, it is not that, but the reaction of Popery that we fear; the result of the education, going on now, of the mind without God. Ours is an age in which science works her miracles, an age in which we measure earth and heaven, an age in which we command the sun to be our painter and bid the lightning go upon our errand: if there is nothing in our souls but that, know you the result? If to that there be added nothing, the end inevitably must be atheism—an atheism in which God shall be dethroned from His place within our hearts, and the adoration of the Creator be succeeded by self-worship, mammon-worship, ease, luxury; and from that all the wisdom in the breast of Solomon cannot, and will not, save us.

II. We now consider the transcending superiority of the spiritual wisdom of Christ.

There is a contrast drawn—"a greater than Solomon is here." Had not our Master drawn the contrast, we should not have dared to do it. To draw a contrast between the human and divine, between Solomon and Christ, would savor of irreverence; but as His blessed lips have done it, there can be no irreverence in our following it out in detail.

Observe, the contrast between them does not lie in this, that Solomon was human and Christ divine, for that is too manifest. There are two points in which we believe in the divinity of Christ: the divinity of His nature, and that of His character. Divine by nature, the Eternal Word made flesh, the Everlasting Son of the Everlasting Father manifested here on earth; that is, as it were, His physical divinity. But He was also divine because in Him was the manifestation of the divine character; and that is His moral divinity. Now, it is in that respect that the contrast is here drawn between the characters of the two wisdoms; and, therefore, what we have to say on this point shall divide itself into these two branches—the contrast between Christ the teacher and Solomon the teacher, and the contrast between Christ the King and Solomon the king.

First, the teaching of Christ was not what we call intellectual teaching; the very mention of such an expression seems to us a kind of irreverence, from which we shrink. His superiority did not consist in that He taught deeper truths of science than Solomon. Solomon spake of the cedar of Lebanon and of the hyssop springing out of the wall. So spake also Christ, but in a different tone and manner. He spake of the grass that to-day is, and to-morrow is cast into the oven. His heart and eye were open to the sky: He saw the bright burning red of evening, that foretold the fineness of the future day. He saw the glorious sun come forth in his majesty. He spake of the splendor of the Oriental lily. He saw the corn of wheat fall into the ground and die, and "yet it abideth not alone." He spake, too, of the corn, and its many lessons—its gradual growth, first the blade, then the ear, and after that the full corn in the ear; also of its various lots and vicissitudes, sometimes to be cast on dry and stony ground, sometimes among thorns, and sometimes in the good ground, where it might bring forth fruit abundantly. But in all this He spake not as the naturalist, not as the man of science, but as the Son of God. Where Solomon saw the truths of nature, the Redeemer saw and taught the truths of spirit. If He saw, for example, the rain falling on the just and on the unjust, and the sun shining on the good and bad alike, He discerned in that the character of the Father, and told His hearers to be "merciful, even as their Father also is merciful." If He saw the corn of wheat fall into the ground and die, He discerned there the great principle of self-sacrifice. So that herein, brethren, lay the difference—where Solomon taught simply truths, natural facts, and laws, the Redeemer saw and taught truths spiritual.

Again, there is a contrast here between Christ the King and Solomon the king. The apathy of the age for the wisdom of the Redeemer is easily accounted for: for whatever is simple, whatever is really great, requires time before its majesty can be understood. The really great cathedral is not appreciated at once; some gay and gaudy pile will be admired first; and so, too, he who sees a snowy mountain for the first time is disappointed, it is not so large and grand as he expected, it appears as if he could in half an hour attain the summit; but when he tries to ascend it, then he finds its height; it is not till he has gone to a distance, and seen it from some standpoint ten, twenty, or a hundred miles removed, and finds it still there, in all the majesty and purity of its eternal repose, the monarch and the king of all around—it is not till then that he begins to feel for it something like affection. Precisely so, if it may be said with reverence, is the divine character of Christ. There is something almost amounting to blasphemy in the tone with which we dare to call Him God. God, yes! but to an extent and with a depth of reality which that expression does not reach. There are, perhaps, few of us who do not remember what we thought of Christ when we were young. He seemed to us then as something commonplace; there was a poorness and a lack of brilliancy, for His was not the victory or the triumph of the senator or of the conqueror; and in our boyish love of enterprise this simple life of Christ seemed to us tame and cold. But life has gone on, and we begin to understand, when disappointment has saddened the heart and grief has sobered it, when we have comprehended the littleness of all here below, when, after weary struggles, we find ourselves infinitely below one single thought that ever passed through His mind—we begin to understand that there is a depth in that expression, "A greater than Solomon is here." We leave the men of the world to marvel and wonder at the Solomon of intellect and wealth, of success and influence; we have found a shrine at which our souls may worship the King whom we revere, the God whom we adore.

Now, in conclusion, I have two or three things to say. First, from this let us learn the error of those who are inclined to sneer at intellectual illumination. The Queen of Sheba was praised for coming to hear this wisdom. The language which some men use would almost leave it to be supposed that the less a man knows, the nearer he is to God; if so, then the best soil in which religion can grow is the soil of ignorance.

And, secondly, we learn the error of those who make intellectual illumination all in all. Here has been taught us a sad and solemn lesson: remember this, intellect may be cultivated at the expense of heart. There is an awful expression following the text—"The light of the body is the eye, therefore when thine eye is single, thy whole body also is full of light; but when thine eye is evil, thy body also is full of darkness." If the intellectual eye within us be made diseased or feeble by unbelief or impurity, the light is turned into darkness. The deepest darkness is that which follows the brilliancy of the lightning flash at night; the deepest darkness of the soul is that which follows the illumination of the mind. It leads to God, say you, but it will be through darkness and degradation, the fearful price which Solomon had to pay. If it does lead a nation, it will be through anarchy and reigns of terror. The illumination of the understanding must be joined to the training and discipline of the heart by God's Holy Spirit.

XXIII.

THE LAW OF SELF-SACRIFICE EXEMPLIFIED IN THE DEATH OF CHRIST.

Brighton, August 3, 1851.

"Jesus answered them, saying, The hour is come, that the Son of man should be glorified. Verily, verily, I say unto you, Except a corn of wheat fall into the ground and die, it abideth alone: but if it die, it bringeth forth much fruit. He that loveth his life shall lose it; and he that hateth his life in this world shall keep it unto life eternal. . . . Now is my soul troubled; and what shall I say? Father, save me from this hour: but for this cause came I unto this hour. Father, glorify thy name."—John xii. 23-28.

I HAVE read all these verses, because to have separated them would have broken the connection of the thought; taken together, they contain a history of one of the mental struggles of the Redeemer. The occasion of the utterance was this: certain Greeks, who had come up to one of the annual feasts, entreated for admission to the presence of the Lord. Now, in this request there was something exceedingly unusual, for they were Gentiles, and on them apparently as yet no impression had been made.

The verses I have read contain the reply of our Lord to this announcement. At first sight there is no connection between the announcement and the reply; but on looking more closely we perceive a most intimate connection. Had our Redeemer been a mere man, intelligence like this would have produced joy, for it told of success and popularity. But the Son of God looked deeper, and saw in the approach of these Greeks the first coming of the Gentile world; and together with that thought came also the remembrance of the condition without which the ingathering could not take place, that condition being the Redeemer's own death. For the Spirit, we read, could not be "given until Jesus had been glorified;" the Divine life which was in Jesus could not expand itself so as to become the world's life till the shell in which it was contained was broken down: according to His own simile, the corn of wheat must die before it can bring forth fruit. Then began one of those inward struggles of the Redeemer of which we read two or three times; preludes, as it were, to the Garden agony; the idea of death vividly presented.

And now, brethren, we will endeavor to examine this in a real way. We are about to enter on the real history of a real spirit. We are in the habit of shrinking too much from the investigation of the mental struggles of Jesus, because it seems as if it were profanation to believe that the laws of His mind were the same as those of ours. But in this we commit two errors. First, by this method we entirely lose the notion of the proper humanity of the Saviour—a humanity which did not consist alone in having flesh and blood like ours, but in this, that He had a mind governed, like our own, by the laws of association, and that He had a heart and sympathies which throbbed as ours. It contains also another error, that it is a false conception of true reverence. It is reverential to be cautious of approaching too closely the secrets of an earthly sovereign, because to approach too near would only produce familiarity, and make us feel that he, like ourselves, is but a frail and sinful man. But the majesty of Jesus requires no precaution like this; it requires not to be defended by earthly rules of distance. The nearer we approach to Him, the more we track His thoughts and feelings, the more we feel the truth of His Divine majesty. Nay, it is only so that we can believe in Jesus as the Son of God; only so far as we love and understand the character of Jesus as the Son of man shall we be able to feel, and therefore to adore, Jesus Christ as the Son of God.

We divide these verses into two branches:

I. The law of the atonement; and,

II. The mental struggles through which that law was accepted by the will of Christ.

I. In the law of the atonement the first thing that these verses tell us is the gloriousness of suffering. The Saviour does not say, " Verily I say unto you, The hour is come that the Son of man should die," but, " The hour is come in which the Son of man should be glorified."

There are two ways of looking at every act: the one is to look at the appearance, the other at the reality. And hence it comes to pass that that which to man seems mean is often inwardly glorious; and that which, as regards external circumstances, is surrounded with glory, in the sight of God is mean and miserable. Let us take an instance of this from common life: the soldier dies a ruffian's death, the lineaments of humanity crushed beneath the tramp of the war-horse. There is nothing in the outward circumstances of his death to distinguish them from a mere ignoble brawl; but over the soldier's death is shed the glory of that cause for which his life was offered, and so that which seemed outwardly mean becomes a glorious death. Precisely in this way, only in a far higher and deeper sense, was the death of the Redeemer, in external circumstances, a mean thing, but in inward principles glorified by God. In outward circumstances most mean—dragged and driven like a sheep to the slaughter; but through the long vista and the lapse of ages all the meanness of these circumstances has disappeared, and now we behold only the Divine love, and truth, and obedience which prompted to that death; so that even the circumstances themselves become glorious. The very cross, which was associated with an idea no more noble than that which is now connected with the scaffold and the gallows, has become to us the most glorious word in all our language.

Now, we observe that that which in the sight of God glorified the death of Christ was not the outward pomp of circumstance, for of this there was none; but it was the spirit of that death; and so we say of every life and death, that it is not the outward circumstance, but the inward spirit, which makes it mean or glorious. According to our common human way of speaking, a throne is glorious and a coronet noble; but there is nothing that can ennoble cowardice or meanness or selfishness. According to our mode of speaking, the dungeon and the scaffold and the lower arts of life are base and mean; but the death of the Redeemer has sanctified the cross, and the life of the Redeemer has shed a glory over the trade of a carpenter.

The second thing we are told respecting the law of the atonement is that it is part of the same great law upon which God has constructed the universe—death for life, the death of one for the life of many. The instance selected by our Lord is that of a corn of wheat. If there is to be a crop, there must first be the destruction of the seed. Now, let us not suppose that this is a solitary instance; it is one case out of many. Go where vegetation is the rankest, go where verdure waves the thickest, and there lies beneath decay and death; but out of the destruction that lies below has been deduced the glory of the petals of the flowers. And not only so, but our very daily and hourly life is supported by death. The lives of vegetables and animals are given involuntarily for us. We stand on the graves of the ages that are past. Remember, then, we rest upon a fact; we do not seek to explain the fact, we are content to admit it; but, admitting it, we have no right to be surprised if the Bible tells us of another corresponding with it, that the death of Christ was the life of the world.

Observe, therefore, I pray you, this doctrine of the atonement is no strange, new, arbitrary principle; it is a principle existing all around us; it is not unnatural, but most natural. The world of grace corresponds with the world of nature. The Father who made the law by which the flesh of living things sustains the life of others is the very same Being who made and obeyed the law by which the flesh of Christ is to the world "meat indeed." To enforce this law, Christ finds a parallel for the principle of His own sacrifice in the destruction of a corn of wheat.

The next thing that we remark in the law of Christ's atonement is that it involves the condition of self-devotion. The way in which He states it is this: "He that loveth his life shall lose it, and he that loses his life for My sake shall find it." There is one thing that must have struck us as failing in the parallel we have named. We do not thank the grain of wheat for dying, because its death is involuntary; and therefore, in order to constitute a true and proper sacrifice, another element is needed. When that which exists in nature by a mere unconscious law or by a blind instinct is accompanied by a living will that could reject it if it chose, then you have an idea of proper self-devotion. And this is the law of our highest life, pronounced by Christ to be also the law of His existence. The sacrifice of Christ was a voluntary one, else had it been no sacrifice at all; therefore we read, "No man taketh My life from Me, but I lay it down of Myself," "Therefore doth My Father love Me, because I lay down My life that I might take it again." The death of Christ is the world's life; the flesh of Christ was given to be meat and drink spiritually to us. This is the fact; the explanation of it we do not venture to give. There are many popular explanations, that tell of infinite sin demanding infinite suffering, and assert that the death of Christ saved the world because it was punishment. When men speak thus, they know not what they say; these are human arguments which are not written in the Bible. The Bible says that the death of Christ saved the world because it was the highest instance of that law which makes death necessary for life, and because it was voluntary self-sacrifice. The Bible facts about the atonement we receive with all our heart and soul and mind and strength.

II. Pass we on, secondly, to consider the steps of the mental struggle by which the law of the universe was embraced as the law of the Redeemer's life. For, brethren, it is one thing to understand a law, and another to obey it. There is no truth that our young men have to learn more important than this, that to admire that which is right is one thing, but to do what is right is another quite; and so we read of the young man in the parable who said to his father, "I go, sir, and went not." Now, the Divine life of Christ subordinated innocent human desires to itself by degrees. Had it not been so, His would not have been a real humanity; it would have been an emptying Himself of all human feelings, because He would have then been merely Deity in human shape. The struggle in the mind of Christ is expressed in these words: "Now is My soul troubled; and what shall I say? Father, save Me from this hour: but for this cause came I unto this hour. Father, glorify Thy name." He was literally distracted between two feelings—the innocent feeling, the natural craving after life, and the higher feeling which desired to embrace the will of God; the one is expressed in the first of these prayers, "Father, save Me from this hour;" the other in this, "Father, glorify Thy name."

And now let us perceive the steps through which this victory was won—it was through the efficacy and force of prayer. Prayer is by no means a mere talisman through which we substitute our will for that of God, but it is more truly that communion of the mind with God through which our will becomes at last merged into His will. If there is any condition necessary for the perfection of prayer, it was that of this prayer of Christ, for it was an innocent, humble prayer, one of submission and of faith—"Father, save Me from this hour." But that prayer was not granted, if to grant a prayer be to fulfil the longings of our humanity; but it was answered in a higher sense, for by degrees the wish itself passed away, and the wish of the man became the wish of God. And so there was one entire perfect will, the will of the Father being that of the Son—"Father, glorify Thy name."

Here, then, in conclusion, is given to us the one perfect specimen of a true battle of a human soul, and the soul's true victory; here is given us the one perfect pattern by which we may understand the true efficacy of prayer; and here is also given us the true sacrifice of personal will, the sacrifice of "Him who, through the Eternal Spirit, offered Himself without spot to God." This sacrifice is most truly expressed in the Psalmist's words, "Lo, I come to do Thy will, O God." That is the one atoning sacrifice through which the world's life comes; and that becomes our life when the spirit of that sacrifice has become ours, and we have learned what is meant by the apostle when, writing to the Romans, he beseeches them "to present their bodies a living sacrifice, holy, acceptable unto God, which is their reasonable service."

XXIV.

PURE RELIGION.

(FROM AUTOGRAPH NOTES.)

Brighton, November 2, 1851.

"Pure religion and undefiled before God and the Father is this, To visit the fatherless and widows in their affliction, and to keep himself unspotted from the world."—James i. 27.

This is evidently a protest; pure religion in opposition to impure or corrupted religion.

There were perversions of the Gospel in early times, such as that of licentiousness, of which we spoke last Sunday. In St. James's time God's sovereignty was corrupted thus: "He is the Cause of everything, therefore of sin. Sin is His plan to salvation. Sin, therefore, is a phantom, a nothing. Don't make yourselves uneasy about it. If a man's person is accepted, his acts do not signify. Christians are free from all restraints on the affections of the heart." This was evidently the doctrine to which St. James refers when he says, "Let no man say when he is tempted, I am tempted of God; for God cannot be tempted with evil, neither tempteth He any man." Observe how arguments are sought for sin: it honors God; or God has decreed it; or our nature is weak!

Now, St. James's answer was an appeal to first principles, for this doctrine outrages them: "Do not err, my beloved brethren. Every good gift and every perfect gift is from above, and cometh down from the Father of lights, with whom is no variableness, neither shadow of turning." And there is no other answer. If you choose to say, "I am fated," there is no reply. God foreknows it; it will be; therefore it must be. But we can appeal to conscience; and every healthy conscience says there is a flaw in the reasoning, though no reason can show you where the flaw is. I appeal to those principles which govern common life. Make that defence before a judge. If you make it insolently, you are condemned; if in earnest, you are put in a mad-house.

So in religion. And remark, whatever encourages sin or makes light of it is not religion. All these fine boastings about being the elect of God are vain:—"If any man among you seem to be religious, and bridleth not his tongue, but deceiveth his own heart, this man's religion is vain. Pure religion and undefiled before God and the Father is this: To visit the fatherless and widows in their affliction, and to keep himself unspotted from the world." St. James comes down to the practical.

And now beware of tampering with that difficulty. It will be a snare leading to ruin. We lay the blame on God; we say, "Why had we these appetites except for gratification?" I have a firm conviction that this thought, when yielded to, treads down all distinction between right and wrong. We think we are fated, and we charge God with our sins.

Let us recur to the deepest feeling of the heart, which says, "Good is from God."

St. James shows us religion in two branches: benevolence and self-government.

I. "To visit the fatherless and widows in their affliction."
Here is Charity.
II. "To keep himself unspotted from the world."
Here is Purity.

I. Duty of Charity.

1. Its first principle is benevolence. Now, benevolence is always

active. I lay stress on the word "visit." Observe the necessity of interpreting Scripture according to its spirit, and not its letter. This, in the letter, would be impossible. It would cut off from religion the afflicted and the young, who, from want of experience, and because of the offensiveness of visiting, could not. Besides, imagine the time of sadness taken up in condolences; the poor man's house made a public receptacle for rich folk practising benevolence. Therefore, interpret this passage in its spirit. Go to seek, do not wait till affliction offers itself. This is the peculiar spirit of Christian philanthropy. It is illustrated by the example of the *Sœurs de Charité*, of Howard, and of Ashley.

The time is coming when the warrior's wreath will be seen to be blood-dabbled, and the law-lord's coronet only a homage to talent. Real bravery is active goodness. These are the grander walks. But on a large scale or a small, this is your principle: "Be active in good."

2. The second principle of charity is sympathy.

"*Visit:*" do not relieve, do not advise. There are times when relief is an impertinence and advice an insult; times when pressure of the hand and a glistening eye are more eloquent than gold.

Observe the exquisite delicacy of Job's friends: "They made an appointment together to come to mourn with him, and to comfort him. . . . They sat down with him upon the ground seven days and seven nights, and none spake a word unto him, for they saw that his grief was very great."

Visit; that is, acquaint yourselves with suffering. What we want is more *sympathy*. Let us do the rich of this country justice. They are not oppressors, hard, exacting; all their duty is not done, but they do much, and are willing to do more. What, then, do we want? It is a fatal fact that the rich and the poor know nothing of each other. Hence such things as "pepper-water," advice in times of famine on the one side, and bitter indignation on the other side, as if the rich were mocking. It is hard to feel with people when we are not in the same circumstances. We preach temperance when we neither toil nor thirst; cleanliness when we know not what it is to return jaded to a home in disorder; frugality—have we ever computed a laborer's expenses? We say the peasant should not be a poacher or a pilferer. Why! is the rich man never tried for theft? Oh, we say, sin leads to misery. Do we remember misery leads to sin?

Now this is sympathy. To feel with the poor, we must understand them first. Don't think it always necessary to go with your purse or your advice. "Visit" as a friend.

3. The third principle of charity is condescension; "Visit the fatherless and the widow."

The widows and the fatherless were defenceless in Judea.

Condescension has two branches; considerateness for the desolate: condescension to the friendless.

For an illustration of considerateness, take Christ's example. He is found by invitation in the rich man's house; He is found by choice at Bethlehem, in Bethesda, at Bethany. Especially mark Him at Simon's house, in His intercourse with the desolate, degraded one. This is considerateness. So in society. Seek not the great. See the awkward one in the corner, the man of no birth, wealth, or pretensions—Christ would have drawn that one out. This delicate Christian considerateness is to be shown not merely for those whose misery is gross and palpable, but for those who suffer in a more subtle form, from neglect.

To illustrate condescension, take Christ at the well in Samaria. Observe, condescension is not difficult from the highest to the lowest. The rich landlord can give his hand to his tenantry at the annual feast, and get credit for it. Condescension flatters our love of influence; we stoop from a height.

But condescension is difficult between those with whom we are in constant intercourse, such as our servants; and difficult also with those who are in a grade near us. Ancient noblesse is shy of parvenus; the gentleman of the tradesman; the rich tradesman of the second-rate. Here, then, is the test. If you have the spirit of visiting the fatherless and the widows, you would stoop to those lower than yourself. It is just the difficulty that was between the Jew and the Samaritan. The Jew could afford to condescend to the Gentile, for the law separated him from them. But when Christ broke through the wall of partition between the Jew and the Samaritan, it was genuine condescension.

And, observe, condescension does not lower. Mistake not. We draw the veil of mystery and etiquette to protect ourselves. Evil lowers, and vulgar familiarity, and coarseness; but not condescension. You may be affable and yet have a sacred spell of dignity around you that none would wish to break through.

Was the Godhead lowered by condescension? "Wherefore

God also hath highly exalted Him, and given Him a name which is above every name." So with us. Haughtiness and reserve leave the heart barren. Condescension is the true dignity of man.

II. Duty of Purity: "To keep himself unspotted from the world."

St. James specifies a distinct form of evil, the world; not other forms of evil.

Let me define what the world is. It is not this beautiful world, which weaves for God the living garment in which the Invisible has robed His mysterious loveliness. Drink in beauty and heaven as much as you will from that. Yet a narrow mind has sometimes been tormented with a scruple about the lawfulness of enjoying the world, even in this sense.

Nor, again, does the world mean domestic affections. Let us guard against a common mistake. Men tell us when we love our children they will be taken from us. Awful picture of a tyrant God! When we weep, they bid us dry our tears; they forget that Jesus wept. We love little enough; let us bring in no cold, desolating, stoical theory to make that little less. Desecrate not the sacred home of love by the name of the forbidden world.

The world that spots is the spirit of evil around us. Wherever men congregate for pleasure, business, or amusement, there is evil. It belongs to the town rather than to the country; to large societies rather than to small. A mixed, strange, many-headed monster is it. It is like the miasma of a marsh. Each single pleasure is harmless in itself till the noxious juices are drawn out. It differs in different ages; persecuting and soft, money-making, infidel and superstitious—a torrent which we must stem.

Observe, distinct effort is required in a man to "keep himself unspotted from the world." You are spottable; the world can spot you—"*keep*" yourself.

Moreover, we may not decline the danger. We must go right through. Christians must be soldiers, tradesmen, citizens. There can be no luxurious shutting ourselves up with our devotional books. The snow-river flows through the lake without imbibing its warmth. We must transmute the evil.

Out of the innumerable influences of that multiform evil we select only three.

1. The world's tainting influence upon delicacy of heart.

This tendency is universal. There are manufactories where the evil and the well-disposed mix in dangerous proximity for hours together; bold vice and modest virtue. Go higher still. Enter gay society; look at young persons at the end of two seasons. Observe the influence upon them of newspapers, novels, and conversation in producing familiarity with evil. They have tasted of the "tree of knowledge," and have gained knowingness. Oh, the degradation and agony of a heart which feels itself naked! When the drapery is torn from life, we know what lies beneath.

All this comes from the world; not from your own heart only, but from the miasma of many hearts. In a marsh each single plant is harmless; the festering, noxious juices come out of the many. The retired life is safe; in the crowd danger straightway rises.

This is the natural tendency, unless it be counteracted by the effort here spoken of—"*Keep* yourself unspotted from the world."

2. The world's power to make artificial.

Define the world as the not-natural. Picture the man of the world seeming to be what he is not—a well-bred person with every emotion under control, with features immovable. We are as sure of meeting consideration from him as if he were influenced by the Gospel. Yet all this bland courtesy is on the outside; it is the smoothness of coin caused by friction in the purse. The edges, the corners, the salient points, all individuality rubbed away. This species of worldliness begins early. The boy at school dares not speak of his mother and sisters; at last he becomes brutalized enough to ridicule his home. It is an unnatural control, as well as an unnatural affectation of feeling. So in afterlife. The world honors riches; we are feverishly afraid of being detected in poverty. If our fortune be diminished, we adopt meanness and artifices at home, that we may seem the same abroad.

The world honors politeness; hence compliments and flattery. Oh, the crushing sense of degradation that comes from it!

The world honors feeling; hence sentimentality.

The world honors high birth; hence the attempt to seem familiar with good society.

This is the world. Men and women who have not kept themselves unspotted from the world are not what they seem. Hollow and unreal, their affectation appears everywhere in accent, motion, and sentiment.

And, do what we will, we imbibe this. Dikes intended to keep out salt water still admit some. The precept to be natural makes us unnatural; we affect nature.

Now, there is no remedy for this but what St. James gives. Firstly, some familiarity with suffering; and, secondly, intercourse with God. We must live "before God the Father;" live in the splendors of the next world till this world is dim. The man living in sunshine is not dazzled by the oil-lamp. One who hears in his inmost soul the harmonies of everlasting harps will not mistake the discord of this world for music. One looking out for death and judgment to come will not heed the judgments of this world. Feel the powers of the world to come; that is the secret of keeping one's self unspotted from this world.

3. The power of the world to destroy feeling.

It is a common expression to speak of the heartlessness of the world. Let us trace the history of the decay of feeling. We passionately crave a more lively life. Life generally is a dull, vegetating existence. There are times when we get out of this; when the blood runs fast, and thoughts and imaginations crowd and hurry and precipitate, as if we had gigantic energy. It is the delightfulness of animal exhilaration. There are the different excitements of conversation, society, music, or of the stimulant of wine; all those things which the world offers; "all that is in the world, the lust of the flesh, and the lust of the eyes, and the pride of life, is not of the Father, but is of the world." There is the craving of the drunkard. Life would be robbed of its exhilaration, so he cannot give up drink. Now, this is the consequence: unsettlement and deadening of feelings.

So in the body. In the tropics man is matured early and decays early. He is old at thirty; the sensations of life are all felt early.

Similarly in the heart. Early maturity of feeling is premature decay of heart. Existence does not depend on time. One man at twenty-five has lived longer than another at fifty.

Observe, all God's pleasures are simple ones; health, the rapture of a May morning, sunshine, the stream blue and green, kind words, benevolent acts, the glow of good-humor. It is the time when you need nothing stronger than bread and water to be intoxicated with happiness.

But look at other excitements. The great calm presence and beauty of creation does not come forth to the sorceries of artificial excitement. Stimulate the jaded senses with town life, and then there is no radiant wisdom left in the simplicities of life.

This is the lesson we press upon the young. Keep unspotted from the world. The keenness of wonder is by degrees lost early, and is followed by exhaustion of feeling; and men become *blasé* of life.

Oh that the young would learn from the experience of those who know it. Remember Solomon's state. Is there anything whereof it may be said, "See, this is new?" Ye that live in pleasure, to this you are coming!

There are peculiar features in the present time. The world is moving fast, and we with it. There are a multiplicity of pleasures; a cheapness in their purchase, and change in their variety. Thousands see foreign lands now. There are the excitements of railways, speculation, and literature. These produce exhaustion of feeling and of interest. Compare the patriarchal times, and we find the man of one hundred and fifty had not lived so much as the man of forty now. Let Christians, therefore, be on their guard. They have need of calmness. They have the power of the Gospel and duty to soothe them. Remember the Cana feast. Would you have your best last? Avoid stimulus; live plainly. You will drink the rich body of heavenly wine, and feel the refreshment of its sacred joy.

And now a word of application.

St. James gives a distinct view of religion. It is practical charity and purity. God's sovereignty and eternity are nothing without this. You are no favorite of Heaven to be exempt.

And, observe, both charity and purity are joined together, not kept separate. There is a difficulty in their union; but observance of the one cannot excuse neglect of the other.

The active must be worldly.

The strict, pure, quiet, dreamy, must be active.

External benevolence and inward purity go hand in hand.

XXV.

THE PROGRESS OF REVELATION.

(1.)

Brighton, Advent Sunday, November 30, 1851.

"Of which salvation the prophets have inquired and searched diligently, who prophesied of the grace that should come unto you: searching what, or what manner of time the Spirit of Christ which was in them did signify, when it testified beforehand the sufferings of Christ, and the glory that should follow. Unto whom it was revealed, that not unto themselves, but unto us they did minister the things which are now reported unto you by them that have preached the gospel unto you, with the Holy Ghost sent down from heaven; which things the angels desire to look into. Wherefore gird up the loins of your mind, be sober, and hope to the end."—1 Pet. i. 10–13.

It is plain that the Apostle Peter in these verses speaks of two epochs of God's revelation to the world—one that has been, another that is to be. The prophets, he tells us, of the elder dispensation dimly and indistinctly foresaw a coming day, a day of glory, preceded by human suffering. Similarly St. Peter announced the approach of another day of grace and glory, far more blessed and glorious than any that earth had yet seen. The anticipations of the first were realized in that which is called the first coming of the Redeemer; the anticipations of the second dispensation shall yet be realized in what we call the glories of His second advent. We are led, from the text, to assume an analogy between the two dispensations: the first did not come without expectation; and, according to analogy, we are entitled to expect that neither shall the second come on us without anticipations of its approach. It is with this as with the dawning of the natural day; you see not the landscape in its detail, but yet the general outline of the whole is visible, though it is in part dim and indistinct.

Our subject, then, this morning is an extremely large one, so far as it can be contained or sketched in the limits of a single sermon; it is no other than this—God's plan in His revelations to the world. It divides itself into these two branches:

I. The mode of that dispensation which was imperfect and is past.

II. The dispensation of that revelation which is yet to come.

I. First, then, we remark that the former dispensation was based on a system of mediation. Putting aside all theological terms, let us endeavor to understand this. A mediator is simply one who acts between two parties as a medium; a mediator is one who through things visible conveys instruction on things that otherwise would be misunderstood. Now, God's revelation to man is mediatorial; it could be none otherwise. Human nature being as it is, God could not, or, to speak more reverently, God did not, reveal Himself singly to each individual. But His plan was this: He took a single nation, that through that nation He might reveal Himself to the world—a nation that of all others was at the outset the rudest and the coarsest, for God would begin from the very beginning; and one of the objects in so training that nation was that out of it the choicest spirits might be formed, becoming the teachers, first of the Jewish nation, and through them of the world: it is these men whom St. Peter calls the prophets.

And, now, before proceeding further, let us endeavor to gain a distinct notion of what we mean by inspiration. An inspired man is a higher kind of man; he is one whose aspirations are more generous, more unselfish, more pure, than those of ordinary humanity. The difference between him and common men is this: that of the twofold nature in which we all participate, the fleshly and the spiritual, the lower predominates in others, but in him the higher, the heavenly and the spiritual. What they felt feebly, almost unconsciously, he felt mightily and consciously.

Now, let us take a few instances in which this marvellous contrast between inspired and uninspired men is shown. When the whole nation of Israel were content to remain in bondage, if they might only have the flesh-pots of Egypt, the voice of God came to one among them telling him that the life of freedom, even though the way to gain it lay through the wilderness, was so immeasurably superior to every other life that no sacrifice could be too great to secure it. Again, when the people trembled at the blaze of the lightning from Mount Sinai, and feared when they heard the trumpet voice of thunder, among them there was one heart which desired to see God face to face, and to gaze undazzled on His intolerable splendor. When the pleasure-loving crowd sat down to eat and to drink, Moses came down from the mount where he had been with God, struggling and wrestling for Duty and Right and Law; and when he saw what they were, and felt how immeasurably his aims were above theirs, and how hopeless the distance, the prophet dashed the tables to the ground. Take another instance from the case of an inspired warrior. When Nahash the Ammonite offered peace to the besieged inhabitants of Jabesh-Gilead, it was on terms of obloquy and disgrace. They asked a respite of seven days, in which they might send the message to all the coasts of Israel; the craven people, when they heard the message, lifted up their voices and wept. But there was one heart in Israel which looked for better things for God's nation: when Saul heard it, the Spirit of God came upon him, and he sent back this message to the men of Jabesh, "To-morrow by that time the sun be hot ye shall have help." And when the morrow came and the inhabitants looked out, suddenly beneath the walls of Jabesh-Gilead the battle-cry of Saul was heard, and the rays of that sun were flashed back by the swords of the thousands that he had brought, burning to avenge their country's wrongs, led on by one noble inspired heart. This, brethren, is what the Bible calls inspiration. There are different kinds of inspiration—that of the lawgiver, as Moses; that of the artisan, as Bezaleel and Aholiab; that of the warrior, as Saul and Gideon and Barak, men who delivered their country, not by brute courage, but by inspired valor. Lastly, there was that of the prophets, whose office was not so much to predict future events as to interpret the present. They did not read the fate and fortunes of empires as mere soothsayers, but it was given to them, with burning hearts, to reach grand first principles which are true to-day and forever. They were partakers of the larger humanity of Christ, just as the Apostle Peter here says, "They were searching what, or what manner of time, the Spirit of Christ which was in them did signify."

Now, the means whereby they arrived at that perfect knowledge of the future were twofold: first, the materials of the revelation that had been already given to them were with others as well as with them; the difference lay in the spirit that was within them. Let us look at their materials; manifestly they were the

Jewish Scriptures. God's revelation to the world is God's education, for "what revelation is to the race, that education is to the individual." A revelation begins, as education does, with the first elementary principles. The elementary principles taught directly to the Jewish nation were few; the direct truths might almost be compressed into these—the unity of God, the holiness of God, the blessedness of doing good, and the misery of doing wrong. It was long before lessons as simple even as these were learned. How long was Israel in learning the unity of God! how many times is it repeated, "Hear, O Israel, the Lord our God is one Lord!" Though the power of God was so plainly shown to be superior to that of the Egyptian gods, yet still idolatry continued in Israel for long years, and it was not till after the Babylonish captivity that they were entirely weaned from it. This will show us why other truths were not taught, for so childlike a nation was as yet unable to bear them.

Immortality was but indirectly taught to Israel. I say not that in the Old Testament Scriptures immortality is not named, but in the primitive revelation of the five books of Moses it is not directly spoken of; for all the system of Moses rested on temporary rewards and punishments: if they were obedient, they were to eat the fruit of the land into which they were led; if disobedient, the nations among whom they dwelt were to be pricks in their eyes and thorns in their sides. Contrast the two revelations. St. Paul says, "To them who by patient continuance in well-doing seek for glory and honor and immortality, the reward shall be eternal life;" Moses says, "Honor thy father and thy mother, and thy days shall be long in the land." Yet though not directly taught, it was taught indirectly. Just as in the elementary book of the child the higher truths are neither shut out nor distinctly told, but are implied, so it is with God's revelation. In the Book of Genesis we find it written that man was made of the dust of the earth; and God breathed into his nostrils the breath of life: not one word here of immortality. Now consider how a pious Jew must have reasoned on this when he stood by the grave of some beloved one; would not this have been his inward reasoning? Dust to dust, yes, but the breath of God breathed into his nostrils, what has become of that? I give to you now the actual reasoning of an inspired man on this subject. In the Book of Ecclesiastes we find Solomon saying, "The dust shall return to the earth as it was, and the spirit shall return to God who gave it." Again, when God spake to Moses in the bush, He said, "I am the God of Abraham, of Isaac, and of Jacob." That was not to teach immortality; the direct object of it was to encourage Moses in his mission to Pharaoh with the assurance that the God of his forefathers would be with him. Nevertheless, consider once more how an earnest and religious heart would reason on that: God is the God of Abraham, Isaac, and Jacob. Where then are they? Are they no longer in existence? Is this the God of love? Can annihilation be His reward to those who have served Him best? Does He say to His most faithful servants, "Return to the nothingness from which you came?" Our hearts demand it of us that an immortality there must be. And this was precisely the mode of reasoning our Lord used when asked by the Sadducees concerning the resurrection of the dead. He produced no direct testimony to immortality, because there was none found in the writings of Moses. The proof he produced was an indirect one, even this, that God is the God of the living, not of the dead. And when, brethren, you add to this the many other passages in which the same thing was implied, passages such as that common formula by which death was described when it was said that a man was "gathered to his fathers," passages by which the Jew was forced to live out of the present and for the future, and to familiarize himself with that which was to come, it will then become evident to us that through all the system God was preparing the highest minds by hints, and by imperfect expressions, for that revelation, in after-ages to be made manifest, when life and immortality should come to light through the Gospel. These were the materials on which the imaginations of the prophets had to work.

There was, however, another source from which they derived their knowledge, that which St. Peter calls "the Spirit of Christ which was in them," the Jewish Scriptures, and these Scriptures interpreted by spiritual hearts.

"The Spirit of Christ" is, in other words, the spirit of self-sacrifice; for, just in proportion as a man is great and good is that spirit strong in his soul. The measure of a man's goodness is the measure of his self-devotion. These men turned to the Jewish Scriptures, and found there the principles of Jewish sacrifice, the externals of which differed not much from those of heathen sacrifice, for the gross Jew had probably much the same notion as the heathen concerning it; he felt that God was angry, and congratulated himself that another had felt the pain of punishment instead of him. To the prophets it was not so, for it gave them a desire to dedicate themselves to God. And so, when we turn to the Psalms or the Prophets, we find passages with which we are familiar, and in which they speak indignantly of mere sacrifice: "Thou desirest not sacrifice, else would I give it Thee; Thou delightest not in burnt-offerings." "The sacrifices of God are a broken spirit; a broken and a contrite heart Thou wilt not despise." And, again, "Sacrifice and offerings Thou wouldest not, but a body hast Thou prepared me." Thus the deep desire of the soul was replied to and expressed by the faithful in the Jewish sacrifices.

II. We now pass on, secondly, to consider the dispensation of the day of grace and glory which is yet to come.

Now, first, brethren, I have to observe, as before so now, that God's plan of revelation is partly by truths direct, partly by truths indirect. The direct truths of the Christian revelation are those which in the Jewish were indirect; for instance, immortality and self-devotion. But there are indirect truths also, which in the fulness of time shall be revealed hereafter. Take the testimony of our Blessed Lord: "I have many things to say, but ye cannot bear them now." Consider the testimony of Moses: "A prophet shall the Lord raise up unto you like unto me." Christ is spoken of as a prophet, but in what sense, if not as preparatory to a greater revelation? Again, the text says, "Be sober, and hope to the end." In other words, it is that which it is our business to celebrate to-day—our anticipation of the glory of the revelation of Jesus Christ.

Now, let us take an instance of these truths. The first we give is one which in the early ages of Christianity was indirect, but has become direct now; it is the doctrine of the admission of the Gentiles; not distinctly taught by Christ, but taught by implication, for it was long before the apostles themselves perceived that it followed from the doctrine He had taught. In process of time it was admitted, with reluctance, by the Apostle Peter; but it did not become a direct truth until proclaimed in all its breadth and fulness by St. Paul—"There is neither Jew nor Greek, circumcision nor uncircumcision, barbarian, Scythian, bond or free, but Christ is all and in all."

Next, we come to a subject more delicate, the consideration of some of those truths which are to be revealed hereafter, and of which we have now only a dim foreshadowing. Out of the innumerable thoughts that here crowd upon us, I have selected but three. First, there is given us in the Scripture this hint, "One is your master, even Christ, and all ye are brethren." That, we dare to say, has not in almost any sense or form yet been realized in a world where power and wealth produce hatred instead of love, and the religion of Christ is a sword instead of peace. But is there, to an earnest and a loving heart, no pregnant intimation of a human brotherhood yet to come, more deep, more broad, and far more spiritual than has ever yet been exhibited in this world?

Again, in the history of the early Church we find that "no man said that aught that he possessed was his own." On these words the wildest schemes of socialism have been founded; but is there here no hint, no intimation, of a system far more generous than any we have yet conceived? Does it not tell of a mode of life higher far than our present system of rivalry and competition?

Take one hint more. In the beginning of the Gospel we read this declaration to Mary: "Hail! thou that art highly favored, the Lord is with thee; blessed art thou among women." Upon that hint the Romanist has elaborated Mariolatry—the worship of one single woman. There are many among us who can sneer at Mariolatry, but it is not from the sneerer that the deepest truths are learned. Instead of sneering, let us look at the truth so miserably caricatured by Rome. Out of these pregnant words, the blessing of the Virgin, is there no hint given? Remember these were new words in this world of ours. The masculine qualities, courage, wisdom, strength, had been revealed, but now was given to the world a representation of the divine character of purity, modesty, and self-devotion; are there in these words no anticipations to give the Christian heart a hope of a coming day when woman shall yet be what her Creator designed she should become?

Now, let us close this subject with the two practical pieces of advice that the Apostle Peter gives: "Be sober, and hope to the end." First, a lesson of hopefulness, then of sobriety.

There are dark views held by many respecting the future of the race. Men talk gloomily of a flood of Romanism and Rationalism; but the only question we ask is this, whether God is guiding the race or not. If He guide it, then it is on its way to good, and not to evil. The Apostle Peter, in the midst of persecution, encourages the disciples with these views and with strong faith in God. Let men sneer, call these dreams, ask for something practical—it is good to get away into God's future from our own selfish interests and hopes. This, then, is the remedy for all our fears for the future, to trust with unwavering faith in the God who guides the destiny of our humanity.

The other lesson impressed on his converts by the Apostle Peter was sobriety: "Be sober." For be assured that we know little except in outline of that which shall be hereafter. The tree of our humanity has blossomed once, but the fruit is yet to come; it is not for us to anticipate and prematurely grasp that fruit—it will ripen in God's good time.

Hints are given for us to ponder on them, and to hope in God, not to scheme and rave.

"God is His own interpreter,
And He will make it plain."

XXVI.

THE PROGRESS OF REVELATION.

(2.)

(FROM AUTOGRAPH NOTES.)

Brighton, Advent, December 7, 1851.

"Wherefore the law was our schoolmaster to bring us unto Christ, that we might be justified by faith."—Gal. iii. 24.

IT may be well to follow out the subject of last Sunday.

The principle laid down last Sunday was that the plan of God's revelation to the world has been to teach some truths directly; others indirectly, by implications, hints, allusions. So that the indirect truths of one dispensation become the direct truths of the next. For instance, immortality and self-sacrifice, which were the indirect truths of Judaism, are now the direct truths of Christianity.

The services of the day seem to invite us to examine this subject further. In the Collect we pray that "we may in such wise read, mark, learn, and inwardly digest the Holy Scriptures, that by patience, and comfort of Thy Holy Word, we may embrace and ever hold fast the blessed hope of everlasting life, which Thou hast given us in our Saviour Jesus Christ." And, again, in the epistle we read, "Whatever things were written aforetime were written for our learning, that we, through patience, and comfort of the Scriptures, might have hope." Therefore, the subject offered for our contemplation by the Church is the Holy Scriptures as furnishing a guide, a hope, a consolation preparatory to Christ's second advent. This seems the leading thought which regulated the selection of the services of the day.

The Epistles to Timothy, the last Paul wrote, are of a darker shade of thought than his earlier ones. He sees perilous times coming, for the grace and love of Christianity would be received by men of undisciplined hearts. It became evident that the Advent was not near, but far off, and that the conflict between good and evil would go on for a long time. And yet in the midst of all this there is one ground for consolation. St. Paul is assured that Timothy would struggle against the evil in his day; and this because he had from a child known the Holy Scriptures, which were able to make him wise unto salvation: knowing the truth, he would be resolute in contending for it.

The objection raised by the Jews against Christianity was that it contradicted the earlier revelation. And, in truth, there was much to favor this objection. For, in the first place, Judaism declared the Jews to be God's chosen people; whereas Christianity entered into the world proclaiming God to be the universal Father. And even Christ's teaching seemed to corroborate this view: "Ye have heard it was said by them of old time"—that is, by Moses—"an eye for an eye, and a tooth for a tooth; but I say unto you that ye resist not evil, but whosoever shall smite thee on thy right cheek, turn to him the other also."

St. Paul replies to such an objection in the text. The reply amounts to this: The human race had been under a system of education, and the spirit of Christianity was not more contradictory to that of Judaism than the duties, the treatment, and the education of a man are contradictory to those of a child: "The law is our schoolmaster." This, then, is our subject, God's preparation of the world for the first advent of the Redeemer.

We divide it into two branches on the present occasion. The law is our schoolmaster—

I. As giving precepts in which principles were involved, but not expressly taught.

II. As teaching inadequate and not perfect duties.

I. The law gives precepts, not principles.

Every wise teacher begins so. He gives rules, not principles. And the first duty of the pupil is blind obedience. At length, when the pupil discerns the principle, he may dispense with the rule or not, as he pleases.

Of the mode of teaching in the Jewish law the first instance we select is the second commandment. It runs thus: "Thou shalt not make to thyself any graven image, nor the likeness of anything that is in heaven above, or in the earth beneath, or in the water under the earth. Thou shalt not bow down to them, nor worship them."

According to this law, the Israelite was not only not to worship a graven image, but not even to make one. The possession of an image or a statue was unlawful. Those adornments of our houses and cities, which we freely use, were forbidden him. Yet we all know it was not this, but idolatry, which the law was intended to forbid. The *spirit* of the second commandment is the prohibition of idolatry; the *letter* is, thou shalt not make a graven image.

Idolatry is the worship of anything as the Highest which is not the highest—the admission of any conception of God which is either false or else unnecessarily inadequate. For example, to worship God as cruel would be idolatry, because false. Such is the worship of Juggernaut. To worship God as the mere source of life is idolatry, because it conveys an inadequate idea of God. Such was the Egyptian worship, which reverenced life in its lowest forms. The idea was not false: God is the Principle of Life; but then God is much more.

But here observe. It is only idolatry when *unnecessarily* inadequate—that is, when the man might and ought to have had higher views. All conceptions of God are inadequate: that of the highest Christian is inadequate to represent the All-perfect truly. But it is one thing to think inadequately of God because the powers are feeble, and another to think so when light is given to form nobler conceptions and to think more justly. The conception of the Jew was an imperfect mental image, because he knew not God as Love; but it was not idolatrous, because there was a kind of "it must needs be" in the inadequateness.

But if a Christian were now to acknowledge as his Highest an image of God as vindictive, jealous, partial, or lax, or as a mere Creator, when He has been revealed as Love, he would tread on the very verge of idolatry, because he might have a higher image in the Divine Humanity of Christ, who is the "express Image of God's Person." And so a Protestant who quotes the second commandment against the Romanist, to prove the Romanist idolatrous because he reminds himself of God by graven images, may be himself idolatrous in a deeper sense; he may think of God as partial—loving him and his small sect only. The Romanist breaks the letter of this second commandment, many a Protestant the spirit of the law.

Now, what we are concerned to observe is that the Jew was not *taught* this principle of idolatry; he was trained to it by a precept. He was not to make images, like the Egyptian, of the ibis or the crocodile, because it was degrading to the idea of God; nor images, like the Assyrian, of those strange winged human figures which we see in the Museum, because they are inadequate; nor images like the devil-gods of the Philistines, because they were a slander upon God.

And thus, by degrees, excluded from all lower forms, the Jew would reach that state to produce which the law was given—the state in which he could form a worthier conception of the Almighty. Then he would be no longer under a schoolmaster. Having reached the spirit of the law, the law would be no longer binding on him.

Do you think any intelligent, wise Christian considers that law in its letter binding upon him? Is there any but the narrowest mind who would quote the second commandment to a Christian, "Thou shalt not *make* to thyself a graven image," as forbidding sculpture and imitative art? Yet it *was* forbidden by the second commandment.

The second instance of this principle which we allege may be found in the law of Moses is, "Thou shalt not muzzle the mouth of the ox which treadeth out the corn."

Consider for a moment the not uncommon interpretation of

this law. There is a favorite mode of interpreting the Old Testament Scriptures, especially among Puritan divines, which looks on them as a collection of oracles or types out of which a recondite meaning was to be developed. The spiritual sense of Scripture is regarded as the hidden connection of these types with some Christian mystery, and the spiritual interpretation of Scripture is the discovery of such a resemblance. On this principle, because St. Paul extracts out of this command the duty of the Christian Church to make provision for its ministers, therefore, under his guidance, they say oxen were the type of Christian ministers; and wherever the word occurs, so they read it. The oxen supporting the brazen sea were types of a Christian ministry; and their looking east, west, north, and south was typical of the universal spread of Christianity.

For one moment let us stop to think. All the Old Testament Scriptures were intended to teach some one. For whom, then, was this command given? Was it for the Jews of old? Could it be that the Jews were from this to guess that in after-times a Christian ministry were to be supported? And if so, what was that to them? Or was it to teach Christians? Can the plain duty be left to be spelled out of a recondite and debatable enigma? The danger of this mode of interpretation is that it turns Scripture into a collection of trifling littlenesses, makes it a set of riddles, and the expounder of it a riddle-guesser. And just as the eye loses its power by ever looking through a microscope, so does the mind lose the comprehensiveness of its grasp by straining after these infinitesimal littlenesses.

The true spirit of the law is this, the ox is a toiler for man's good. God says, Muzzle him not, he has a right to feed. But observe the principle involved. The ox has a right as a laborer, not as an animal. Then it follows that "every laborer is worthy of his hire." The minister is worthy because a laborer; not because of a Scriptural type, but because of a Christian principle. It is thus that St. Paul reasons: "Doth God take care for oxen?" That is, is this law merely meant to inculcate benevolence to animals, or is there a principle in it? "Saith He it altogether for our sakes? For our sakes, no doubt, this is written."

Now, many a man who would accept this application of the principle because it was made by Paul, might miss the great teaching of his principle. For, read it only as a type, and then many a man who would scrupulously pay his minister, because commanded by a Bible type, would be severe and rigorous on his laborers. In that case he would be a slave to the letter, instead of being made a freeman by the principle.

II. We pass on to consider the second way in which the law was education by a schoolmaster.

It was so because it prescribed inadequate duties—a part instead of the whole, which was to develop into the whole.

Of this we select three instances.

1. The institution of the Temple worship.

The Jews were to hallow the place which the Lord should choose to put His name there. The place where the ark rested, and where the Temple stood, there God was—there were men to worship.

Now, this might mean either of two things.

It might mean that God was more there than elsewhere. This idea lay at the bottom of that miserable question between the Samaritans and the Jews—Which was holier, Mount Gerizim or Mount Moriah? And this lies at the root of all modern wrangling as to whether a church be holier than a hill-side—whether the consecration by a bishop imparts actual intrinsic sanctity to stones and walls. And, observe, exactly in proportion as one place becomes more holy in our eyes, others become less holy. When God is confined to one spot, He is banished just in that proportion from all other spots. To sanctify your church, you profane God's world. Whatever peculiar degree of acceptableness you add to the prayer offered up in one place, you take from the prayer offered up in all other places.

But, again, it *might* be that God was teaching the Jew this: that if He put in a claim to part, He had a right to the whole; that if God were in Jerusalem, He was also in the desert. And assuredly God did teach the Jew this. For there were times when, driven from his country, the partial truth was insufficient, and he was forced to realize the more adequate one. So Daniel, exiled in Babylon, prayed; the old feeling still clinging to him, his windows therefore open to Jerusalem; but still persuaded that, although far away from Jerusalem, yet that God was hearing him. In a very touching psalm David yearns after the ordinances and the Temple service he had once enjoyed : " As the hart panteth after the water-brooks, so panteth my soul after Thee, O God." But before the psalm is finished he realizes the truth that even in his banishment God will "command his loving-kindness in the daytime, and in the night his song shall be with me, and my prayer unto the God of my life;" and that he may therefore pray from "the land of Jordan, and of the Hermonites, and from the hill Mizar."

When faith was well-nigh extinct and forms dead, there was one man at least in Israel who from the localized worship had extracted the deeper truth. The iron-hearted Baptist goes into the wilderness, and with no temple but the sky, no symbols but the solemn trees, the moaning night-winds, and the roll of Jordan, an emblem of the eternity into which his soul was passing, feels that God is there as truly as in the Temple of Jerusalem. And the Son of Man Himself said, "The hour cometh when neither in this mountain nor yet at Jerusalem shall men worship the Father. God is a Spirit, and they that worship Him must worship Him in spirit and in truth, for the Father seeketh such to worship Him." Thus, then, through a most inadequate truth, the Jew was led on to the larger truth that God is here, and therefore to be worshipped. But then God is everywhere, and his true temples are infinite space and the soul of man.

2. The second instance is taken from the fourth commandment, "Remember that thou keep holy the Sabbath-day."

So runs the law, one seventh of all time is God's. But see how inadequate this is. It is a truth, but only a part of the truth. For if that one portion be exclusively God's, then just in that proportion the rest of time is not God's. This is what Pharisaism, ancient and modern, perpetually tends to. It purchases the sanctification of the one seventh by the profaning of the six sevenths. The Sabbath is God's, then Monday is not God's, but yours and the world's.

Assuredly, this was not God's teaching by that Divine institution of the Sabbath-day. But, just as now a "right of way" is often secured to the proprietor by shutting up a road one day in the year, not to declare it his only on that day, or more on that day than others, but simply to vindicate his right in it for every day; so did God shut up one seventh part of time, that it might be understood that all belonged to Him.

Accordingly, when we come to the New Testament, we find

that revealed which had been so long implied. St. Paul says, "Let no man therefore judge you in meat, or in drink, or in respect of a holy day, or of the new moon, or of the Sabbath-days. One man esteemeth one day above another; another esteemeth every day alike. Let every man be fully persuaded in his own mind. Ye observe days and months, and times and years. I am afraid of you, lest I have bestowed upon you labor in vain." As if the whole labor of the past had been in vain, so long as they were still cleaving to the inadequate truth, instead of embracing the higher and expanded one, that *all* time is God's; every day of life to be consecrated to Him.

3. The third instance we adduce is that of the third commandment: "Thou shalt not take the name of the Lord thy God in vain, for the Lord will not hold him guiltless that taketh his name in vain."

This is commonly quoted as prohibiting blasphemy and cursing; but originally it had nothing to do with this. To take the name of God in vain was to use it in asseveration, to call God to witness, and then, by breaking the oath, to make that invocation vain or void, and thus render the name of God a worthless and frivolous thing. It was equivalent to "Thou shalt not forswear thyself, but perform unto the Lord thine oaths."

In this spirit the whole Jewish law was framed. If a man was put upon his oath by the priest, he was bound to utter truth, under tremendous penalties: "And if a soul sin, and hear the voice of swearing, and is a witness, whether he hath seen or known of it; if he do not utter it, then he shall bear his iniquity."

It was in obedience to this law that Christ responded to the high-priest's question. At first He held His peace, but when "adjured by the living God" to say if He were the Son of God, He immediately replied, "I am."

Thus, then, the lesson God taught the Jew was truth, but truth inadequate, truth under certain circumstances. It was an exceedingly inadequate exposition of duty: truth when the priest was by, truth when God was present, or when God's name was invoked. Now here, too, the limitation of the command was most dangerous. In proportion as a Jew thought himself peculiarly bound to be true when on his oath, he would feel freed from obligation when not on oath. So, now, men who would shudder at perjury, think comparatively little of untruth.

Nevertheless, though originally inadequate, see how this law taught deeper views of truth. So long as the Jew believed that God was limited to one seventh of time, or limited to a portion of space, so long, of course, was the duty of truth limited too: truth only where God is—you must not lie on the Sabbath, nor perjure yourself in the court of justice. But when the Jew learned that all time was God's, and all space—that He is ubiquitous in time, omnipresent in space—then the lesson he had been learning came into a more extended application. And the pious Jew must have reasoned thus, "I was taught to be true where God is; but God is everywhere, therefore woe is me if, in the Awful Presence that fills each moment of time and every corner of space, my lips or heart should utter an untruth."

And precisely such was the expansion which Christ gave to the third commandment: "Ye have heard that it was said by them of old time, Thou shalt not forswear thyself, but perform unto the Lord thine oaths: but I say unto you, Swear not at all: neither by heaven, for it is God's throne, nor by the earth, for it is His footstool; neither by Jerusalem, for it is the city of the great King." In other words, God is everywhere, heaven His throne, earth His footstool—the very hairs of your head are counted by Him. And so in Christianity the sin of lying is equal to the Jewish crime of perjury. The Christian word is as sacred as the Jewish oath, being fenced by sanctions precisely the same. You speak in God's presence, speak where you will. And hence the Christian "yea" is to be "yea, indeed," and the Christian "nay," "nay, indeed."

In the application of this subject we have three things to say.

1. The first truth at which we arrive is this: revelation is education. We ask no better definition than this of St. Paul's. The human race has been under a schoolmaster. What education has been to the individual, that is revelation to the race. God is revealing Himself to His world.

And herein lies the difference between the atheistic and the Christian view of the progress of the human race. Atheism infers it from the qualities of the pupil, Christianity from the love of the teacher. Atheism—that atheism, at least, which puts God out of the question—talks of the majesty of the human intellect, counts up the triumphs of past discoveries, and infers the future from the past. But it is not so, we reason. We begin with God, not man; we do not say, man will reach all truth, but God will teach him all truth; not, man will find out God, but God is seeking man. In other words, we believe in revelation.

2. The second thing we arrive at is that revelation is progressive.

Understand what we have in the Bible. Not truth absolute, but truth relative. If we think that inspiration means the communication of the highest spiritual truth, or the power of communicating it, we utterly confuse the meaning of inspiration. If we think that Moses, Job, David knew, except most dimly, what we know, we confound the different ages of revelation. Or if we suppose that even the truths we have now are aught but the dimmest dawn of that blaze of truth which shall be in the coming revelation, we lose the doctrine of this text. For there is no revelation but the ever-continuing.

3. Lastly, let us learn that the training of the character in God's revelation has always preceded the illumination of the intellect. The truths I have spoken of are contained in a few sentences: God fills all space, all time. To have low notions of God is idolatry. God being everywhere, man's life should be everywhere true.

But it took God four thousand years to teach these truths to the human race. And here again, therefore, we are in diametrical opposition to the modern systems. It is the fashion now to rely upon the illumination of the intellect for the perfecting of the character. God's way from old time has been to rely upon the training of the heart and habits for the illumination of the understanding.

You may teach a child these truths in ten minutes; but to teach them as God would have them taught, to teach them in any way that shall not be worthless, that demands a long, holy, obedient, humble life.

XXVII.

CHARACTER AND MISSION OF THE BAPTIST. (I.)

(COMPILED FROM AUTOGRAPH NOTES FOR TWO SERMONS.)

Brighton, December 24, 1848, and *December* 14, 1851.

"Then said they unto him, Who art thou? that we may give an answer to them that sent us. What sayest thou of thyself? He said, I am the voice of one crying in the wilderness, Make straight the way of the Lord, as said the prophet Esaias."—John i. 22, 23.

To those who merely accept a truth because it is written, the life of John the Baptist presents nothing much more significant than the fact that it pleased God, we know not why, to send a prophet to prepare the way for Christ.

But to those who love to realize the Past, to bring it near, and reproduce it with the same distinctness in which it would have been seen had they lived in it, not only is the figure of the Baptist one of the most striking of all which stand out in Bible history, but also the necessity of his appearance is most intelligible, and his life one with the peculiarities of which they can most deeply sympathize.

We say John had a special mission. Let us understand what we mean by that mission.

God's missions are not like ours. It is not the office which makes the man, but the man whose character creates the office. The office arises out of the circumstances which mould the character. Looking at him, when life is done, in a worldly point of view, men would say his life was the result of all the circumstances which made him what he was. Looking at the same facts, religion says, True, circumstances made him; but circumstances are God's appointment. This is what we mean by a mission—God sent him.

The significance of the Baptist, his life, the place he occupies in the world's history, the peculiarities of his character, we shall never understand by merely referring them, with seeming piety, to an arbitrary fiat of the Most High. We must understand the day before we can comprehend the man. We must understand the circumstances which made him what he was before we can comprehend in what sense God "sent him."

Our subject will therefore divide itself into three branches:

I. The circumstances which made the man.
II. The man John.
III. His mission.

I. The circumstances which made the man. John was the exhibition of his age—the transition point between the old and the new.

The symptoms of an old religion breaking up were evident; unity was succeeded by diversity. We may compare with it the state of Catholicism when St. Bernard's voice moved Europe to the Crusades. When a multiplicity of sects arose, previous to the Reformation, men might know that reformation was near. The "fulness of the time was come," visible to all who observed the signs of the times.

There were four divisions of society in Judea: Pharisees, Sadducees, Essenes, and Herodians.

1. The Pharisees.—The Pharisees were the formalists of their day. Consequently, their religion had slumbered into habit. They mumbled prayers, bowed their heads, quoted maxims having lost principles, and had a sharp-defined creed. The inner life of conscience had passed into the life of outward habit.

The Pharisees endeavored to keep religion alive by scrupulously and reverently retaining the past. God did not speak to them, but He had spoken to rabbis of past days. Their faith amounted to this: that for four hundred years God had been silent; that since Malachi, He had not inspired the sons of men. But inspiration was real once. It was a kind of antique reverence for the symbols of a faith which once was, but was evidently extinct now. These were secular, scheming, worldly politicians, joining great zeal for religion with laxity in duties.

It is an evidence of something gone when antiquarians collect and prize relics of the past. Strong symptoms of an expiring religion are seen when men value the printed Word of God more than His Living Voice, when they worship the Bible instead of the God of the Bible.

Pharisaism is the religion of habit.

2. The Sadducees. — The Sadducees were of another order. Theirs was the cold heart and clear intellect. They were the rationalists of their day. Sadduceeism is the reaction of Pharisaism in every age. Wherever there is an unquestioning formalism or a wild fanaticism, there a spirit will rise asserting the rights of the understanding. Rationalism is a dry, critical, negative spirit. It is Protestantism merely. It protests against all that cannot be proved. It reduces everything to an intelligible system. So the Sadducees said, " We can find no proofs of the authenticity of any books beyond the five of Moses; consequently, we reject them. We will hear of no veneration for antiquity; that is mere feeling, and books are not to be received on the authority of feeling." They cut books and chapters out of the canon ruthlessly; examining them as coolly as they would some old record—not with a patient, reverent criticism, but with a cold-blooded sneer. They took their stand on a narrow creed indeed. Again, they said, " We can find no proof of immortality. We throw on you the burden of proof. It may be; we do not know. These are simply aspirations of your own; the belief of good and wise men before you. All well, but possibilities are not proofs."

Here, observe, was the religion merely of the intellect.

3. The Essenes.— There was a third party in Judea at this time, the Essenes. There were some who could not bear this formalism or this scepticism. That life-weariness which is found in refined ages—scarcely known in earlier, but felt when men begin to look in as well as out—sent many into the desert, to lead a simpler, calmer, austerer life. They could not bear the awful blank which the Sadducees had made by cutting out of the canon all the spiritual words. They could not feed their souls on the trifling fripperies which made up Pharisaic religion. They tried to find God in contemplation. They were what we should call mystics. They felt the infinitude of all truths, and recoiled from the sharp dogma which would put truths into words. They retreated into the inner shrine of our humanity, and said, God must be felt, not talked about, nor understood. Nay, even the steady, consistent life of practical duty was merged by them in vague feelings, tender or mysterious.

There have always been such tendencies. Protests against what is hard. Glorious assertions of that which is boundless and deep, and imaginative and awful in the soul. Such is the silent quietism of the Quakers, who wait mutely for the effluence of the Spirit; and such the source of that profound stillness which breathes through Thomas à Kempis.

Here, then, was the religion of feeling.

The defect of such religion is that its tendency is to lose at last the actual *fact* of outward truth—God, religion, all, become a feeling, not a fact.

4. The Herodians.—Respecting them we know little. They were probably a political party, who desired to make Herod king. Their existence tells, of course, of a large number of men who had turned aside from questions merely ecclesiastical and religious, to those which concerned man's social and political existence.

And such there will ever be: men of active mind who seek realities, and to whom religious subtleties seem shadows. Men of stern Roman integrity, like Gallio, who will bend all their energy upon causes of property or wrongs, but if it be a matter of questioning about your matters, will say, "See ye to it, for I will be no judge of such matters." Men who are weary of disputes between Pharisees and Sadducees, and turn their attention to facts of science, on which they can find firm resting-ground. Such a one, perhaps, was that mental giant of modern times, Humboldt, who, almost alone of men, was capable of writing a history of the universe; and who has told us—a sad, memorable confession—that in the pursuit of science only can the mind find refuge from the mysteries of Being and the pain of questions which are insoluble.

Thus, then, Jewish society had separated itself into four departments, the religion of habit, of feeling, of intellect—formalism, scepticism, mysticism—and of interest respecting the affairs of this present life.

Now, religion is meant to impregnate all of men. But there ever is a tendency in our religion to narrow itself into one of our faculties, and then exhibit itself as only habit or feeling or intellect. The consequence of this tendency was that Jewish society was rent into fragments and fractions, and therefore was its unity lost.

II. The man John.

Now, consider how it was impossible for a man like John to find a home in any of these parties.

Should he join himself to the Pharisees?

How, with his impatience of all that was unreal and the iron earnestness of his nature, could he belong to those whose life was droned away in litanies and frittered into genuflexions?

Or the Sadducees?

Can you conceive him resting in mere protesting negations; satisfied with their cold intellectual system; pleased to hear some protesting orator demonstrate how superstitious and idolatrous the Pharisees were?

Or, again, should he become one of the Essenes?

That iron man, with his practical sense of duty, his terrible sense of wrong; whose words fell from him like a warrior's, with soldier-like brevity, sharp and trenchant, every sentence a half-battle! Think you he could go and dream life away in contemplation, in stillness, and in sickly feeling?

Well, then, the Herodians?

Surely, for one so real, a patriot's life offered what was wanted. A Jewish patriot to emancipate his people. Was not John the man for the hour?

But this was equally impossible. What his spirit burned and yearned for was, not a mere civil liberty, nor a polity, but a kingdom of God on earth. What was it to him whether a licentious emperor or a licentious viceroy sat on Israel's throne? What to him whether his province groaned on still beneath the Roman yoke, or that rebellion should succeed, and popular excesses and popular vices follow imperial despotism and royal vices?

He loved humanity almost more than men. He felt his country's degradation. But his was one of those spirits to whom God is dearer than humanity. And, therefore, for such a one in mere political existence there was no career, among such parties there was no home for him. No wonder he stood aloof from all.

It is only by a consideration of such circumstances that the Baptist's peculiar life becomes intelligible.

III. Let us now consider: The mode of preparation, and its effect on the mind of John—this latter first.

i. The effect produced on the mind of John by his dwelling in the wilderness.

This was not a desert of rocks and sand, but wild, uninhabited forest-land. Amidst such scenes the spirit of John was disciplined for his peculiar work. He was there thirty years, "till his showing unto Israel." Think of this! Thirty years' preparation for one year's work. So natural was this that when he came into the world of men, his last hour soon struck.

Consider the testimony of such a life as his to the existence of another world. I do not mean one future, but present—around us; a world of thought, feeling, contemplation. "Man does not live by bread alone;" a man's life "consisteth not in the abundance of the things that he hath." Look at John's childhood. From his birth this had been his choice: "The child grew, and waxed strong in spirit, and was in the deserts until the day of his showing unto Israel." We live feebly; we cannot believe except we have truths echoed again and again. From Sunday to Sunday is too long to believe in God without evangelical props and means of grace. There are souls which God has made who can expatiate in that invisible world where others can scarcely breathe; growing like hardy plants upon the rock, like the heather in the sand.

In the wilderness the child shrank not from the awful solitude. He was not alone: all around him were the types of the Invisible. The river flowing by, the storm-shaken trees above, and the grass not bent beneath, breathed into his soul a deep peace. He had no forms to worship by; but the world was the great form which shaped his ideas of God. And then, beyond, beyond, the Presence " whose dwelling is the light of setting suns."

Observe the effect produced on such a mind by the conventionalities of society. Pharisees and Sadducees came to him—the men without a faith, and the men without a heart; and indignation, as of an ancient Hebrew prophet, awoke against them. Rapacious publicans, the discontented populace, the haughty soldier of the Roman armies, came to hear of a higher life. And he showed them all how false their life had been. Then came his life at the court of Herod; all around he saw a conventional, artificial morality. There sin that was condemned in the poor publican was considered venial in the great man. But John knew no such distinctions. He had been living alone with God, reading his Bible, looking at the heart of things, hoping for the kingdom of God; and this was no kingdom of God at all. So, of course, all fell away from him: such a man was not fit for life. Accordingly, when he came into the world and spoke of things by their real names, the end soon came.

So is it always. No one sees how the battle goes while he is in it: no one ever understood the world except by getting out of it from time to time. How a short contact even leaves us in levity and earthliness, how we find ourselves acquiescing in its false maxims! And we return to wonder how hollow and false a thing our life has become.

Observe, again, how the Spirit of God in such a mind passes into life.

Had John died before his thirty years were over, he had discharged no mission. But he differed from the Essenes in the practical character of his call; it was not to meditation, though he was an anchorite himself. So the Spirit of God, buried in the heart, passes out into action. This is Christian life. Beginning in the resolution of a firm, solitary heart, passing into life, ending in deep peace: it brings the desert into the world, the hermit into life, and sends him, with a strong, self-conquering heart, through the manifest duties of life—in the world, but not of the world.

John was prepared for his work in the loneliness of the wilderness.

From a very early age the young soul began to ask those deep questions which are deepest. But he got no help from rabbi or scribe; so he went into the desert, to be with God—alone.

Losing the solaces of an earthly home, he found in God his everlasting portion. Like a single trunk of an alpine tree rising solitary from between the interstices of some lonely rock and throwing its branches over the cataract. You look for soil, there is scarcely any to be seen; and yet that gnarled root has fastened its tenacious grasp on the bare stone, and tossed its green branches in the air, as if it needed nothing but the breath of heaven for its support. So this soul flourished where less hardy spirits would have starved, and he breathed freely the atmosphere of heaven while yet on earth.

Then consider the reality of his life. His food, locusts and wild honey; his dress, camel's-hair and a leathern girdle; his drink, the chance brook. These are the simplicities of life that force men to be real.

On two previous Sundays I spoke of the Advent in reference to the development of our humanity—God's education of the race, and God's education of the individual. For religion deals not only with man the social, but with man the individual besides.

Christianity is a church—God's relation to humanity; but it is also a religion—a matter of personal experience. We stand alone, separate from all other beings. We partake of common influences. But our individuality, separated from all other, lies based deeply in that.

And this is one of the great lessons taught by the Baptist's life: the solitary character of the relation between God and the soul.

It is a mournful prospect for the man who is timorously asking the formalist and the ritualist to tell him what it is reckoned by the majority safest to believe, which is the right Church, and such-like questions.

Mournful, too, for the spirit who is trying by sharp intellect to cut into the heart of truth, and finds layer after layer and covering after covering taken off, till he comes to the central nothing; who is trying to penetrate the mystery of being with subtle intellect, clear and sharp, and finds truth after truth untenable and unprovable.

Then, in the hour when the timorous are dismayed, when habit is broken by some shock, and the intellect darkened, the brave soul of faith dares to look into the Awful Darkness and feel God.

Believe in God—your own soul and God. Dare to be alone. Dare to be as Christ was. Do not go about asking what this man believes, and what that. Dare to enter into that solitude which is peopled by the spirits of "just men made perfect." Be sure that God is nearer than you think. Be true to Him, and brave. One thing real amidst a world of shadows.

The second lesson taught by that life is the necessity of falling back on first principles.

Consider the simplicity of John's life and creed. He had enough to supply life, and no more. From artificial pampered life he falls back on the fact, "Man wants but little." His creed was simple as his life—"Repentance," and "judgment to come."

The deepest truths are always the first and simplest.

In this age the real questions are, not the frivolous ones discussed in religious journals—baptism, surplices, and such like—but, What is God, and where? What is human life? Whither are we tending?

Be sure that in a dying hour the questions will narrow into a very few: God—Eternity—the Soul—Judgment—and the Cross.

ii. The mode in which John prepared the way for Christ—his mission.

1. John calls himself a voice.

A voice is the utterance of a meaning sound—an articulate expression. The wind is called God's voice, which "shaketh the cedars"—where a meaning is fancied. John was the world's voice. Four centuries had passed, and yet no man could speak the word. Simple enough it seems: "Repent," if God's kingdom is to come. Regenerated society comes not from regenerated institutions, but from regenerated hearts. Changed hearts will produce changed character and changed institutions. But none till John had found the tongue to express this, though all acknowledged it when it was spoken. The dim, vague longing, the restless tossing of that age, had found a voice at last. John spoke out what it wanted; felt deeply what all were feeling. What we want, said he, is not political reformation, nor a more accurate creed, nor more liberty, but alteration of heart and life—in one word, Repentance. So spake the Voice of the Age—in articulate tones at last.

There is a great distinction between eloquence and fluency; fluency is command of words, eloquence of words which express thought. Fluency John had not; short, sharp, decisive words were his—no ornament or trick of oratory there. Let us never covet fluency; it is a fatal gift. Let every man covet eloquence. It is to speak the right thing at the right time, in the right way. And that is done sometimes in a way which it seems a contradiction to call eloquence. Silence may be eloquence, and stammering lips may be eloquent. Let a man be earnest and true. The heart will feel the expression of itself. Those very few words of John were not spoken to the world in vain.

And this was the secret of his marvellous success. Pharisees and Sadducees came. How little you would have thought this was the voice that spake what they wanted! And yet they came.

John himself marvelled—why were they there? The Pharisee, satisfied with himself, what had he to do with "repentance?" The Sadducee, satisfied with the present, what did he care for "wrath to come?" "One touch of nature made the whole world kin."

Reality had fronted them, and the veil fell off. We are not happy, they said; we are miserable. Prophet of the Invisible, what hast thou to tell us?

2. John was "the voice of one crying in the wilderness, Prepare ye the way of the Lord, make His paths straight."

The metaphor is drawn from the custom of Eastern kings sending heralds and pioneers before them to clear a road.

At the period of the Jews' return from captivity, we hear the sublime language of Isaiah: "Prepare ye the way of the Lord, make straight in the desert a highway for our God. Every valley shall be exalted, and every mountain and hill shall be made low."

The King was coming, all obstacles were to be removed. Observe, there was to be *levelling*. There was to be an elevation of that which had been unduly depressed, a depression of the unduly exalted.

There was the mountain of Caste. The Jews prided themselves on their hereditary descent from Abraham: "We have Abraham to our father." Yes; they were of Abraham's family, without Abraham's faith. The voice of the herald spoke: "I tell you, God is able of these stones to raise up children unto Abraham;" and then that mountain fell.

There was the mountain of Religious Sectarianism. The Pharisee stood on an elevation. He was above others, on the strength of certain formulas of expression, of breadth of phylacteries, of length of prayers. Then the voice spoke, "O generation of vipers," and another mountain fell—that of religious separatism, on which a man exalts himself above his fellows.

There was the mountain which gave impunity to wrong-doing. Herod took his brother Philip's wife. In a common man—a poor publican—Herod's offence would have been great. Many a wretched sinner was condemned by Pharisaic sanctimoniousness. But Herod being in power, great allowance was to be made for his sin. Therefore spake again the same dauntless voice that never quailed before the face of man: There can be no kingdom of heaven on earth while this is allowed; sin is sin, wrong is wrong, in the greatest as well as in the smallest. Covered by the imperial purple of Rome and surrounded by the fasces of authority, sin is vile, just as much as in the unfriended and outcast. The stern voice of the prophet says to the king, "It is not lawful for thee to have her."

Thus before John's teaching all mountains went down. The mountain from which a man looks down on others in virtue of derived worth, or that from which he claims distinction by a correct creed, or that of rank and station.

But, observe, the Gospel did not teach abolition of distinctions, but established them on a true basis. It depressed the proud, it elevated the humble. The time had come when the "vile man was no longer to be called liberal, nor the churl bountiful."

Jesus once stood at the Temple gate. He saw the rich men cast in their offerings and a widow cast in a farthing: "Honor to the splendid offerings of the rich," was the world's cry; "Glory to the widow's mite," was the voice of Christ.

Note, again, the wondrous way in which this preaching did level. All were humbled together. The awful voice proclaiming judgment to come had levelled all in the dust before God. For when man comes to front the Everlasting God, the dream of self-righteousness, the fine-drawn logic of scepticism and infidelity, what can they do for him? When sorrow touches the false heart and the strongest totters, how shall they stand? Ask the waves, when they are swept flat before the hurricane. What is all in front of the blaze of our God, who is as a Consuming Fire?

Now let us apply this.

Such was John's mission—terrible, searching, levelling. He was not the king of love, but of law. His office was not to give God as a Father. He preached Him as he knew him—the All-holy, All-just. The Father was preached afterwards—revealed through the Son, our elder brother.

Meanwhile observe, this must be the order ever. The baptism of John must precede the baptism of Christ: the baptism of water unto repentance that of the Spirit unto life.

Lastly, just in proportion as the work of repentance is deep, the work of grace is permanent. Peter and John were disciples of the Baptist before they became disciples of Christ.

XXVIII.

CHARACTER AND MISSION OF THE BAPTIST. (2.)

Brighton, December 21, 1851.

"And he came into all the country about Jordan, preaching the baptism of repentance for the remission of sins; as it is written in the book of the words of Esaias the prophet, saying, Prepare ye the way of the Lord."—Luke iii. 3, 4.

These words, my Christian brethren, quoted by John the Baptist, had been spoken seven hundred years before by Isaiah himself. Nearly three hundred years after that, Malachi closed the canon of Scripture with these remarkable words: "Behold I will send you Elijah the prophet before the great and dreadful day of the Lord; and he shall turn the heart of the fathers to the children, and the heart of the children to their fathers." Then intervened a period of four hundred years, during which the voice of prophecy was mute, and all that was left to guide the Israelite was that of which Malachi reminded him in the previous verses: "Remember ye the law of Moses my servant." And then, when these four hundred years were closed, suddenly, immediately before the Messiah's advent, there appeared in the wilderness a wonderful man, living a life like that of Isaiah and Elias, applying to himself this prophecy of Isaiah, and having applied to him by Christ that of Malachi concerning Elijah.

I propose as the subject for this day's contemplation to endeavor to return an answer to these two questions: first, by what right and in what sense are these two prophecies, the one originally spoken by Isaiah of himself, and the other distinctly marking out a particular man, Elias, referred to John the Baptist? and, secondly, in what sense was John the forerunner of the Redeemer, preparing His way before Him?

I. Now, to understand on what principle these words are applicable to John the Baptist, we must carry along with us the leading principle of prophecy: it is not merely a prediction of separate events, but, far rather, an announcement of principles. Through the interpretation of the present, the prophets predicted the future; for the announcement of every principle connected with a fact is a prediction of all future events that shall occur under similar circumstances. For instance, the astronomer, in the announcement of the eclipse, has so plainly discovered the principles that regulate it as to be able to foretell without a doubt the very moment of its return. Again, when a philosopher lays down any law, such as that of gravitation, he may say that every stone falls to earth—there he announces a principle; or he may make it a prediction and say, every stone shall fall. And, again, when the physician traces the laws that have regulated pestilence and marks out the course on the map that it has taken, in announcing the facts he is predicting the course of every future pestilence that may occur under similar circumstances. Now, thus it was that our Lord and the prophets applied their prophecy. The prophet Malachi uses the name of Elijah, and says, before another great and dreadful day come, another man shall rise up in the same spirit as Elijah. If you take it as a prediction, then you are driven into those endless questions which have occupied commentators so long, as to whether Elias shall himself return to earth; or else are compelled to criticise the correctness of the Redeemer's application of it to John. Therefore there remains for us another way to understand these words, as an announcement of a principle.

Now let us look at past times. When Israel had fallen from God, another such as Elias appeared, Isaiah demanding justice, mercy, truth. The prophet Malachi therefore tells us that before every such judgment of the Lord, before every such event called in Scripture a "day of Christ," when artificial civilization is succeeded by a great reformation and social reorganization, before every such time there will be a falling back upon first principles. The call for a simpler and a purer life is made sometimes by a single individual, such as Elijah, Isaiah, or John the Baptist, men who have felt more deeply than others the wants of their nation and their age, and have dared to stand out alone, separated from the mass, demanding a reformation; sometimes, again, it has been made not by an individual, but by a spirit pervading all classes.

Now, our Blessed Lord applies this prophecy to John the Baptist. Some came and asked Him, "Master, why say the scribes that Elias must first come?" He told them that "Elias truly shall first come and restore all things." But that the Elias that was to come was not the Elias they had expected, but one in the spirit and power of Elias, who should turn the hearts of the fathers to the children, and the hearts of the children to their fathers. He thus reminded them that what the prophet meant was not a resurrection of the man, but of his spirit.

Brethren, we live in an age which in many respects is parallel to the times of Elias, Isaiah, and John the Baptist; a day in which manifestly we are on the eve of great and mighty changes—changes perchance more deep and radical than any the world has yet seen; a day in which the margins of old parties are melting into each other, and those few who have remained steadfastly attached to some old principles are becoming more bitter against others—a manifest proof of the decrepitude of an opinion. What that coming day shall be none but a prophet can decide; some tell us that it will be an age of warfare and convulsion, others are looking merely for an age of light. The significance of the Baptist's message can never pass away. Therefore it becomes us to ask what that message meant, and what steps must be taken to prepare for the coming advent.

II. In the next place, we return an answer to the second question proposed, in what sense was John the forerunner of Jesus to prepare His way? It is quite plain that the expression of the prophet is a figurative one. It alludes to a custom well known in those times. It appears that in Eastern countries when a monarch desired to pay a visit to a distant part of his dominions, he was accustomed to send his messengers before him to demand of the inhabitants of every part through which he was to pass that they should make his road easy by filling valleys and cutting through hills. Precisely in the same way was John the Baptist to prepare the way for Christ; he came proclaiming a King, he came declaring the conditions without which the Kingdom could not come, and without which the King could not reign. Now, the first of these conditions was this: he prepared the way for Christ by declaring private righteousness preparatory to public reformation.

Brethren, a message most significant! He did not announce this Kingdom thus: "There is a Kingdom coming whose internal regulations shall be so perfect that misery and vice shall be banished, and happiness shall come without any effort;" instead of this he says, sharply, "There can no Kingdom come to you without the preparation of the heart." And herein do the expectations of the Church of Christ and the predictions of Christianity differ from all other anticipations and expectations whatsoever. The peculiarity of Christianity is not the expectation of better times, for every one—the whole world—looks forward to something of that description. But the difference lies in the order in which the millennial glory is expected; the world expects better times through the alteration of institutions, the Church expects better times through the alteration of individuals; the one begins from without, the other from within.

Now, to take an example: there are none looking forward to better times more earnestly than the working classes, and they are taught to expect it through the instrumentality of government; their leaders tell them that all their miseries come from bad government, and that Parliament is omnipotent to convey to them all the blessings of which they have been so long deprived. To them the message of John the Baptist must be again and again repeated, the old severe message, that kings and law and governments can do little, almost nothing; and that the advent of better times for the working classes depends on their own personal reformation, chastity, sobriety, and self-control. But then it will be said, is this your message to the poor—this severe, heartless message? Yes, even so; the laws of the universe are very stern, alter them you cannot. It would be far more easy, far more palatable, to lay the blame on their oppressors rather than on them: the only objection to such a course is the stern unalterable law of God's universe. The law of life is this: no man can be good or great or happy except through inward efforts of his own, sustained by faith and strengthened by the grace of God. The message of the Baptist must be repeated, "Change yourselves, or to you at least no kingdom of God can come."

Let us take for example an expectation much talked of now. It is held by enthusiastic men that half the evils of the world come from rivalry and competition; and if we could substitute for this the system of love, we might then have blessedness. Brethren, we deny not that beneath all this there is a truth; but we say the Baptist's words remain true, and that if we get rid of rivalry we shall have selfishness remain.

Again, it is the hope of numbers that science will do for them what politics cannot do. We are told to expect that science will by degrees banish superstition, and that it will do away with all those maladies and miseries which come from popular ignorance. We honor science in its place, we honor it as the discoverer of many of the laws of the creating God; but we must remember that it has its own place. No man could have stood last summer in that structure where all the works of man were exhibited in one place, without hoping great things for the human race. But, brethren, again, let not these expectations go too far; let us remember the Baptist's message; science can do something, but science cannot bring us God's kingdom. Wherein consists the misery of life—in sickness, or in selfishness? Science may by degrees banish superstition; it will at last banish among Romanists the belief in miracles and relics, and among Protestants the belief in the magical power of the baptismal water; but can science answer to the heart suffering alone, can science give to that aching heart a home, a faith? If not, then what we want is not a kingdom made comfortable by art and science, but a kingdom of the Redeemer, a kingdom of the cross and of humbleness. Therefore, to the philosopher we tell of a wisdom wiser than his own, we speak to him of one whom in his wisdom he would despise—that stern, uneducated man who led a simpler, humbler, and purer life, and whose whole life's philosophy uttered itself in one expression, which was the voice found for our humanity, "Repent, for the kingdom of heaven is at hand."

The next manner in which John prepared the way for the advent of the Messiah was by a simple assertion that right is right, and wrong is wrong. In the text we find it written as the characteristic of that preparation that "the crooked shall be made straight, and the rough places plain." In John, at least, there was no crookedness; he was plain and straightforward at all times; he called things by their right names. You remember the stern fidelity with which he dared to say, in most uncourtly phrase, "It is not lawful." You remember the stern fidelity with which he dared to say out to the popular religious party of the day, in language which to ears polite must have seemed strange indeed, "O generation of vipers, who hath warned you to flee from the wrath to come?"

One of the evils ever attendant on human progress is that of over-civilization, a tendency to make life artificial, and from that which is artificial to pass on to that which is false. Let us look to our own time; we scarcely know how deeply our own common life is saturated with falseness. Our very language is false: we address one another as if plural; it would be considered an insult to any one to address him in the singular number; we write to one another, signing ourselves "humble," "faithful," "devoted;" we accept the social falsehood of permitting it to be said that we are "not at home," because we are, perhaps, too tender to the feelings of our friends plainly to deny them, and are too occupied or too unwell to see them. I say not these are absolute falsehoods, but they are on the road to it; and so our standard comes at last to measure sins by their publicity, and not by their turpitude; and then comes the time designated by the prophet when "the vile man is called liberal and the churl is said to be bountiful." We start at the vices of the poor; while among the rich licentiousness is denominated by the tender name of wildness, we say it is a bad habit contracted in youth. O brethren, it is notorious that the standard of our society is not that of the life of Christ.

Now you will observe that that which prepared the Baptist to be so true was the simple, austere life which he led in the wilderness. Had he identified himself with any of the parties of which we spoke last Sunday, then doubtless he would have been so accustomed to their evils that he would have been unable to see them as he did, and would have felt so bound up with one party or another that, had he spoken, he must have hurt the feelings of a friend. But, standing aloof from all, he could protest in the wilderness against all the vices of the age.

And now, brethren, if there be any of us who would desire to see these things in their true light, the principles of the Baptist's life must be his; something of solitariness, of loneliness, and something that forbids us to identify ourselves with any faction or party—a willingness to stand by and see the game of life played without us. Then, and only then, alone with God, determining to view things as Christ would have viewed them, can man be real and true.

The last way whereof we have to speak in which the Baptist prepared the way for the Messiah was by teaching simple truths, falling back upon first principles. We find in the chapter from whence the text is taken that when John spoke to his nation, by degrees the people came and asked him, "What shall we do then?" To which he said, "He that hath two coats, let him impart to him that hath none; and he that hath meat, let him do likewise." When the publicans asked the same, the reply was only this: "Exact no more than that which is appointed you." And to the same question from the soldiers he replies, "Do violence to no man, neither accuse any falsely, and be content with your wages." You will say it needed not a prophet to tell them these things, nor can we call this a revelation. And yet such have ever been God's revelations, to call men back to simple, first, forgotten principles. You marvel that a prophet was required to tell them these things, but let us remember what life then was. If you had asked a man what was religion, he would have said that it consisted in daily services, in fastings, and in giving alms. Nay, if the same question were asked now, would not the answer be greatly similar? Conceive, then, with what a sense of marvellous astonishment men must have listened to that simple prophet of the wilderness, saying to them, in a voice of thunder, These are not what God requires at the hand of man; His service is "to love mercy, to do justly, and to walk humbly with his God." In other words, religion and goodness are things identical. Such words must have come to these artificial men with a strange freshness and novelty.

Brethren, observe that this was to prepare the way for Christ —it was preparatory to Christ, but not Christ. We draw the distinction between the baptism of John and the baptism of Christ; that it is one thing to bathe the soul with the laver of duty, another to bathe it in the laver of self-sacrifice. And yet in all ages of the world the baptism of John must precede the baptism of Christ, the baptism of repentance and of an altered life must go before the baptism of self-surrender. There are two things which are apparently Christianity, but not really so, the spirit of devoutness and the spirit of moral uprightness. Take the conduct of the upright judge Gallio as an instance of this: he was a strenuous supporter of all things pertaining to law and order, but when it came to matters of religion, he cared for none of those things. Devoutness also may exist separate from morality, as we find in the case of Jacob, who sought the blessing of God at the same time that he was defrauding his brother. It is even so now with the enthusiasm of those who will applaud denunciations of Rome in the morning, and spend the evening in calumny and slander. Brethren, the history of John the Baptist seems to tell us that it is not a matter of indifference which of these two comes first in order; it is not a subject for the self-congratulation of a parent if his child exhibit strong symptoms of devotion unaccompanied by right feeling, or if he show great love for his Bible, and is yet a lying, false, undutiful child. God's order is the opposite, "not first that which is spiritual, but that which is natural, and afterwards that which is spiritual." Better to begin with those qualities which are apt to be derided by the name of worldly qualities and virtues, such as simple truth and integrity, than to begin with the warmest enthusiasm.

This, brethren, is the preparation of the way for Christ, to begin at the beginning; a man must have learned to be just before he can be liberal, honorable before he can be generous; he must have learned self-denial before he dare to use the word self-sacrifice. The foundation of the cross must be laid deep—deep in these simple worldly virtues of honor, integrity, justice: then, and only then, is the way made smooth for the Redeemer to enter into our hearts; then, and only then, virtues now inconceivable will become not only possible, but absolutely familiar.

XXIX.

CHRISTIAN FORGIVENESS.

(FROM AUTOGRAPH NOTES.)

Brighton, March 28, 1852.

"Then his lord, after that he had called him, said unto him, O thou wicked servant, I forgave thee all that debt, because thou desiredst me: shouldest not thou also have had compassion on thy fellow-servant, even as I had pity on thee?"—Matt. xviii. 32, 33.

THE subject of this parable is the danger of the indulgence of a vindictive spirit.

The necessity of enforcing its lessons arises from the fact that Christian forgiveness is not the natural growth of the heart, but an exotic in an unkindly soil.

It also arises from the circumstance that the whole temper of the world around us thwarts that spirit. The natural stiffness of persons who are at variance, and their unwillingness to be reconciled, are so encouraged by the condolences and sympathy of mistaken friends that our society in one cardinal point exhibits few lineaments of the Church of Christ.

The occasion of this parable of the unmerciful servant was Peter's question, "Lord, how oft shall my brother sin against me, and I forgive him? till seven times?"

Now this was the language of human nature, somewhat modified. The Rabbinical law of forgiveness was until three times. Peter doubled this; and gave, as he thought, large latitude for the Messiah's more loving system.

Now, remark, this was exactly the principle of modern honor. A court of honor would decide, as Peter did, points of etiquette and satisfaction. Up to a certain point, forgiveness; beyond that, revenge. Blows, for example, must be wiped out with blood. The question put to such a court would be, What is satisfaction?

This allows something to Christianity. There is to be forgiveness. But something is due to personal rights; therefore forgiveness is to be limited. And hence our modern honor, great as it is in the way of advance over old heathen or savage codes, the law of the woods—over such a proverb as that chanted in old times, "If Cain shall be avenged sevenfold, truly Lamech seventy and sevenfold"—yet can only be called half heathen, half Christian.

To this question Christ replied, "I say not unto thee, until seven times; but, until seventy times seven."

Now here we have the very essence of Christianity. Christianity is a spirit, not a set of rules. "Seventy times seven" is a Hebrew expression. It is not a definite, but an infinite number—a number impossible. Love refuses to be trammelled. Can you prescribe to a parent the number of embraces he shall give his child? Love dies in captivity, as the caged bird of open air pines. Love is free as the expanse of God's own heaven, unlimited and illimitable.

In illustration of this, Christ spoke the parable of the unmerciful servant.

Let us collect what it suggests respecting—

I. The Christian duty of confession.
II. The principle of Christian forgiveness.

I. Confession is of three kinds:

Confession to God of sins committed against God.

Confession to man of sins committed against man.

Confession to man of sins committed against God.

It is only of the two first that this parable says anything. The lord of the servant represents God, and the acknowledgment of the debtor to him is parallel to confession to God of sins against God. But the acknowledgment of the second debtor to his superior servant of a debt owed to him is parallel to confession made to man of sins committed against man.

1. Duty of confession to God.

The necessity for confession arises from the *load* of unacknowledged guilt. As it is expressed in our Church Service, "The remembrance of them is grievous unto us, the burden of them is intolerable."

Let me appeal to you. You cannot move unforgiven; you cannot resist temptation; you cannot pray. Is it not so? A spell holds you, night after night, that will not let you kneel?

But do not fancy yourself safe and forgiven because you *feel* no burden. There is such a thing as a laden slave sleeping on his burden. The first stages of mortification alone are painful; after that, the benumbed senses cease to warn. The frost-bitten man is warned by strangers. So is it in paralysis of conscience—in the benumbed heart.

Now, there are two ways in which confession relieves.

First, by confession we sever ourselves from our sin, and we disown it. We say, "I put it from me, I repudiate it. Not I, O Lord, but sin that dwelleth in me. I plead to Thee against myself. I struggle to the foot of Thy cross, though I be bound in chains." Such was the immediate relief of David: "I have sinned." Instantly does the answer come: "The Lord also hath put away thy sin; thou shalt not die." Such the relief of the publican: "he went down to his house justified."

Next, confession relieves by giving a sense of honesty. So long as we retain sin unconfessed we are conscious of a secret insincerity.

When we have made a clean breast, we feel, "I can do no more; all rests now with God. At least I am true, not trying any longer to appear what I am not." Just as a captain, bringing his ship into port, is sleepless and restless till he has put the helm into the pilot's hands; but then folds his arms and stands aside, responsibility no longer resting with him. He may perish, but it will be with no self-reproach. He has done all he can.

Therefore, let confession be instantaneous. We are tempted to procrastinate. We say that we cannot confess yet; we will wait till we are better.

Now see the lesson of this parable. The servant had one warm moment, infinitely precious, before imprisonment. He seized that. With warm, urgent, impetuous feeling, he pleads: "Lord, have patience with me, and I will pay thee all."

And such, in the strange history of the human soul, is the moment for mercy or hardness, brief as the interval in which the dark cloud in passing shows the moon's disk; when it is once past, all is dark. Seize the moment of strong conviction, of tenderness, of apprehension. Quick! quick! it will not come again.

2. Confession to man of sins against man.

The inferior servant freely acknowledged his debt. Observe a peculiar feature in the case; the other "took him by the throat, saying, Pay me that thou owest." It might have seemed that injury cancelled obligation, or that acknowledgment gave an ungenerous foe a legal hold upon him. Yet still he admits the debt.

So in quarrels. It often happens that he who has offended most is not the one who has offended first. Whereupon the first offender thinks himself exonerated from the duty of acknowledgment. And this makes the real difficulty of mediation. The case is complicated. There are intricacies and recriminations; the first simple aspect is changed.

Now, the plain Christian rule is, the man who has done wrong has no right to consider consequences. Have you wronged; repair. Have you erred; apologize. You may put a weapon into an ungenerous adversary's hand of which he will make unfair use. You may have been injured beyond the injury you did. It is galling to humble yourself to a man who has you at advantage; yet still a Christian man has one thing only to consider. His *Christian* honor can only be tainted by what he does, not by what has been done to him.

Now contrast with this the principle of modern honor.

To that principle which is called honor let us do all justice. It was an immense gain and step beyond the old heathen and savage life, which said, Revenge when and how you can. It was a great gain to say, Revenge only . . . And commendable, too, in that it taught courage, and made life second to honor. For in all its forms courage is to be honored. A brave man has risen above some of the most besetting weaknesses of our nature. None but a brave man can be a good man. The very tenderness of the coward will be pitiful. Even when it only bares its breast to an adversary's sword, honor courage.

But now look into this world's honor. A man of honor resents the charge of meanness. He will not refuse to pay a gambling debt, but he will live extravagantly when he cannot pay his debts. He is indignant at an imputation on his courage; but he will injure in lower ranks of life where redress is too expensive to be possible, and no father's or brother's bullet can avenge the injury.

These are the laws of honor! These be your men of gentle blood! This is the personal dignity at whose shrine lives of others are to be sacrificed, and the blood of God's creatures to be held cheap—personal dignity separated from personal worth—of which the Gospel of Christ knows nothing.

Now, with this modern honor contrast the spirit of Gospel honor; the honor which feels itself degraded by an acknowledgment of error with the honor which teaches through the Cross that wrongs *received* cannot shame — that nothing can disgrace but wrongs *done*.

Contrast the courage which can risk life with the courage which, for Christ's sake, dares to be called a coward and bear shame.

The first noblest attitude of man is innocence; the second noblest, apology. The manliness of saying, "I have done wrong, forgive me," is as high above that of a mere man of honor as the brilliancy of heaven's sun transcends the glitter of an earthly lamp.

II. The principle of Christian forgiveness.

God's forgiveness is a type of ours: "O thou wicked servant, I forgave thee all that debt, because thou desiredst me."

First, it is a free thing: "he had nothing to pay," "and the lord was moved with compassion, and forgave him the debt." This is precisely our state.

The sum was enormous—ten thousand talents; the revenue of a province, the upper servant being a viceroy. It was a sum in comparison with which offences of any man against us are as nothing.

And oh, that coming to account! Opening the debtor's books, and finding how much we owe! Yet one day the reckoning must come.

Next, God's forgiveness is suspended on the condition of our forgiveness.

This pardon was cancelled. Here is a difficulty. How can we be really pardoned if the past is remembered, after all? How can salvation be by grace if there be a condition?

First, let us prove the fact. All forgiveness is conditional: " If ye forgive men their trespasses, your Heavenly Father will also forgive you; but if ye forgive not men their trespasses, neither will your heavenly Father forgive your trespasses." Now, then, proceed to understand it, remembering it is a fact, whether we can explain it or not.

Forgiveness implies two things, favor and remission of punishment. God forgives if He heals with favor, and also if He remits punishment. You may be in favor, and yet punished. David was forgiven, but the child died. Sins of youth are visited on the justified Christian. Or you may be excused punishment, and still not be forgiven. As Ahab, who "went softly," and the penalty did not fall; but still he was not finally accepted. The tree in the parable was condemned, and yet respited.

So we are alive by sufferance. Is not that forgiveness? You have escaped danger, sickness, death; and you are treated as God's child—a favor or forgiveness that would be eternal if not forfeited.

Next, observe that a condition is not a merit. A condition is only that without which something else cannot be. The tree cannot be struck without thunder, but thunder is not the cause of the tree's fall. Man cannot be saved without forgiveness, but his forgiveness is not the cause of his salvation. Without holiness no man shall see the Lord, yet holiness is not merit. Man is not saved by them, yet not without them.

And in this particular case it is quite intelligible. Salvation is a state of love. An unforgiving, vindictive heart *is* in hell. How can it be saved? It *is* "delivered to the tormentors."

Our forgiveness, therefore, is to be:

Unlimited even as God's, "seventy times seven." There is no

sin which man can do which may not be pardoned. The Gospel is built on unlimited forgiveness.

We say every night, "Forgive us our trespasses, as we forgive them that trespass against us." Think what the revengeful man ought to feel when he prays thus. Ten thousand talents! such are my transgressions against God, and yet God has forgiven. But there is a man who has injured me not a thousandth, not a ten thousandth, part: and I will take him by the throat, and say, "Pay me that thou owest." And now, O Lord, forgive me my transgression and my sin!

Observe now the qualifications.

1. It is supposed that he has acknowledged his fault. You are bound to be ready for a reconciliation. But there is a just anger which you are not commanded to relax against an impenitent man. "If thy brother trespass against thee, go and tell him his fault between thee and him alone; if he shall hear thee, thou hast gained thy brother. But if he will not hear thee . . . and neglect to hear the Church, let him be unto thee a heathen man and a publican."

2. God forgave David. He suffered retribution without wrath. Yes, and it may be that although forgiving a man we cannot receive him as before, with perfect, hearty, entire forgiveness. He has forfeited a right to friendship, and is refused admission to your home. You have no rankling feeling. You would do him a service. But you have no foolish, weak sentiment which would let off the criminal or break down boundaries.

XXX.

THE LIGHT OF THE WORLD.

(FROM AUTOGRAPH NOTES.)

Brighton, Christmas-day, 1852.

"That was the true Light, which lighteth every man that cometh into the world."—John i. 9.

OUR subject is the Incarnation of Christ. On this day the WORD was born into the world; but the text forbids our supposing that He existed then for the first time. This chapter speaks of a Word which had been forever with God; which had created the world; which was Light; which had illumined all men, specially one class whom it calls "His own;" which at last appeared in Humanity, and was "made flesh," and was seen, "We *beheld* His glory, the glory as of the only begotten of the Father, full of grace and truth."

According to this view, the history of God's human race is the history of His revelation of Himself. He has revealed Himself through that portion of His essence which is called the Word—that which, like the Reason in us, expresses itself sometimes in a word, sometimes in a symbolic act. But the Revelation has been ever clearer, nearer, truer.

There has been a threefold revelation of the Word:

I. Through Nature: "He was in the world, and the world was made by Him, and the world knew Him not."

II. Through Man: "That was the true Light, which lighteth every man that cometh into the world."

III. Through the Incarnation: "And the Word was made flesh, and dwelt among us (and we beheld His glory, the glory as of the only begotten of the Father), full of grace and truth."

I. The Revelation of the Word through Nature.

"In the beginning"—before the world was, before there was ear to hear, or mind to understand—the Mind of God was speaking with Itself. There was a Word.

Then the Word is spoken of as mediating between the Creator and the creation; bringing the world into being, fashioning it, giving the world its laws; dwelling in brute unconscious matter as a living force; in lower creatures as a life and instinct; imparting reason and conscience to the higher beings.

God's Word found utterance in the material world, in Creation. The time came when He had to speak to others, and take them to share His secrets. God said, "Let there be light;" and, as the seal impresses its own self on the wax, light thrilled through the universe.

He spoke a world into existence.

Now, observe, truly this is a word: "Without Him was not anything made that was made." A word is an expression or a work. But there are many kinds of words. The most expressive of all words are not those which the lips speak.

The American sculptor gazed upon the sky on a summer's morning, which had arisen as serene and calm as the blue eternity out of which it came; he went about haunted with the memory of that repose; it was a necessity to him to express it. Had he been a poet, he would have thrown it into words; a painter, it would have found expression on the canvas; had he been an architect, he would have given us his feelings embodied, as builders of the Middle Ages embodied their aspirations, in Gothic architecture; but being a sculptor, his pen was his chisel, so he threw his thoughts into marble, and said that was his word to his fellow-creatures: here the words and syllables were of stone.*

So this world is God's sculptured work, whereby He speaks out Himself. Every night the curtains are rolled away, and we see what daylight had hid. Every morning the curtains of light are drawn again, and we look down on a world of speaking beauty.

And, observe, this creation is represented as a pervading immanence. "He was in the world," an indwelling of Deity in matter, which is unconscious of His presence. Creation was by indwelling. I ask you to remark how this stands contrasted with the unscriptural conception of creation which men often have. What do people mean generally by Creation? They mean that God made the world as a watchmaker makes a watch. The watchmaker makes the watch, winds it up, goes away from it, and leaves it to go by itself; all connection between him and it then ceasing, except when, from time to time, he regulates and repairs it. Just so God made the world, wound it up, and then projected it from Himself, and left it to go on by itself; interfering now and then in great emergencies called miracles. And so at some spot far distant from the whole the great Maker sits! Very different is the view of creation which Christmas-day presents. God is "in the world," the Life of all that is, the Vital Force; not giving laws, but Himself the Law. And it is the very fault of brute materialism that it does not recognize this august Presence—the "world knew Him not."

See the practical value of this truth. All have learned to talk of the beauties of Nature; but with most men it is a mere sentiment. If they loved Nature, they would seek her. But they descant upon her; and then show their love of Nature by going away

---

* Extracted from Lecture I. on "Influence of Poetry." MS. contains only the words "American sculptor."

from her to the more congenial atmosphere of the ballroom. And, indeed, to any one who does not feel God everywhere, Nature ought to be repulsive. Have we not felt it? Do we never remember a time when, in lonely wood, on seashore or wide plain, far from human dwellings, we shrank from Nature as from a dead, soulless machinery, plunging rather into the crowds of men and the crowded street, because in the one place there was deathfulness and in the other life?

Well, now, the Bible reveals that Christ, the Eternal Word, is in Nature. This world is but the form, of which Christ is the Personality; the body, of which the soul is God; the outer appearance, of which the reality is God, and which mediates between God and us. Beneath it all is Life, and that Life is God. The beauty of the sea-shell and of the field-flower is the loveliness of God; the Force which moves the waters everlastingly is the mighty movement of the One Living Being; the instinct which brings the wild birds in long lines through heaven at the appointed season is the order of the mind of God in them even though unknown to them, "He is in them, and they were made by Him, and know Him not."

And hence we find that in those passages of Scripture which many have explained away as figurative there is a deeper, truer meaning. All Nature has a voice, every created thing is a syllable or sentence of the Word: "The heavens *declare* the glory of the Lord, and the firmament showeth His handiwork." They are the mediating Word of the Father. It is the Living Word which dwells in them, and makes them eloquent of God to us. This world is an everlasting anthem hymning God's secrets.

II. The Revelation of the Word through Man.

The Word was revealed through man universally and specially—universally, "the Light which lighteth every man;" specially, "He came unto His own."

1. Universally.—"The Light which lighteth every man." Through the senses Christ mediates in the world; through man in the reason and the conscience He mediates between us and God. Remark, this was not a limited revelation, it is to "every man." Just as the sunlight shines on all—more intensely in the tropics, more feebly at the poles, yet still shines on all—so Christ speaks to all who are sane.

Now, here we are apt to speak atheistically. We talk of Nature, Natural Reason, Light of Nature, etc., as if these were contrasted with the light of revelation, contradicting it, and were not themselves from God. It is not so that Scripture speaks: "Every good gift, every perfect gift, is from above, and cometh down from the Father of lights." The light in you, whence did it come?—Your reason and your conscience, what are they but the God within you?

Thus the old Fathers, when considering Plato and the wiser heathens, spoke of their wisdom as the unconscious Christ within them. And thus, too, in the Old Testament, rulers and judges are called "gods:" "If David called them gods unto whom the word of the Lord came, and the scripture cannot be broken, say ye of Him whom the Father hath sanctified and sent into the world, Thou blasphemest, because I said, I am the Son of God?"

To the Society of Friends has been granted the honor of vindicating this truth with more prominence than any other body. Their apostle, Fox, took his stand on this text: "The true Light that lighteth every man that cometh into the world." He asserted a universal Light. And it is only at our peril that we deny it. Rightly do we pray, in the Communion Service, "Cleanse the thoughts of our hearts by the inspiration of thy Holy Spirit."

2. Specially.—"He came unto His own."

There is here a distinction drawn between those who received the light common to every man and woman, and those who received the special illumination which entitled them to be called "His own." These, we know, were the Jewish people—His chosen, His own—the nation which had the Light, the inspired people.

Here, then, we reach at once the great question of Inspiration. It has been of late years the fashion to talk of the inspiration of genius, to recognize the poet and the inventor as inspired men. We rejoice that it is so. It is good that men have got out of the old atheism, to recognize all light as from God, and all wisdom as the breath of His Spirit. It is good, therefore, that at the great gathering of nations last year the prayer of the archbishop, in presence of all the marvels of human invention, expressly acknowledged them as the results of Divine Inspiration.

But, still, let us clearly keep in view an essential difference. God acts *out* of the spirit, in Nature—*within* the spirit, in the soul. All He breathes there is inspiration. Yet, still, what we peculiarly mean by inspiration is God's acting on man's higher spirit—his worship, his reverence of moral excellence and beauty. Genius is from God; so is invention, reason, imagination; but a man of genius is one thing, a prophet is another. In this peculiar sense, the Jewish was the inspired nation. The Jews were not great statesmen, artists, men of science. But the thought of God, the sanctity of duty, moral and spiritual truth, were in them as in no other nation on earth. Hence they are called God's chosen people—"His own."

There is a "Light that lighteth every man," and there is a special light from God's Spirit, which does not make them more clever, nor more eloquent, nor wiser, but holier men than others.

III. Revelation of the Word through the Incarnation. "The Word was made flesh."

A time came when, not in outward form and sound, but through the life of man, God was to speak: "The Word was made flesh." From that moment the life of a man was God's expression of His mind to us. It is not what Jesus said, argued, proclaimed—but what Jesus did. The eloquence of a Life, not of mere syllables; nor yet the system of theology which you can make out of His sayings. The one perfect WORD which earth has heard, her Creator's Voice. "The Word was made flesh."

Let us distinguish the doctrine of the Church on this subject from other doctrines resembling it. In the Old Testament we read of certain mysterious appearances; as when God appeared in the form of flame—in Exodus this is called the Lord; in Hebrew speech, the angel or messenger of the Lord. Again, a man appeared to Abraham, yet it is said Abraham began to commune with Jehovah. Now what these appearances were we do not know—whether material or visionary—but certainly they were not incarnations. The form of flame or of humanity so assumed was only assumed, and that for a temporary purpose. Certain early opponents of Christianity taught this as the doctrine of the Incarnation. They said that Christ was an Appearance of God; that He came in phantom or vision, not in actual flesh and blood, not with a human soul.

Again: in the Old Testament we read of God localizing Himself for a time in the Temple as a Shechinah of glory: and in the pillar and the cloud. We read, too, of His dwelling in human beings, in Prophets, with a transient and irregular inspiration, so that sometimes they spoke of themselves fallibly; sometimes of God infallibly. Certain early heretics taught this as the doctrine of the Incarnation. They said that God dwelt in Christ as an individual, precisely as in the Shechinah, or as in the prophets. But that the Eternal Word and Jesus were two distinct beings, separable; and that when the Word was gone, the man was left to die.

And again: in the Old Testament we read of the term "god" given to men because of their performances. Thus, Jah added to Oshea became Joshua; and thus in Psalm xlv. 11, addressed to a royal bride, her husband is spoken of: "He is thy Lord God, worship thou him." And also in Psalm lxxxii. 6, "I have said [of judges] ye are gods." In the same way, some early heretics affirmed that Jesus was God only in this sense; that He was called God because of His spiritual and godlike excellence.

The doctrine of the creed which we read to-day* contradicts each of these views. It says that He was "God of the substance of the Father begotten before the worlds," *i. e.* He had not merely a nature holy like God's, but He was the Word with a human body and soul. It says that He was "man of the substance of His mother," *i. e.* He was not merely a phantom or angelic vision. It says that though He was "God and Man," yet He was "not two but one Christ," *i. e.* the Eternal Word did not enter into Him and depart, but the Human and the Divine are one forever, just as the reason, body, and soul are one complete man. This is the doctrine of the Incarnation.

Now see the application of it.

1. All that can be known of God is through a *Revelation*. What is the doctrine of these verses? An Eternal Word within unfelt or felt, and an Eternal Word external to us, making the Word within felt consciously, and kindling it into higher life.

For the light of Revelation is not contrary to the light of Nature, but the completion of it. It is no more contrary than flame is contrary to heat. Heat within takes fire and blazes when external flame is applied. So the Life of God within is kindled by the Life of God manifested without in Christ. And this is the great doctrine of St. John. An inward susceptibility of life made

* Athanasian.

alive: an inner Light kindled by an outer Light. "Christ in us" developed by Christ manifested without. "As many as received Him, to them gave He power to become the sons of God." Observe, they were the sons of God before: unconsciously. But when they received Christ, they got fresh power; they knew themselves God's children, and got strength to live as what they were by right.

2. The character of this revelation of God is that it is progressive.

All history is the account of God's revealing Himself to man. We connect together these three facts—He was in the world: He was with the world: He was made flesh. Remember the gradations. God is in the world, unconsciously in the brute animals, nearer in human beings, nearer still in the higher specimens of the race, nearest—awfully more near—in Christ. And Advent has taught us to look for a nearer revelation still, a day when "we shall see Him as He is."

XXXI.

RIGHTEOUSNESS.

(FROM AUTOGRAPH NOTES.)

"But he answered and said unto them, Why do ye also transgress the commandment of God by your tradition? For God commanded, saying, Honor thy father and mother: and, He that curseth father or mother, let him die the death. But ye say, Whosoever shall say to his father or his mother, It is a gift, by whatsoever thou mightest be profited by me; and honor not his father or his mother, he shall be free. Thus have ye made the commandment of God of none effect by your tradition. Ye hypocrites, well did Esaias prophesy of you, saying, This people draweth nigh unto me with their mouth, and honoreth me with their lips; but their heart is far from me. But in vain they do worship me, teaching for doctrines the commandments of men."—Matt. xv. 3-9.

THE key to the understanding of this passage is sympathy with the heart of Christ. It is impossible to understand this, or any passage, except by realizing the standing occupied by Christ. To understand Christ is to understand Christianity. Misunderstand the life of Christ, and all controversies become unintelligible—word-fights, not realities. You have not got the key.

Now, the exact contrary to the mind of Christ was the mind of the Pharisee. The antagonism between them was complete. They stood opposed as pole to pole. There was sympathy between Christ and misery, between Christ and error, between Christ and the sin-entangled. There was no sympathy between Christ and Pharisaism; because there is none between the real and the unreal, or between the true and the false: "What fellowship hath light with darkness?"

Consequently, the strife between them was to the death. Between His life and theirs there could be no compromise and no quarter. They saw and felt this as well as He. With unerring instinct they discovered their foe. Whatever He did offended them. Every act, every word, was a contradiction of their life—jarred on them—went against the grain.

This particular instance is only one out of many. At the first superficial view it seems only a question respecting the degree of observance due to customs. They complained that He transgressed the Jewish customs, or observed them too little. He said that they observed those customs too much, and superstitiously. But that which lay at the root of the controversy was something deeper. The quarrel was no trifling one of words and ceremonies. It was the great ancient quarrel—properly, the only quarrel—the quarrel between the real and the unreal.

Therefore our subject divides into two branches:

I. The real righteousness which God accepts.

II. The seeming righteousness which, in the sight of God, is vanity and nothingness.

I. Real righteousness, what is it?

In one word, it is surrender to the will of God. The main thing insisted on by Christ is, God commanded.

Now, distinguish well. A duty is commanded by God which is spiritual and eternal. To honor father and mother is an everlasting obligation, spiritual and moral. The essential peculiarity of this commandment is, not that it is written by God in the Bible, but that it is written by God on the heart. God commanded circumcision. But Christ would not have put circumcision on a level with obedience to father and mother. The one was goodness; the other, not goodness. The one, a law of the heart forever; the other, the requirement of a certain institution for a time. The righteousness of forms is not the righteousness of faith.

This, then, is the peculiarity of the righteousness which is evangelical. It is from within; it is life; it is God in the soul of man; it is the life of the spirit. It is not a creed got by heart; it is not a set of habits acquired; it is not a circle of customs scrupulously observed. It is a life within working outwards, as Christ has himself described it—"The water that I shall give him shall be *in* him a well of water springing up into everlasting life."

This is the righteousness which in other parts of Scripture is called the "righteousness which is by faith," or the righteousness which is a "walking in the Spirit." It is not a righteousness done, but an infinite yearning after a righteousness which is ever doing. It is not a self-satisfaction which numbers up its performances, but an infinite humility which reckons its best performances as nothing.

A man righteous in the Christian sense may seem to the world proud, reserved, and distant. But go to him in his secret moments, and overhear his soul pouring out its secret consciousness, and you will hear language startling from the intensity of its self-abasement. Not, "God, I thank thee that I am not as other men;" but, "God be merciful to me a sinner."

Now, observe a peculiarity of this righteousness.

There are times when it can set forms at nought, neglecting them. It can afford to make nothing of them. Christ's disciples neglected the observance of the very honored custom of washing the hands when they ate bread. Consider what might have been urged. This is an old time-honored observance. You owe respect to constituted authorities. Who are you that presumptuously set yourselves up against the customs of your Church and country? Such things were said. But the disciples minded them not, and Christ supported them in their neglect.

Let us understand this. Doubtless it is a duty to comply with customs, social and ecclesiastical. A man who sets them at defiance is a man of a presumptuous spirit. But there are periods when the forms of society become thoroughly false. Then the strong true man breaks through the cobwebs of etiquette, asserting the real courtesies of the heart. And there are times when priests and parties multiply observances till life is trammelled, and make things essential which are not essential. Then it becomes a duty, if we would imitate Christ, to assert Christian liberty, and to refuse to be bound by the cry of custom, modesty, or constituted authority. There is a time when it is right to say, "Don't wash hands."

II. The seeming righteousness, which, in the sight of God, is vanity and nothingness.

The Pharisee placed righteousness in obedience to tradition. Tradition is something handed down, passed on; in other words, sanctified by custom.

Observe, when Christ distinguishes between God's command and tradition, it is not a distinction between written and oral, but between essential and customary. Obedience to parents was an obligation of everlasting life. To wash the hands was an obligation due to venerable custom.

The spirit of tradition says, It is old, therefore it is sacred; it has been, therefore it should and shall be. And so religion becomes stereotyped.

And, again, observe it is not a distinction between ceremonies commanded by God and ceremonies invented by men; but between ceremonies and *life*. Men commanded washing of hands, cups, pots, brazen vessels, and tables. But it was not because men commanded it, but because it was an outward act, that Christ depreciated it. God commanded circumcision and sacrifice. But prophets spoke lightly of circumcision, and Christ abolished it. In his Sermon on the Mount, He spoke as lightly of ceremonies imposed by Moses as of ceremonies imposed by rabbis: "Ye have heard that it was said by them of old time, . . . but I say unto you." A ceremony was not sacred because imposed by Moses, and profane because imposed by a rabbi. A ceremony is but a ceremony, even if imposed by God or Christ. Circumcision was imposed by God, yet St. Paul says, "Circumcision is nothing." Baptism was ordained by Christ; but baptism is sprinkling with water, and it stands forever distinguished from the obedience which is life.

Now, the religion of Pharisaism makes custom paramount to moral and spiritual life. It identifies religion with arbitrary rules and customs of worship. And the steps by which Pharisaism makes the commandment of God of none effect are two:

1. It begins by insisting on obedience to customs as necessary.

Here the first stand is to be made. Here the first danger begins. After periods of irregularity and laxity, reformers begin with restoring customs, insist upon them, lay stress upon them. You cannot insist on them long without leaving an impression that they are essentials.

A Pharisee of former times would have doubted a man's goodness if he did not wash before meals. A formalist of modern times would think the omission of baptism a crime as great as disobedience to a parent.

Now, let it be said plainly, God will not send a soul to eternal perdition because the man was not circumcised; God will not give eternal hell because a man has not been baptized.

2. The second step is to insist on customs as *more* necessary than spiritual life, till gradually they supersede moral obligation.

Let us explain this particular case. There was a habit of devoting property to the priesthood—God's ministers; therefore to give to a rich priest was religion. To give to a poor layman was only moral. To touch the money or property so devoted was sacrilege: it was "corban." At last a curious perversion came. If a man wanted to evade the obligation of supporting parents, he announced his property to be corban. It was then sacred. Thus a distinction was made between the religious and the moral. And the so-called religious superseded the moral duty.

Now, this is a tendency of human nature: it was not Jewish only. Here it is said that Isaiah prophesied it. But that does not mean *predicted*. Isaiah was speaking to the men of his day, not of Christ's day. But because inspiration deals with principles, not with special cases, what he said was just as true in Christ's day. This is prophecy, and prophecy is of all ages. This tendency, then, did not belong to Christ's day only. There is a great proneness in human nature in every age *to evade a duty under pretence of religion.*

[Early mistakes.—Mother at prayer-meetings.—Refusal of a duel.—Requests of charity.]

The results of this Pharisaical scrupulosity are twofold:

1. Moroseness of disposition and censoriousness. The Pharisees were scandalized by Christ's behavior. They held up their hands in pious astonishment: "Why do Thy disciples transgress the tradition of the elders?"

Singular how inevitably Pharisaical scrupulosity ends in a snarling censoriousness! From the days when the Pharisee numbered his observances in the Temple, and turned round on "this publican," until now, it has ever been the same.

Goodness expands the heart and makes it humble. The larger, the better, the nobler your heart is, the more you will be inclined to make allowance for others, and the more you will say and feel, "God be merciful to me a sinner." But the more you indulge the notion that you can please God by customs, be they ever so time-honored, the more you will contract the Pharisaical habit of watching and blaming others. You will go away from church with pious astonishment that some neighbor was not there who ought to have been. You will kneel month by month at the Lord's supper, miss neither Easter-day nor Good-Friday, and go away to wonder what were the reasons for your neighbor's absence. And then your religion will be the religion of the Pharisees. You will be evading the eternal law of charity under the pretence of what you call religion.

2. A second result of this scrupulosity is hypocrisy.

"In vain do they worship Me, teaching for doctrines the commandments of men." In vain—*i. e.* their religion is no religion, but emptiness. As St. James says, "If any man among you seem to be religious, and bridleth not his tongue, but deceiveth his own heart, that man's religion is vain."

Observe, we use hypocrisy not in the modern sense of pretending to be what men know they are not—the Pharisees thought they were religious—but in the sense of wearing a mask, according to the original derivation of the word.

And see how dangerous, then, what the man calls his religion becomes, because it hides him from himself. Faultless in the etiquette of social life, without one omission in those ecclesiastical observances which are to him religion alone, how shall he know that he is not religious in the sight of God? How shall he be made to feel that his religion is a mask which covers his want of goodness?

Religion is goodness. To love God and to love man is Christianity; all else is only husk and shell.

XXXII.

THE PEACE OF GOD.

"Peace, peace, to him that is far off, and to him that is near, saith the Lord; and I will heal him. But the wicked are like the troubled sea, when it cannot rest, whose waters cast up mire and dirt. There is no peace, saith my God, to the wicked."—Isa. lvii. 19, 20.

There was a time when religion was the healthy and the natural state of man's soul. Whatever may be the literal meaning of those strange passages which tell of a garden in Eden, and God walking in that garden, this, at least, is plain, that man's pulse once beat with love to God as naturally as the current of blood ran which carried health and vigor through his frame. And this, besides, is plain, that over all that there has passed a change. Man's religion then was the religion of spontaneous innocence; the only religion left open to man now, the only religion possible, is the religion of penitence. It is this, my brethren, which makes the Gospel from first to last to bear the character of a system of cure. It is not a work of improvement for a nature which is already good, it is a work of remedy for a nature which has become diseased. There is one word in this passage which marks out the peculiar character of the Gospel of Christ: "I will *heal* him." It is a healing process. And it is this which so peculiarly endears the Gospel to every man who is conscious of frailty and inward pollution. For if it be asked in one word what the Gospel is, we answer, it is all that apparatus of remedy by which a weak, erring, and guilty spirit may get back again the strength and the purity which it has lost.

There is one thing which we all want, and one thing which, in different ways, we are all seeking after. When religion passed away from man's bosom, it was only according to the necessities of his constitution that peace should pass away with it. And now the history of all the tumult that this world exhibits is just this, that men are in pursuit of rest. Restless! Why? because not at rest. Rest is the great want and the passionate craving of our nature. We are here in this world tossing about in the dark dream of a most feverish existence; not satisfied with ourselves, and venting our dissatisfaction on the circumstances in which God has placed us. We want something new, and the satisfying toy never comes. That is the history of a life of excitement; that is the history of the gambling earnestness of mercantile speculation; that is the history of every rivalry and every disappointed attachment and every life weariness which this world exhibits. Men want peace, and the world has said, "Peace, peace!" and they find that "there is no peace." And so it comes to pass that we go on, through boyhood and manhood and old age, struggling and hoping and disappointed; ever seeming near to peace, and never placing our grasp upon it, till there is but one chance of rest left—the quiet and the silence of the grave.

And now, brethren, we observe there are two ways of seeking peace; there are two promises made to the craving human heart exactly the same in words, diametrically opposite in meaning. There is the word promised, "Peace, peace," and God answers that, in the words of this text, "There is no peace, saith my God, to the wicked!" and there is, besides that, Christ's promise, "Peace, peace to him that is far off, and to him that is near." The world proposes to fulfil her promise by *gratifying* nature; the Gospel proposes to fulfil its promise by *expelling* nature. The world's method is this, "Gratify the desire that burns within you. So long as it lasts, it is your passion and your torment. Slake it by indulgence, and be at rest. My peace means the satisfying of every inclination." There is a meaning and a truth in that promise, brethren; and if only there were no other world but this, and if only there were no judgment to come, and if only there were no such thing as conscience, the man who denies himself nothing would be the man who gets rest from himself and from the fever that burns within him. It would be wise and well to live as men live on the world principle, "Let us eat and drink, for to-morrow we die." Now, the peace which Christ proclaims is not this peace at all, but another altogether. The world's peace is the indulgence of the heart as if it were in a state of health— "Let nature have her way;" Christ's peace is the healing of a disordered heart. It does not consist in giving the rein to desires, but in mastering them. It consists in placing the whole soul under the discipline of the Cross, and "bringing into captivity every thought to the obedience of Christ." We are "sick to death," sick of our own selfishness and our own unregenerated hearts; and we are here in this world to be cured.

These, brethren, are our only two hopes of rest. The world's peace comes by adding fuel to the fever; Christ's peace comes by curing it. And there is not a man in this congregation who is not resting his faith and his expectation of rest on one of these promises or the other. There is not one who has immersed himself in business, and there is not one who has hidden himself like Adam in the trees of this world's garden of enjoyment, who does not hope to find in his own way the rest which his spirit needs. Through the path of guilt, or through the path of restlessness, we are all seeking rest. In life's retirement or in life's bustle it is the same pursuit in different forms. Seek on we must, till we win or miss forever.

In considering the promise of rest which comes from the lips of God, we shall examine two connected subjects which are contained in these verses:

I. The struggle of an earnest soul towards peace.
II. The exclusion of a guilty soul from the possibility of peace.

I. The struggle of an earnest soul towards peace.
1. Now, the first step in the struggle of man's soul towards peace is made by treading on the ruins of human pride. One source of human restlessness—one reason, at least, why men pass through this world chafing, fretful, and dissatisfied with their lot in life is just this, that they have formed an overweening estimate of self, and they find that neither God nor man treats them as they think that they deserve. And then when a man comes to the close of his existence, he begins to feel as if he had not had justice done him—he has not been rightly valued, he has not been understood, he is not where he ought to be, and so he bears on his countenance the marks of a disappointed man. It is the adoration of self that makes men miserable. It is that strange greediness of praise which gives contempt its power to wound us. For, only let it be known to a proud spirit that one man has sneered, it matters not that the world is deafening him with its admiration, that sneer will shoot a pang of wretchedness through the hour of his proudest triumph.

And now, brethren, the first thing the Gospel does is to crush that spirit of self-esteem. At the foot of the Cross there is no room for pride. The Cross read out this lesson to the world: merit is impossible before God. We are not claimants for reward, we are but suppliants for life—a life which has been forfeited by guilt. Once get that truth by heart that you are nothing, and you can never suffer again from wounded pride. Has this world neglected you, my Christian brother? Has it not appreciated you, not honored you, not given you the position to which you thought yourself entitled? Well, my brother in sin, and what right had you to demand that it should give you anything? Learn this first, how much do you deserve on God's earth? And if it should turn out that you deserve nothing and have received little, then calculate whether you have been defrauded. Oh, my brethren, when we have passed through the first humbling smart of that conviction, and when we are content to stand, as it were, unclothed before God, without one claim upon Him except the righteousness of Christ, there is one step made towards peace, and then our hot, swelling hearts may find rest; and all that burning, seething tumult with which our proud bosoms throb over our fancied slights and our imaginary injuries will be at rest. When first the humility of the Gospel takes possession of our souls, it is the dawn of a morning which goes before an everlasting day of calmness and serenity.

2. The second step which a Christian makes in his progress towards peace is the attainment of a spirit of reconciliation. If there were nothing else to make men wretched, uncertainty respecting their future destinies would be enough. We are going down into eternity, and its waves are rising to ingulf us, every day nearer and darker; and if we have only a "perhaps" to meet it, and all beyond the moment of ingulfment is utter and confused uncertainty, and a most vague ignorance whether the God whom we are to meet for the first time be satisfied or not, I say not that there is not steel and manhood enough in the heart of man to meet that calmly: there is—hundreds are doing it every hour, timid women and resolute men, quietly watching their own decay and fronting death unflinchingly—but I say this, that there is no *peace*, there is no *rest*, in the prospect of eternity unless there is something very much more than a guess that God is loving us. It is one thing to meet death intrepidly, and it is altogether another to meet it peacefully and trustfully.

Now, there is an observation that we have to make respecting this peace of reconciliation. There are two classes of persons who are privileged to feel reconciliation with God; but the character of their peace is somewhat different. Peace is enjoyed by those who have been in covenant with God, as it were, during all their lifetime; and peace is attainable by those who have only received His forgiveness late. There is this difference distinctly asserted in the text, "Peace to him that is far off," and "Peace to him that is near."

In the first place, then, we draw this doctrine from the text, that there is peace for those who have remained through life near to God. Such men there are spoken of in the New Testament as the "ninety and nine just persons who need no repentance." And such a one seems represented to us under the character of the elder son in the parable, who had not wandered from his home to seek his fortunes in the world. There are some in this world whose religious growth has been so quiet, so regular, so steady, that they are altogether unconscious themselves of the vastness of the work that God has been doing in their souls. For the fact is, we are not conscious of those changes which go on quietly and gradually in the soul. We only count the shocks in our journey. And if there has been no sudden conversion, no impetuous and tumultuous feeling of reconciliation, you may speak to such men of what are called religious experiences, but they have very little account to give you. And this is the history sometimes of those who have been nurtured in religious families. They have imbibed the atmosphere of religion without knowing it; and so they go on loving God quietly, unostentatiously, doing simple duties happily, without speaking of them, till duty has become a habit, and religion has become the very element of life. These are not the conspicuous Christians, but they are the affectionate, cheerful, tender ones in the family circle; they are the Christians of that strict integrity, that high-mindedness, which governs hospitality; that scrupulous attention to what some call contemptuously moral duties which more impassioned Christians often fail to exhibit.

Now, there is something peculiar, brethren, in this peace. The peace of men who have been religious from childhood is a very different thing from the keen luxury that attends the return of a prodigal son, but it is the best on the whole. It has more of heaven's deep tranquillity. It has more of childlike intimacy with God. The deepest peace is that which is scarcely conscious of its own peacefulness: "Son, thou art ever with me, and all that I have is thine," but he did not know this till he was told. Oh, there is a great mistake that we make about this. We think this peace a dull thing. We look down upon such men, and smile at their simplicity, and despise the monotony of their existence. There is a purity and innocence of heart, a simplicity, an ignorance of evil, which men who have got their minds enlarged by eating of the "tree of the knowledge of good and evil" look down upon with a contemptuous pity. But, brethren, it is God's best peace, enjoyed by them that are "near." Let us remember this. Serenity and pure-heartedness are the kind of peace that has most of heaven. It is better than religious *rapture*. The rapture that comes from pardoned guilt is like the fire-rocket that streams and blazes through the black sky, making everything brilliant for a moment, and forcing men to look at it; the peace of him that has lived near to God is like the quiet, steady lustre of the lighthouse lamp, startling no one, very easily mistaken for a common light, but never quenched; ever to be found when wanted, casting the same mild ray through the long night across the maddest billows that curl their crests around the rock on which it stands. That is the kind of peace enjoyed by him that is near.

There is another class of men to whom the grant of peace is possible. "Peace to him which is far off, saith the Lord," by which we understand those who have lived for a time in the alienation of guilt from God. Brethren, we claim attention to this. Peace is not the exclusive lot of *consistent* men. It belongs under the Gospel to *guilty* men. It has been said in language somewhat daring that it is almost worth while to have sinned in order to taste the deep luxury of penitence. Rightly taken, those are not rash words. They are not more than Christ has sanctioned by His own declaration, "There is more joy among the angels of heaven over one sinner that repenteth than over ninety and nine just persons which need no repentance." It almost seems as if the joy of returning to God had in it something more rich, more ecstatic while it lasts, than the peace which belongs to consistent obedience. It is just that feast of the fatted calf, with the robe and the ring and the dancing, which disconcerted the elder son in the treatment of his brother. . . . Men who have sinned much, is it not so? Is there not such a thing as loving much, because much has been forgiven? Is there not in God's strange dispensations a kind of balance of blessedness which almost seems to make up to a guilty penitent for the wretchedness that is gone by? And, after all, for most of us, this is the *only* Gospel. One here and there in this congregation there may be who has lived near to God from childhood; but if there is only peace for *him*, we have no Gospel for the mass. We, the majority—we, brethren, God knows, we have lived far enough from God at some period or other of our lives. Things that will not bear speaking of—things that it is well not to think about—belong to the history of our past lives. . . . Shall we be told there is peace for innocence?—peace for those who have received the Spirit and not grieved His intimations? Ah, my Christian brethren, that is not the Gospel for us; we want a Gospel for the guilty. "Peace for him that is near," that we can understand; but the words at which our hearts exult are these: "Peace to him that is far off." Man's noble attitude is that of consistent holiness from the moment that he turns to God; and most of us have forfeited that. Man's noblest attitude is earnest penitence, and that is opened to us still; and with it there is opened "peace."

It is a mercy that the Scripture record of human life is painted to us in such dark colors as it is. It has been the infidel's sneer that the Bible saints are men whom even a novelist would scorn to take for his heroes. It is a small and pitiful sneer. The Bible saints were not the heroes of romance, for then they might have been painted spotless. They were the men of real life, and the details of that life sometimes guilty enough. But, then, life was an earnest thing with them. It was transgression, if you will; but then it was sore, buffeting struggle after that—much toiling and wandering in sharp suffering, that none knew but God: it was the penitence of men bent manfully on turning back to God. And so they fought their way back till they struggled out of the thick darkness into the clear light of day and peace. Let us lay this to heart. It is not the having been "far off" that makes peace impossible. It is not sin—no, not the darkest—that shuts out from restoration: "Being justified by faith, we have peace with God." It is languid indecision, desperate sullenness, anything which keeps a man away from Christ, that prevents peace; but in all this world there is nothing else.

3. The last step in a Christian's progress towards peace is the attainment of a spirit of active obedience. There is a mistake that men make respecting religious unhappiness. They think that it arises only from the fear of punishment. And they suppose that if you could but convince a man of his personal safety before God, if he could but know that his salvation was secure, straightway all religious uneasiness would be calmed; and so men sit down to look into themselves as if the one great question they had to answer were this, "Am I saved or not?" But it is not so. It is not the dread of hell that makes men miserable. That is only a part of human restlessness. There is an eternal law that man cannot be happy except in keeping God's commandments. Make a man sure of heaven, and leave him with a soul not reduced to harmony, not humble, not pure, not obedient, he is a wretch still. There is a corroding, maddening sensation which comes from the feeling of uselessness; there is something that almost amounts to torture in the start with which we sometimes awake to the conviction that life is gliding away and nothing done; there is an uneasy, gnawing self-reproach that comes from duties left unfulfilled. What is misery? It is the boundless law of duty written on the heart, and the accumulated self-reproach of not obeying it. Do we want the picture of a restless heart? Infinite duty, infinite transgression, infinite woe—that is the restlessness of man.

And now let us ask what is the remedy provided by God to heal this restlessness? God's remedy, brethren, is to write His law by the spirit upon the heart, so that we love Christ, and then we love what Christ commands. It has been well remarked, it is not said that *after* keeping God's commandments, but *in* keeping them, there is great reward. God has linked these two things together, and no man can separate them—obedience and peace. And it seems to be for this reason that when the early years of life have been spent in those professions which demand implicit obedience, the religion of riper years so often puts on a character of peculiar brightness. The religious soldier and the religious sailor are generally happy Christians for this reason, it may be, among others, that they have transferred to God's service the habit of unquestioning, prompt, ready obedience which was taught them in their professions. For them there is no speculating about difficulties; there is none of that discursing into the whole world of motives which so often, in men trained to think rather than to act, disconcerts and saddens the whole life. Theirs is a life of action, and what is peace but this: "If a man love me, he will keep my commandments," *and* "I will manifest myself to him?"

But let us place this in the form of direction. Does a man want faith? Let him not excruciate his mind by questionings about his own salvation, whether he is to be saved or not. He may ask that question till he is on the verge of insanity, and get no answer after all. There are two things that a man has to look at in this world—one is, God seen through the cross of Christ: there is no mistake what God means by that; He means that He is reconciled. The other is the duty that lies immediately before him; let him bend himself anxiously and earnestly to that. But as he values peace, let him not look at *self*. It is not well to be too anxious about the certainty of pardon. Pardon would not make you happy. God's law written on the heart makes you happy. There is no argument in all the world by which doubts can be made to pass away except this—action. There is no hope of rest for an infinite soul except in this—earnest obedience.

When a man has attained these three things, a spirit of humility to accept the righteousness of Christ instead of his own, and a spirit of faith to trust in God's reconciliation, and a spirit of activity to do the will of God, there has been fulfilled the promise prophesied to him that is far off and to him that is near.

II. We pass on now to the reasons which exclude the guilty heart from the possibility of peace. There are two reasons assigned in these verses: one is because of the heart's own inward restlessness, and the other is because of the power of memory to visit transgression with remorse. The first reason is given in these words, "Like the troubled sea, the wicked cannot rest;" this is the heart's own inward restlessness. The second is, "Like the troubled sea, there is that within them which casts up mire and dirt;" this is the heart's power of bringing up again what has been sunk.

1. And now with respect to the first of these, the soul's own natural restlessness, "They cannot rest."

This impossibility of rest arises partly from the soul's own majesty. God made the spirit of man like the ocean in its vastness. Ten miles deep the Atlantic depths go down where human plummet never sounded, and the billows that roll their wild tumult above have ten miles of water beneath to heave them up. A pond may be without a ripple; as to the troubled sea, just because it is vast, it cannot rest. And so is it with the soul of man. It is its own magnificence that makes it intensely miserable. Take the meanest and the weakest in this congregation, and in that frame that we gaze on, it may be with contempt, there is a spirit which has a capacity in it for heaven and for hell. Rest! Brethren, shall we talk of a thing like that *resting?* Why, man's soul rocks and billows itself with an eternity beneath it. It is that which makes human suffering a thing of grandeur, because every pang that contracts a human brow, and every quiver that distorts a pale lip, are only indications of what may merge into the unresting doom of infinite wail. When God put man in possession of a self, and made that self immortal, he only made him master of a tremendous heritage of woe.

Partly, again, this impossibility of rest comes from the soul's power of being acted upon by heavenly influences and by earthly ones together. The sea rests not because of the attraction of the heavenly bodies, which keep it in an endless ebb and flow—drawn towards the earth and drawn towards the sky alternately, and obeying neither impulse solely, it *cannot* rest. Know we nothing of this in our own bosoms? There is a tide of feeling which ebbs alternately to heaven and earth. "The flesh lusteth against the spirit, and the spirit against the flesh." We are conscious, surely, of high instincts that tell of God; conscious, besides, of grovelling propensities that drag us down to earth—low wants and lofty longings. So long as these hold man's soul alternately, is rest possible? Nay, brethren, one force must overcome the other before that can be. The love of God must master the world's attraction, or if not, then the soul is "like the troubled sea when it cannot rest."

Partly, once more, the impossibility of rest arises from outward circumstances. There are winds that sweep along the ocean's surface and fret it into agitation. A small gust raises a single wave on the surface of the water, and before that wave has passed over a thousand miles, it has become a swell which may swamp a navy. Something like this man has to make him restless. Besides his own inborn passions, there are circumstances from without in this world to fret and agitate and discompose his spirit—small trials of temper that make up much of the weariness of life ; reverses of fortune ; all that men call annoyances and sorrows. And then we lay the blame on these and ask, "*How* could the man have been otherwise than as he is? He is disappointed, miserable; well, but the circumstances of his earlier years, faulty education, others' neglect, made him so." Ah, my brethren, the man who has not peace in himself cannot get peace from circumstances. Place him where you will, he carries an unquiet heart along with him. Can you keep the ocean from the wind? Can you bid the gust and the hurricane be still, and not play their wild game over the face of the waters? Can you save man from circumstances? Nay. We are here to control the circumstances in which we are placed, and transmute them, and get good and spirituality out of them. It certainly may be true that a man is made restless and miserable by circumstances. It certainly may be that the ocean is ploughed into billows by the tempest blasts, but all that they did was to lash the ocean and show that it was yielding water and not firm rock. All that circumstances have done when they make a man restless is just this, to show that he is not incorporated with the Rock of Ages.

2. The second reason assigned for the exclusion of the guilty soul from the possibility of peace is the power of memory to recall the past with remorseful associations ; and this seems conveyed in these words, " Its waters cast up mire and dirt." It is the bringing to light again what has once been buried. For it is one result of ocean's restlessness that the ravages which it makes are not ingulfed in its depths forever. You may see the surges wear and fret away the basement of the cliff against which they dash themselves, and the mass of broken rock falls into the depth and disappears, and then it is carried away by the tide as it retires. But a thousand miles off there will be shingle and mud to fringe the sea-foam. The fragments may have rolled for many a long month at the bottom of the ocean, ingulfed, unseen, but they are still there, ready to appear at the appointed moment. Navies may sink, and the waters roll above them as if they were to appear no more ; but the wanderer on some distant beach is startled in his ramble to read the dismal tale of shipwreck in the planks that are stranded on the shore.

Now, there is something fearfully like this in the constitution of our souls. Deeds that we have done and thoughts that we have dwelt upon sink like stones into the ocean, and we expect that they will appear no more. But, my brethren, it would seem that a thing once lodged in the memory never can be lost. ·It may sink for a time—long years—as in the ocean depths, but there are tempests which may bring it up again some day. Have we never known those moments of existence when we seemed endued with an unusual, startling power to recall a long train of past occurrences, when the mind seemed almost supernaturally active, not at the bidding of *our* will? By night, alone, when music had touched the string of long-forgotten associations, when conversation had left a strange excitement in the spirit, have we never known what it is to find a marvellous rapidity in the power of thought, and all the past come as freshly before us as if it were yesterday? Brethren, with a mind like that, man is not one moment secure of rest; he is doomed to recollect. A dull and heavy body blinds his senses, and so buries his misery for a time; but it is there, and God can cast it up at any moment in the shape of mire and dirt. This is the misery of remorse—the worst torment of man's stormy mind. It only needs that the body which buries recollection for a time shall be dissolved, and then there begins the eternity of a hell of recollections—when every act of bygone guilt which has not been sunk in the blood of Christ shall be as fresh and vivid before a sinner's eyes as it was at the moment when it was committed.

In conclusion, the first thing, brethren, that has to be urged upon us from this subject is the connection which subsists between peace and cure: "Peace, peace, *and* I will heal him." Peace and cure must go together. No peace for the soul where there is no cure. And now the question is this, If you have peace, what is your peace worth? And the answer to that depends upon the answer to another question: Is the spirit healed of all its malady? There is an absence of apprehension, and there is a freedom from self-reproach, which are not Christ's peace, but only the calm of forgetfulness. There was a time when Herod's spirit was at rest. A single guilty inclination, a single unmanly, unhallowed tenderness stood between his soul and its perfect cure. One man prevented his enjoying that tenderness in peace. Herod removed that man from his way, and then came a calm. What was the value of that peace? Brethren, only this, that the Saviour's preaching, or rather a mere rumor of it, brought back the apparition of John the Baptist to his remembrance, and with it all the unquiet consciousness of guilt. A little silence, a summer's-day calm, and then the ocean cast up again its mire and dirt.

There is a law in this world that sin and sorrow shall be joined together. It may be a long time first, for God has an eternity before Him to strike in, *and He can wait.* There is another law in this world, "There is no peace, saith my God, to the wicked." And there is only one thing in all the universe that interferes with the stringency of these laws. That one thing is the blood of Christ, so applied to the character and so sunk into the affections that the guilty can go free and the sinner be at peace. Brethren, each of us knows what his own past has been. I ask you, will it bear to come up again? Or do your hearts tell you there is meaning of terrible emphasis in these words "mire and dirt?" If so, there is but one way to keep it all hidden in the heart's depths. It is to have it buried there by the transforming, purifying, calming power of Christ. Be healed, and you may be at peace; but if the heart is not cured of its evil, your peace is worth nothing.

We also press this truth—there is no amount of sin that bars from the attainment of saintliness. There is a peace which "passeth all understanding" for those who have kept their garments undefiled; but be this remembered too, God speaks peace —ay, rapture—to those who, having soiled their garments, have made them " white in the blood of the Lamb." The truth is, that when the heart is entranced with unexpected love, and yet the man's head hangs down with more than ordinary shame, he sometimes outstrips in holiness those who have advanced more leisurely. It is the "eleventh hour" with him; and if others may walk, he must run, and so sometimes he more than makes up lost ground. It is the evening of his day; his night is closing in, and there is not a moment to be lost. Brethren, sinful and beloved! if I speak to those whose early years were those of immorality, be this your consolation—it is well to trust in the cross of Christ for *pardon;* but there is a rarer faith, a faith little exercised, to trust in Christ for *strengthening.* Expect much, and you will win much. Where sin hath abounded, there often " grace much more abounds." It is your peculiar prerogative, my erring brethren, to love much, to feel much, to do much. Only remember this, that there is no step of saintliest excellence, and there is no thrill of purest peace, that is impossible to you, if only you have placed yourselves in earnest under the discipline of Christ.

THE END.

ROBERTSON'S SERMONS.

SERMONS PREACHED AT BRIGHTON by the late Rev. FREDERICK W. ROBERTSON, the Incumbent of Trinity Chapel. With Portrait on Steel. Large 12mo, 838 pages, Cloth, $2 00; Half Calf, $3 75.

While hapless Englishmen complain in the papers, and in private, in many a varied wail, over the sermons they have to listen to, it is very apparent that the work of the preacher has not fallen in any respect out of estimation. Here is a book which has gone through as great a number of editions as the most popular novel. It bears Mudie's stamp upon its dingy boards, and has all those marks of arduous service which are only to be seen in books which belong to great public libraries. It is thumbed, dog's-eared, pencil-marked, worn by much perusal. Is it then a novel? On the contrary, it is a volume of sermons. A fine, tender, and lofty mind, full of thoughtfulness, full of devotion, has herein left his legacy to his country. It is not rhetoric or any vulgar excitement of eloquence that charms so many readers to the book, so many hearers to this preacher's feet. It is not with the action of a Demosthenes, with outstretched arms and countenance of flame, that he presses his Gospel upon his audience. On the contrary, when we read those calm and lofty utterances, this preacher seems seated, like his Master, with the multitude palpitating round, but no agitation or passion in his own thoughtful, contemplative breast. The Sermons of Robertson have few of the exciting qualities of oratory. Save for the charm of a singularly pure and lucid style, their almost sole attraction consists in their power of instruction, in their faculty of opening up the mysteries of life and truth. It is pure teaching, so far as that ever can be administered to a popular audience, which is offered to us in these volumes.—*Blackwood's Magazine.*

The reputation of Mr. Robertson's Sermons is now so wide-spread that any commendation of ours may seem superfluous. We will therefore simply recommend such of our readers as have not yet made their acquaintance, to read them carefully and thoughtfully, and they will find in them more deeply suggestive matter than in almost any book published in the present century.—*Church of England Monthly Review.*

They are Sermons of a bold, uncompromising thinker—of a man resolute for the truth of God, and determined in the strength of God's grace to make that truth clear, to brush away all the fine-spun sophistries and half-truths by which the cunning sins of men have hidden it. * * * His analysis is exquisite in its subtleness and delicacy. * * * With Mr. Robertson style is but the vehicle, not the substitute for thought. Eloquence, poetry, scholarship, originality—his Sermons show proof enough of these to put him on a level with the foremost men of his time. But, after all, their charm lies in the warm, loving, sympathetic heart, in the well-disciplined mind of the true Christian, in his noble scorn of all lies, of all things mean and crooked, in his brave battling for right, even when wrong seems crowned with success, in his honest simplicity and singleness of purpose, in the high and holy tone—as if, amid the discord of earth, he heard clear, though far off, the perfect harmony of heaven; in the fiery earnestness of his love for Christ, the devotion of his whole being to the goodness and truth revealed in him.—*Edinburgh Christian Magazine.*

These Sermons are full of thought and beauty, and admirable illustrations of the ease with which a gifted and disciplined mind can make the obscure transparent, the difficult plain. There is not a sermon that does not furnish evidence of originality without extravagance, of discrimination without tediousness, and of piety without cant or conventionalism.—*British Quarterly.*

When Mr. Robertson died, his name was scarcely known beyond the circle of his own private friends, and of those among whom he had labored in his calling. Now every word he wrote is eagerly sought for and affectionately treasured up, and meets with the most reverent and admiring welcome from men of all parties and all shades of opinion. * * * To those that find in his writings what they themselves want, he is a teacher quite beyond comparison—his words having a meaning, his thoughts a truth and depth, which they cannot find elsewhere; and they never look to him in vain. * * * He fixes himself upon the recollection as a most original and profound thinker, and as a man in whom excellence puts on a new form. * * * There are many persons, and the number increases every year, to whom Robertson's writings are the most stable, satisfactory, and exhaustless form of religious teaching which the nineteenth century has given—the most wise, suggestive, and practical.—*Saturday Review.*

As an author, Mr. Robertson was, in his lifetime, unknown; for with the exception of one or two addresses, he never published, having a singular disinclination to bring his thoughts before the public in the form of published sermons. As a minister, he was beloved and esteemed for his unswerving fidelity to his principles, and his fearless propagation of his religious views. As a townsman, he was held in the highest estimation; his hand and voice being ever ready to do all in his power to advance the moral and social position of the working-man. It was not till after his decease, which event created a sensation and demonstration such as Brighton never before or since witnessed, that his works were subjected to public criticism. It was then found that in the comparatively retired minister of Trinity Chapel there had existed a man possessed of consummate ability and intellect of the highest order; that the sermons laid before his congregation were replete with the subtleties of intellect, and bore evidence of the keenest perception and most exalted catholicity. His teaching was of an extremely liberal character, and if fair to assign a man possessed of such a universality of sympathy to any party, we should say that he belonged to what is denominated the "Broad Church." We, with many others, cannot agree in the fullest extent of his teaching, but, at the same time, feel bound to accord the tribute due to his genius.—*Brighton Gazette.*

To our thinking, no compositions of the same class, at least since the days of Jeremy Taylor, can be compared with these Sermons, delivered to the congregation of Trinity Chapel, Brighton, by their late minister. They have that power over the mind which belongs only to the highest works of genius; they stir the soul to its inmost depths; they move the affections, raise the imagination, bring out the higher and spiritual part of our nature by the continual appeal that is made to it, and tend to make us, at the same time, humble and aspiring—merciful to others and doubtful of ourselves.—*Brighton Herald.*

The Sermons are altogether out of the common style. They are strong, free, and beautiful utterances of a gifted and cultivated mind.—*Eclectic Review.*

They are distinguished by masterly exposition of Scriptural truths and the true spirit of Christian charity.—*Morning Post.*

Mr. Robertson, of Brighton, is a name familiar to most of us, and honored by all to whom it is familiar. A true servant of Christ, a bold and heart-stirring preacher of the Gospel, his teaching was unlike the teaching of most clergymen, for it was beautified and intensified by genius. New truth, new light, streamed from each well-worn text when he handled it.—*Globe.*

PUBLISHED BY HARPER & BROTHERS, NEW YORK.

☞ HARPER & BROTHERS *will send the above work by mail, postage prepaid, to any part of the United States, on receipt of the price.*

ROBERTSON'S LIFE AND LETTERS.

LIFE, LETTERS, LECTURES ON CORINTHIANS, AND ADDRESSES of the late FREDERICK W. ROBERTSON, M.A., Incumbent of Trinity Chapel, Brighton, 1847-1853. With Portrait on Steel. Large 12mo, 840 pages, Cloth, $2 00; Half Calf, $3 75.

No book published since the "Life of Dr. Arnold" has produced so strong an impression on the moral imagination and spiritual theology of England as we may expect from these volumes. Even for those who knew Mr. Robertson well, and for many who knew *him*, as they thought, better than his Sermons, the free and full discussion of the highest subjects in the familiar letters so admirably selected by the Editor of Mr. Robertson's *Life*, will give a far clearer insight into his remarkable character, and inspire a deeper respect for his clear and manly intellect. Mr. Brooke has done his work as Dr. Stanley did his in writing the "Life of Arnold," and it is not possible to give higher praise. * * * Every one will talk of Mr. Robertson, and no one of Mr. Brooke, because Mr. Brooke has thought much of his subject, nothing of himself, and hence the figure which he wished to present comes out quite clear and keen, without any interposing haze of literary vapor.—*Spectator*, London.

The Life of Robertson of Brighton supplies a very unique illustration of the way in which a man may attain his highest fame after he has passed away from earth. There are few who make any pretension to an acquaintance with modern literature who do not know something of Mr. Robertson's works. His sermons are indisputably ranked with the highest sacred classics. * * * The publication of his "Life and Letters" helps us to some information which is very precious, and explains much mystery that hangs around the name of the great Brighton preacher. It will be generally admitted that these two volumes will furnish means for estimating the character of Mr. Robertson which are not supplied in any or all of his published works. * * * There was no artificiality or show about the pulpit production, no half-utterances or whispers of solemn belief; but there was the natural restraint which would be imposed by a true gentleman upon his words when speaking to mixed congregations. Many of us wanted to know how he talked and wrote when the restraint was removed. This privilege is granted to us in these volumes. * * * There was no romance of scene and circumstance in the life of Frederick Robertson; but there was more than romance about the real life of the man. In some respects it was like the life of a new Elijah. * * * A more thoughtful, suggestive, and beautiful preacher never entered a pulpit; a simpler and braver man never lived; a truer Christian never adorned any religious community. His life and death were *vicarious*, as he himself might have put it. He lived and died for others—for us all. The sorrows and agonies of his heart pressed rare music out of it, and the experience of a terribly bitter life leaves a wealth of thought and reflection never more than equalled in the history of men."—*Christian World*, London.

Mr. Brooke has done his own work as a biographer with good sense, feeling, and taste. * * * These volumes are of real value to all thoughtful readers. For many a year we have had no such picture of a pure and noble and well-spent life.—*Morning Herald*, London.

There is something here for all kinds of readers, but the higher a man's mind and the more general his sympathies, the keener will be his interest in the "Life of Robertson."—*Athenæum*, London.

With all drawbacks of what seem to us imperfect taste, an imperfect standard of character, and an imperfect appreciation of what there is in the world beyond a given circle of interest, the book does what a biography ought to do—it shows us a remarkable man, and it gives us the means of forming our own judgment about him. It is not a tame panegyric or a fancy picture. The main portion of the book consists of Mr. Robertson's own letters, and his own account of himself, and we are allowed to see him, in a great degree at least, as he really was. * * * It is the record of a genuine spontaneous character, seeking its way, its duty, its perfection, with much sincerity and elevation of purpose, many anxieties and sorrows, and not, we doubt not, without much of the fruits that come with real self-devotion; a record disclosing a man with great faults and conspicuous blanks in his nature.—*Guardian*, London.

Mr. Brooke has done good service in giving to the world so faithful a sketch of so worthy a man. It would have been a reproach to the Church if this enduring and appropriate memorial had not been erected to one who was so entirely devoted to its service; and the labor of love, for such it evidently was, was committed to no unskilful hands. * * * Mr. Robertson's epistolary writings—gathered in these valuable volumes—often unstudied, always necessarily from their nature free and unrestrained, but evidencing depth and vigor of thought, clear perception, varied knowledge, sound judgment, earnest piety, are doubtless destined to become as widely known and as largely beneficial as his published Sermons. It is impossible to peruse them without receiving impressions for good, and being persuaded that they are the offspring of no ordinary mind.—*Morning Post*, London.

As no English sermons of the century have been so widely read, and as few leaders of religious thought have exerted (especially by works in so much of an unperfected and fragmentary character) so penetrating and powerful an influence on the spiritual tendencies of the times, we can well believe that no biography since Arnold's will presently be possible to be compared with this, for the interest excited by it in the minds of readers who consciously live in the presence of the invisible and eternal, who feel the pressure of difficult questions and painful experiences, and who seek reality and depth, and freedom in the life and activity of the Church of Christ. * * * Mr. Brooke has produced a "Life of Robertson" which will not unworthily compare with Dean Stanley's "Life of Arnold," and which, with that, and Ryland's "Life of Foster," and the "Life of Channing," is likely to be prized as one of the most precious records of genuine manly and godly excellence.—*Nonconformist*, London.

The beautiful work which Mr. Brooke has written contains few, if any, romantic episodes. It is the life of a man who worked hard and died early. * * * Mr. Brooke has acted wisely in allowing Mr. Robertson to speak so fully for himself, and in blending his letters with his narrative, and arranging them in chronological order. These letters are in themselves a mine of intellectual wealth. They contain little of table-talk or parlor gossip; but they abound with many of his best and most ripened thoughts on multitudes of subjects, political, literary, and scientific, as well as theological. We wish we could present our readers with extracts from them; but even if we had space, it would be unfair to the writer to quote disjointed fragments from a correspondence which now belongs to the literature of the country. * * * Mr. Brooke has performed his responsible task as a biographer and an editor in a spirit of just and discriminating appreciation, and with admirable ability.—*Morning Star*, London.

PUBLISHED BY HARPER & BROTHERS, NEW YORK.

☞ HARPER & BROTHERS *will send the above work by mail, postage prepaid, to any part of the United States, on receipt of the price.*

www.ingramcontent.com/pod-product-compliance
Lightning Source LLC
Chambersburg PA
CBHW021802230426
43669CB00008B/609